# WORLD FOOD CRISIS: AN INTERNATIONAL DIRECTORY OF ORGANIZATIONS AND INFORMATION RESOURCES

WHO'S DOING WHAT SERIES: 4

# World Food Crisis: An International Directory of Organizations and Information Resources

*Edited by*
THADDEUS C. TRZYNA
*with the assistance of*
JOAN DICKSON SMITH
*and*
JUDITH RUGGLES

**Public Affairs Clearinghouse
Claremont, California**

Published by Public Affairs Clearinghouse,
P.O. Box 30, Claremont, California 91711

ABOUT THE PUBLISHER
Public Affairs Clearinghouse, which edits and
publishes reference works on national and
world problems and on state affairs in the
United States, is a program of the Center for
California Public Affairs. The Center,
established in 1969 and affiliated with The
Claremont Colleges, is a nonprofit foundation
for research, publishing, and public service.
It is concerned primarily with the character,
public problems, and future development of
California. A catalog of publications issued by
the Center and the Clearinghouse is available
on request.



Represented outside North America by George Prior
Associated Publishers, Ltd., Rugby Chambers, 2 Rugby
Street, London WC1N 3QU.

1      2      3      4      5

L C 76-4270,

ISBN 0-912102-21-7

# CONTENTS

# INTRODUCTION

Providing enough food to meet the needs of an ever-increasing world population is one of the greatest challenges mankind has ever faced. Half the world's population, 2 billion people, suffers from chronic malnutrition, and at least 460 million people are actually starving — they do not get enough calories of dietary energy. What is being done about this problem, and who is doing it?

The purpose of this book is to help answer that question by providing in convenient reference form a central source of information about organizations concerned with the world food problem, their programs and activities, publications, and other information resources.

Emphasis is on organizations of international character and those based in the United States and Canada, although some key organizations of other countries are also listed. The major organizations working in the field are given more detailed treatment.

The main focus of this book is on the food needs of poor countries. However, we have also listed groups interested in hunger, malnutrition, and overconsumption of food in the richer countries.

The world food crisis has many dimensions. Included here are organizations concerned with direct food relief, nutrition, rural development, the international food trade, research and training in agriculture and fisheries, climate change, religious and ethical questions, finance, preservation of genetic resources, soil conservation, public education, pest control, fertilizer, and alternate diets. The stress is on groups working on problems of basic foods, especially grains and fish.

Food and population are two sides of the same coin. A companion volume, *Population: An International Directory of Organizations and Information Resources* (Public Affairs Clearinghouse, 1976) deals with the other side of the coin.

The book is divided into six major parts. *Part 1,* the "User's Guide to Who's Doing What," is a unique feature of this series, designed to help readers identify organizations concerned with broad areas of interest, such as fisheries or education.

*Part 2,* "Intergovernmental Organizations," lists agencies whose members are national governments. United Nations agencies are listed first, followed by other intergovernmental organizations. *Part 3,* "International Non-Governmental Organizations," lists groups of international scope that are not affiliated with governments.

*Parts 4 and 5,* respectively, describe U.S. and Canadian organizations, listing federal government agencies first, and then non-governmental organizations. *Part 6* lists some key organizations of countries outside North America. *Indexes* of organizations, acronyms and initialisms, and subjects begin on page 125.

As with any such first effort, this directory has faults and limitations. Suggestions for improving the book as a whole, as well as specific corrections and additions, will be appreciated. These should be addressed to the editors at Public Affairs Clearinghouse, P.O. Box 30, Claremont, California 91711.

The information in this book was collected by questionnaire from the organizations listed and from current secondary sources, mainly publications of limited distribution, unpublished material, or documents of U.S. or UN agencies.

We appreciate the help of the many organizations which replied to our letters, often in great detail, or filled out questionnaires. Special thanks are due to the Canadian International Development Agency; the Food and Agriculture Organization of the United Nations; María José Galrao, Inter-American Center for Agricultural Documentation and Information; International Union of Nutritional Sciences; National Association for Foreign Student Affairs; New Internationalist Publications, Ltd.; Jayne Millar Wood, Overseas Development Council; Technical Assistance Information Clearing House of the American Council of Voluntary Agencies for Foreign Service; Office of Food for Peace, U.S. Agency for International Development; Foreign Agricultural Service, U.S. Department of Agriculture; and Irene A. Smith, World Council of Churches.

We hope that this book will contribute to better public awareness and understanding of the world food problem. We also hope that it might encourage readers to get involved in working on the problem, perhaps by joining one of the many citizens' organizations that are listed here.

# Part 1.
# User's Guide to
# Who's Doing What

This User's Guide is designed to direct readers to organizations concerned with specific problems or subject areas; references are to page numbers.  It is organized as follows:

# BROAD INTERESTS

Listed here are the major organizations having a broad interest in the world food situation. <u>See also</u>: Relief and Development Agencies; Financial Institutions; Public Opinion.

<u>INTERNATIONAL</u>: The World Food Council (5) has responsibility for overall coordination of United Nations activities related to the food situation.  Other key agencies in the UN System are the Food and Agriculture Organization (11-14), especially its Committee on World Food Security; and the International Fund for Agricultural Development (10).

Other UN agencies with broad interests include: ECOSOC (3) and the UN regional economic commissions (3-5); United Nations Institute for Training and Research (8); United Nations Research Institute for Social Development (8); United Nations Environment Programme (8); United Nations University (9); UNESCO's Man and the Biosphere Programme (16); and the Consultative Groups on Food Production and Investment in Developing Countries (10) and International Agricultural Research (10). The UN World Food Conference of 1974 is described on page 19.

Outside the UN System, the key intergovernmental body is the Organisation for Economic Co-operation and Development (27), especially its Development Assistance Committee, which is a central source of information on development aid from all sources.  Other intergovernmental organizations with wide food interests are the Organization of American States (28), especially its Inter-American Committee for Agricultural Development and its Inter-American Institute of Agricultural Sciences; and the autonomous International Commission for Agricultural and Foodstuff Industries (24).

International non-governmental organizations having broad interests in the field include: International Council of Scientific Unions (36); International Federation of Agricultural Producers (37); International Union of Food Science and Technology (42); World Association for the Struggle Against Hunger (46); and World Council of Churches (46).

The Society for International Development (45) is the major international professional association concerned with development problems. The new International Food Policy Research Institute (39) promises to have an important role in analyzing food policies.

The Club of Rome (33) and the International Federation of Institutes for Advanced Study (38) conduct interdisciplinary studies on relationships among food, population, and other factors.

The International Institute for Environment and Development (39) and the International Union for Conservation of Nature and Natural Resources (42) are concerned with sustaining the natural environment as a life-support system.

<u>UNITED STATES</u>:  In the U.S. Government, the Department of Agriculture (49-52) has broad concerns with domestic food problems and foreign agriculture and food trade particularly as they affect U.S. agriculture.

The Agency for International Development (54) carries on a large program of development and relief activities related to food and agriculture. U.S. international food policies are developed by the State Department's Office of Food Policy and Programs (54).

Other U.S. Government agencies having broad interests in the world food situation are the Office of Technology Assessment (49); Board for International Food and Agricultural Development (49); and National Academy of Sciences-National Research Council (57).  The Development Coordination Committee (49) advises the President on all U.S. development assistance programs.

The following U.S. non-governmental organizations are involved in education and/or research on broad issues related to the world food situation: Agricultural Development Council (59); American Enterprise Institute for Public Policy Research (61); Community Nutrition Institute (71); Earth Metabolic Design (75); East-West Food Institute (75); Hudson Institute (79); Institute for Policy Studies (80); Institute on Man and Science (80); Iowa State

USER'S GUIDE - BROAD INTERESTS

University's World Food Institute (82) and Center for Agricultural and Economic Development (82); the M.I.T. System Dynamics Group (84); Michigan State University's Institute of International Agriculture (84); National Planning Association (89); Philadelphia Macroanalysis Seminars (91); Resources for the Future (93); Stanford University's Food Research Institute (95); the University of California Task Force on World Food Problems (98); and Worldwatch Institute (101).

The following groups are concerned mainly with sustaining the natural environment as a life-support system: Acres U.S.A. (58); the Environmental Fund (75); Friends of the Earth (78); and the Sierra Club (94).

Professional societies with broad interests include: American Chemical Society (60); American Society of Agricultural Consultants (63); and Institute of Food Technologists (80).

The Center for Community Change (66) provides management and fund-raising services to other groups. The Interreligious Task Force on U.S. Food Policy (81) coordinates activities of Jewish, Protestant, and Roman Catholic organizations. The National Council of Churches (86) has broad concerns, including coordinating food-related efforts of Protestant and Orthodox denominations.

Other U.S. private groups with broad concerns include the Ford Foundation (77); Friends Committee on National Legislation (78); New Directions (90); Overseas Development Council (91); Rockefeller Brothers Fund (93); and Rockefeller Foundation (93).

CANADA: In the Canadian Federal Government, the Department of Agriculture (105) has broad concerns with domestic food problems and foreign agriculture and food trade particularly as they affect Canadian agriculture.

The Canadian International Development Agency (105) and the International Development Research Center (106) carry on overseas relief and development programs related to food and agriculture. Canadian international food policies are developed in the Department of External Affairs (106). The Science Council of Canada (107) is concerned with food policies.

Non-governmental organizations in Canada with broad interests include: Association Quebecoise des Organismes de Cooperation Internationale (107); Canadian Council for International Cooperation (108); Canadian Council of Churches (108); Canadian Institute of Food Science and Technology (108); Canadian Inter-Church Committee for World Development (108); and Latin American Working Group (109).

OTHER COUNTRIES: France's Office de la Recherche Scientifique et Technique Outre-Mer (ORSTOM) (115) carries on research and development projects around the globe. The Future Shape of Technology Foundation in the Netherlands (119), and the Swedish Association for Future Studies (121) carry on research into the future of the food situation as it relates to other resources and factors. The Institute of Development Studies at the University of Sussex in England (123) is a national center for research and education.

# RELIEF AND DEVELOPMENT AGENCIES

The following organizations conduct or support programs of food aid and/or food-related development assistance in developing countries. See also: Cooperatives; Education and Information; Financial Institutions; Nutrition.

FOOD RELIEF: Many of the agencies listed in this section, both public and private, include some direct assistance in the form of food to people in the countries in which they operate, although the emphasis is increasingly on attacking the root causes of hunger, rather than simply feeding people.

The largest food relief programs are the UN World Food Programme (5) and the Food for Peace Program of the U.S. Agency for International Development (54). The latter program includes sales to countries as well as food donations made through the World Food Programme, U.S. voluntary agencies, and governments of developing countries. The Foreign Agricultural Service of the U.S. Department of Agriculture (51) assists in developing Food for Peace sales policies. The Department's Commodity Credit Corporation (50) determines the availability of commodities to be sold under the program.

Emergency food aid is provided by both the UN High Commission for Refugees (9) and UN Relief and Works Agency for Palestine Refugees in the Near East (9).

The International Council of Voluntary Agencies (36) maintains a Commission on Emergency Aid to assist in coordination of its members' relief, including food relief, projects.

The Cooperative for American Relief Everywhere (CARE) (72) probably has the largest privately-operated feeding program; some 20 million people are fed by CARE daily.

RELIEF AND DEVELOPMENT: INTER-GOVERNMENTAL AGENCIES: Major inter-governmental agencies involved directly in food-related development and relief projects are the United Nations Development Programme (6); the UN World Food Programme (5); UN Children's Fund (7); Food and Agriculture Organization of the UN (11); World Bank (14); World Health Organization (17); Colombo Plan (21); and the European Development Fund of the European Economic Community (23).

The Inter-American Institute of Agricultural Sciences (28) operates development projects in the Western Hemisphere. The Afro-Asian Rural Reconstruction Organization (20) has a modest program.

The Consultative Group on Food Production and Investment in Developing Countries (10) coordinates programs of various agencies.

Among the major donors to food relief and development programs are the new International Fund for Agricultural Development (10); League of Arab States (26), which administers the Special Arab Fund for Africa (26); Organization of Arab Petroleum Exporting Countries (OAPEC) (29); and Organization of Petroleum Exporting Countries (OPEC) (30).

RELIEF AND DEVELOPMENT: NATIONAL GOVERNMENT AGENCIES: U.S. Government agencies involved are the Agency for International Development (55); ACTION (56), which operates the Peace Corps; and the Inter-American Foundation (56).

The Canadian Government agencies concerned are the Canadian International Development Agency (105) and the International Development Research Centre (106).

Other national government development agencies listed are: Australian Development Assistance Agency (113); Belgium's Ministry of Development Cooperation (113); the Danish International Development Agency (115); French Ministry of Cooperation (115); West German Ministry of Economic Cooperation (116); Israeli Ministry of Foreign Affairs (117); Japan International Cooperation Agency (118); Netherlands Ministry of Development Assistance (119); Norwegian Agency for International Development (120); Swedish International Development Agency (121); and British Ministry of Overseas Development (122).

RELIEF AND DEVELOPMENT: INTERNA-TIONAL NON-GOVERNMENTAL AGENCIES: The following groups are primarily concerned with coordinating international development activities of various non-governmental organizations: Caritas Internationalis (33), Roman Catholic charities; World Council of Churches (46), Protestant and Orthodox agencies; and International Council of Voluntary Agencies (36), voluntary efforts of all types.

Other international non-governmental agencies include: Africa Committee for the Rehabilitation of the Southern Sudan (33); Brothers to All Men (33); Friends World Committee for Consultation (34); HEED Bangladesh (34); International Cooperative Alliance Development Fund (36); Lutheran World Federation (43); Oxfam (44); Pan American Development Foundation (44); Salvation Army (46).

RELIEF AND DEVELOPMENT: U.S. VOLUNTARY AGENCIES: Some 90 American voluntary agencies involved in food-related relief and development activities abroad are listed in this book.

The following groups are concerned with coordinating the work of other organizations in this field: American Council of Voluntary Agencies in Foreign Service and its Technical Assistance Information Clearinghouse (TAICH) (60), which includes most of the major groups; the Joint Strategy and Action Committee (82), which includes several major Protestant denominations; the National Council of Churches (86), which includes Protestant and Orthodox denominations; and Private Agencies Collaborating Together (PACT) (92).

Several other organizations offer consultation to other groups in such areas as fund-raising and public relations.  These include Coordination in Development (CODEL) (72); Friends of the Third World (78); and some of the organizations listed in this User's Guide under Public Opinion.

Major denominational agencies are: American Baptist Churches (60); American Friends Service Committee (62); Baptist World Relief (65); Catholic Relief Services (66); Christian Church (68); Christian Reformed World Relief Committee (68); Church of the Brethren (69); Church of God (69); Episcopal Church of the United States (75); Lutheran World Relief (83); Mennonite Central Committee (84); Presbyterian Church in the U.S. (92); Seventh-Day Adventist World Service (94); Unitarian Universalist Service Committee (96); United Church of Christ (96); United Methodist Committee on Relief (96); United Presbyterian Church in the U.S.A. (97); and Southern Baptist Convention (95).

The National Council of Churches (86), which links Protestant and Orthodox denominations, carries on a range of interdenominational aid activities through Church World Service (87) and Agricultural Missions (87).

Other U.S. voluntary agencies involved, many of them religious in nature, are: Accion International (58); Africare (58); Agricultural Missions Foundation (59); American Institute for Free Labor Development (62); American Jewish Joint Distribution Committee (62); American Kor-Asian Foundation (62); American Near East Refugee Aid (62); American ORT Federation (62); Andean Foundation (64); Asia Foundation (64); Christian Children's Fund (67); Christian National's Evangelism Commission (68); Church Women United (69); Columban Fathers (69); Community Development Foundation and Save the Children Federation (70); Consortium for International Development (71); Cooperacion (71); Cooperative for American Relief Everywhere (CARE) (71); Direct Relief

Foundation (74); Divine Word Missionaries (74); Dooley Foundation (75); Farmers and World Affairs (76); Foster Parents' Plan (77); Ford Foundation (77); Fund for the Peoples of the South Pacific (78); Friends of Children (78); The Gleaners (78); Heifer Project International (79); Holy Cross Foreign Mission Society (79); International Development Foundation (81); International Educational Development (81); International Executive Service Corps (81); International Independence Institute (81); IRI Research Institute (82); Iran Foundation (82); Kellogg Foundation (82); Kettering Foundation (83); Maryknoll Fathers (83); Maryknoll Sisters (84); Meals for Millions Foundation (84); Medical Assistance Programs (84); Mill Hill Missionaries (84); Missions Health Foundation (85); National Association of Evangelicals (85); National 4-H Foundation of America (89); Near East Foundation (90); New World Coalition (90); Oxfam America (91); Partners of the Americas (91); People to People Health Foundation (Project HOPE) (91); Plenty (92); Public Welfare Foundation (93); Rockefeller Foundation (93); Salvation Army (94); Self-Help (94); Sudan Interior Mission (95); Technoserve (96); Utah State University (98); Volunteer Development Corps (99); Volunteers for International Development (99); Volunteers in Technical Assistance (99); World Education (99); World Neighbors (100); World Vision International (100); YMCA (101); YWCA (100).

RELIEF AND DEVELOPMENT: CANADIAN VOLUNTARY AGENCIES:  Anglican Church of Canada (107); Canadian Catholic Organization for Development and Peace (108); Canadian Hunger Foundation (108); Canadian University Service Overseas (108); Christian Reformed World Relief Committee of Canada (108); CARE of Canada (109); Food for the Hungry (109); Lutheran Council in Canada (109); Mennonite Central Committee (Canada) (109); Presbyterian Church in Canada (110); Unitarian Service Committee of Canada (110); United Church of Canada (110).

<u>RELIEF AND DEVELOPMENT: VOLUNTARY
AGENCIES IN OTHER COUNTRIES:</u>

<u>Australia</u>: Australian Council of Churches (113);
 Community Aid Abroad (113)
<u>Belgium</u>: International Cooperation for Social
 and Economic Development (113)
<u>France</u>: CIMADE (116); United Towns Organi-
zation (116)
<u>Germany</u>: Arbeitsgemeinschaft fuer Welt-
 mission (116); Christoffel Blindenmission (116)
<u>Iceland</u>: Icelandic Church Relief (117)
<u>Japan</u>: OISCA International (118)
<u>Netherlands</u>: Interchurch Coordination Com-
 mittee for Development Projects (119)
<u>New Zealand</u>: CORSO, Inc. (119); National
 Council of Churches (119)
<u>Norway</u>: Norwegian Church Relief (120)
<u>Sweden</u>: Swedish Missionary Council (121)
<u>Switzerland</u>: HEKS (121)
<u>United Kingdom</u>: Christian Aid (122); Bible and
 Medical Missionary Fellowship (122); Help
 the Aged (122); Leprosy Mission (122);
 Regions Beyond Missionary Union (123);
 Tear Fund (123); War on Want (123); Volun-
 tary Committee on Overseas Aid (123).

# AGRIBUSINESS

The following organizations have a special
interest in the role of business corporations,
particularly multinational agribusiness, in the
world food and nutrition situation:

The Food and Agriculture Organization of the
UN has an Industry Cooperative Program (12).
The Economic and Social Council of the UN (3)
and various of its subunits have been interested
generally in the problems of transnational business corporations.

U.S. nongovernmental organizations concerned
include: Agribusiness Accountability Project
(59); Center for Science in the Public Interest
(66); Council on Economic Priorities (73);
Council on Religion and International Affairs
and its Carnegie Center for Transnational
Studies (73); Interfaith Committee on Social
Responsibility in Investments (80) and its
Corporate Information Center (73).

In Canada, the Taskforce on the Churches and
Corporate Responsibility (110) is concerned

with this area, as are the British Haslemere
Group (122) and Counter Information Service
(122).

Two organizations focus on nutritional problems caused in developing countries by promotion of commercial baby food: Baby Foods
Action Group in the U.K. (122); and the
National Komitee voor Gezonde en Rechvaardige
in Belgium (114).

# ALTERNATE DIET

Every year, millions of tons of grain and
other sources of protein - enough to improve
the diets of all the world's hungry people -
are used to feed livestock that is slaughtered
to feed the rich. It takes up to 22 lbs. of
animal feed, for example, to produce 1 lb. of
protein in the form of prime beef. While
many of the religious organizations listed in
this book work to encourage less consumption
of meat and other wasteful foods, the following
organizations - both religious and secular -
are specifically concerned with promoting
alternate diets and simpler lifestyles on moral,
humane, or health grounds:

Vegetarian groups have led in this field for
many years. They include: International
Vegetarian Union (43); American Vegan
Society (64), which promotes total vegetarian-
ism; American Vegetarian Union (64), which
promotes abstinence from fish, flesh, or fowl;
Vegetarian Society of New York (99); London
Vegetarian Center (122); The Vegetarian
Society (123).

Bread for the World (65) has published "An
Alternative Diet for People Concerned About
Hunger." The Joint Strategy and Action
Committee (82); National Beef Boycott Committee (85); and Citizens' Association to Save
the Environment (109) in Canada have also
been active in this area.

The Shakertown Pledge Group (94) and its
contacts in Australia (113), Germany (116),
Jamaica (117), and the U.K. (123) promote
a simple life style, as does Jochgruppen Haus
(121) in Switzerland.

Alternate, or unconventional, sources of protein have received much attention from many of the relief and development agencies listed in this directory.  Those specifically concerned with such sources include: World Health Organization (17); Office of Nutrition in the U.S. Agency for International Development (56); International Seaweed Symposium (42).

The American Corn Millers Federation (**60**) promotes CSM, a blended corn-soy-milk food product used widely in food relief programs. Battelle Memorial Institute (65) conducts research on vegetable-protein meat substitutes.

## AQUACULTURE AND SOILLESS CULTURE

Organizations specifically concerned with these fields include: International Working Group on Soilless Culture (43); the U.S. Sea Grant program and its National Aquaculture Information System (53); American Fish Farmers Federation (61); and Battelle Memorial Institute (65).

## CLIMATE AND WEATHER

The following organizations are concerned with the impacts of climatic change, weather, and weather modification on agricultural production:

The World Meteorological Organization (18) is the key international agency involved in this field.  The UN Environment Programme (8) is concerned with monitoring and analysis of climate change.  UNESCO's Ecological Programme (16) also has an interest.

The Environmental Data Service in the U.S. National Oceanic and Atmospheric Administration (52) collects, analyzes, and disseminates data on climate and weather worldwide.

Other groups concerned are: International Society of Biometeorology (42); the University of Wisconsin's Climate/Food Project (98); and the International Federation of Institutes for Advanced Study (38), which has a project on the impact of climate change.

## COOPERATIVES

While many of the relief and development agencies listed in this book are active in promoting farmer, fishing, and consumer cooperatives in developing countries, the following groups focus specifically on the cooperative as a means of dealing with food problems in both industrialized countries and the Third World:

The UN Research Institute on Social Development (8) has done studies on cooperatives. The International Cooperative Alliance (36) is the global umbrella organization for the cooperative movement.

Other groups involved are: International Research Centre on Rural Cooperative Communities (41); the Farmer Cooperative Service in the U.S. Department of Agriculture (52); Agricultural Cooperative Development International (59); Asian-American Free Labor Institute (64); Cooperative League of the U.S.A. (72); Credit Union National Association (74); Food Conspiracies (76); Food Co-op Directory (76); Food Coop Project (76); National Council of Farmer Cooperatives (88).

## DOMESTIC PROBLEMS

Hunger and malnutrition are not limited to the less developed countries.  The following organizations are concerned with domestic hunger and food issues and programs in the U.S.:

The Office of Technology Assessment in the U.S. Congress (49) has been concerned with national food policy generally.  The Food and Nutrition Service in the U.S. Department of Agriculture (51) administers federal domestic food programs, including food stamps and school lunches.

Non-governmental organizations involved include:  Academy for Contemporary Problems (58); Bread for the World (65); California Food Policy Coalition (65); Center for Community Change (66) and its Hunger and Development Program; Center for Science in the

Public Interest (66), which sponsors the annual Food Day; Chicago Grey Panthers (67); Community Warehouse (71); Exploratory Project for Economic Alternatives (76); Food Conspiracies (76); Food Co-op Directory (76); Food Coop Project (76); Food Research and Action Center (77); The Gleaners (78); Gray Panthers (78); Hunger Task Force (80); Hunger Workshop (80); Interreligious Taskforce on U.S. Food Policy (81); National Beef Boycott Center (85); National Coalition for Land Reform (86); National Conference of Catholic Charities (86); National Council of Churches (86) - especially its Working Group on Hunger, National Farm Worker Ministry, and Delta Ministry; National Council on Hunger and Malnutrition in the U.S. (88); National Food Stamp Information Committee (89).

# EDUCATION AND INFORMATION

Many of the organizations listed in this User's Guide under Broad Interests or Relief and Development Agencies conduct educational and training programs for people working in the field of food and rural development, or provide specialized information services of various kinds. The following groups are particularly active in this area. (Those involved with public education are listed under Public Opinion.)

EDUCATION AND TRAINING: United Nations agencies involved are the Food and Agriculture Organization (11-14); the United Nations University (9); the UN Development Programme (14), which has an Economic Development Institute; and the World Health Organization (17), which sponsors training of medical and other professionals in nutrition.

Other groups concerned with education and training include: the OECD Development Centre (28); International Institute of Protein Food Technology (39); the U.S. Department of Agriculture (49-52), which trains foreign nationals in the U.S., as does the autonomous Farm Credit Administration (56); the U.S. National Science Foundation (57), which provides study grants to U.S. scientists and engineers; Agriservices Foundation (60); and the International Association for the Exchange of Students for Technical Experience (80).

The Arca Foundation (64) funds educational and communication projects. U.S. university activities are coordinated by the Association of U.S. University Directors of International Agricultural Programs (64). The Institute of International Education (80) promotes and services educational exchange programs. The National Association for Foreign Student Affairs (85) facilitates study by foreign nationals at U.S. universities and colleges.

The special programs listed of the following universities are involved in varying degrees in training students, as well as conducting research and other projects: Columbia (69); Cornell (73); Iowa State (82); Michigan State (84); Stanford (95); California (98); Chicago (98); Wisconsin (98); Utah State (98). The East-West Food Institute (75) also trains postgraduate students.

INFORMATION: Major global sources of information about food and related topics are the Food and Agriculture Organization of the United Nations (11-14), whose numerous information services include the International Information System for the Agricultural Sciences and Technology (AGRIS) (12); the several Commonwealth Agricultural Bureaux (21), which publish scientific information services used in all parts of the world; and the U.S. Department of Agriculture (49-52), whose Foreign Agricultural Service (51) is the basic source of agricultural commodity information for the world, and whose National Agricultural Library (50) has a special Nutrition Information and Educational Materials Center, and publishes the "Bibliography of Agriculture."

Other important information sources include the Development Reference Service in Paris, operated by the Society for International Development (45); the Economic Research Service (51-52) of the U.S. Department of Agriculture, which stores and disseminates data on agricultural technology relating to developing countries; the U.S. National Technical Information Service (54); the League for International Food Education (83), which is a clearinghouse for nutrition information and personnel; the Smithsonian Science Information Exchange (94); and the International Liaison Service of the Canadian Department of Agriculture (106), which publishes reports on the world food and agricultural situation.

The International System of Scientific and Technical Information in Agriculture and Forestry (25) serves the Comecon countries of Eastern Europe and the USSR. The Inter-American Association of Agricultural Librarians and Documentalists (35) promotes information exchange in the Western Hemisphere. The Institute for World Order (80) has a University Food Resource Center. Volunteers in Technical Assistance (99) maintains a Technical Information Service for development workers. There is an International Food Information Service (122) in the U.K.

## FERTILIZER

While many of the relief and development agencies listed in this book have projects involving production or distribution of fertilizers or instruction on their use, these groups are particularly concerned with fertilizer: the Food and Agriculture Organization of the UN (11-14) in general, and the FAO/Fertilizer Industry Advisory Committee of Experts (12); the FAO/IAEA Joint Division of Atomic Energy in Food and Agriculture (18); the International Fertilizer Development Center (38); the International Potash Institute (41); the Agricultural Research Service of the U.S. Department of Agriculture (49); and the Fertilizer Institute (76).

## FINANCIAL INSTITUTIONS

The following organizations concentrate on making loans or investments, rather than outright grants of money, for food-related projects in developing countries: International Bank for Reconstruction and Development (World Bank) (14) and its affiliates; Asian Development Bank (20); Caribbean Development Bank (21); Colombo Plan (21); Inter-American Development Bank (24); Pan American Development Foundation (44); International Foundation for Independence of the International Independence Institute (81).

The FAO Investment Centre (12) identifies and prepares projects for financing. The Consultative Group on Food Production and Investment in Developing Countries (10) is a coordinating mechanism sponsored by the World Bank, UNDP, and FAO.

The U.S. Farm Credit Administration (56) trains nationals of developing countries in agricultural credit. The Credit Union National Association (74) of the U.S. helps develop credit unions in the Third World.

## FISHERIES

See also Aquaculture. In the United Nations System, the Food and Agriculture Organization (11-14), especially through its Committee on Fisheries and various fisheries commissions, is the main agency concerned with fisheries as a food source. Under FAO are the Indo-Pacific Fisheries Council (13) and the General Fisheries Council of the Mediterranean (14). Other UN agencies concerned are the UN Environment Programme (8), which works to conserve life-support systems of the oceans; and UNESCO's Office of Oceanography (16).

Regional intergovernmental bodies set up to conserve fish resources and regulate harvesting (usually on an advisory basis) include the East African Freshwater (22) and Marine (22) Fisheries Research Organizations; the Inter-American Tropical Tuna Commission (24); the International Commissions for the Conservation of Atlantic Tunas (24), for the Northwest Atlantic Fisheries (25), and for the Southeast Atlantic Fisheries (25); the International North Pacific Fisheries Commission (25); the North-East Atlantic Fisheries Commission (26); and the South West Atlantic Fisheries Advisory Commission (30).

The International Whaling Commission (25) is concerned with regulating the harvesting of whales, which are mammals, not fish, but which are a source of food used in some countries, particularly Japan.

Other organizations especially concerned with fisheries are: the OECD Committee on Fisheries (27); Gulf and Caribbean Fisheries

Institute (34); and National Fisheries Institute (88).

The International Union for Conservation of Nature and Natural Resources (42) has a special interest in the marine environment and its resources. The U.S. Government's National Marine Fisheries Service (53) and Sea Grant program (53) are concerned with both domestic and global fish resources. The American Fisheries Society (61) is a major professional organization in the field.

In Canada, the Fisheries and Marine Service in the Department of the Environment (106) is the main federal agency involved.

# GENETIC RESOURCES

Preservation of genetic resources in danger of extinction and collecting, cataloging, and storing genetic material are crucial to present and future development of improved crops.

The principal organizations involved are the International Board for Plant Genetic Resources (35); the various institutes sponsored by the Consultative Group on International Agricultural Research (see list, page 10); and the Agricultural Research Service (49) of the U.S. Department of Agriculture.

Also concerned are the International Union for Conservation of Nature and Natural Resources (42); International Seed Testing Association (42); and American Seed Research Foundation (63).

# LIVESTOCK AND DAIRY FOODS

The main international organizations concerned particularly with livestock and dairy products, including poultry and egg products, are the Food and Agriculture Organization of the United Nations (11-14), which has specialized groups devoted to this field; the UN Conference on Trade and Development (6), whose new commodities program includes meat; the International Center of Tropical Agriculture (25), which deals with livestock on the tropical lowlands of the Western Hemisphere; the International Laboratory for Research on Animal Diseases

(40), which concentrates on Africa; and the International Livestock Center (40), which focuses on tropical Africa.

The Commonwealth Bureaus of Animal Breeding and Genetics (21), of Animal Health (21), of Animal Nutrition (21), and of Dairy Science and Technology (21) provide information services in the field.

Other international groups include: Dairy Society International (34); International Dairy Federation (37); International Veterinary Association for Animal Production (43); World Association for Animal Production (45); and World's Poultry Science Association (46).

U.S. non-governmental organizations concerned include: Agriservices Foundation (60), which holds an International Stockmen's School; American Dry Milk Institute (61); American Sheep Producers Council (63); Dairy Research, Inc. (74); Heifer Project International (79); National Dairy Council (88); National Food and Conservation through Swine (FACTS) (89); and Poultry and Egg Institute of America (92).

# NUTRITION AND HEALTH

INTERNATIONAL: The key groups in the United Nations System are the Food and Agriculture Organization and its various subunits (11-14); the World Health Organization (17); and the FAO/WHO Committee on Experts on Nutrition (12). The Protein-Calorie Advisory Group (10) advises several UN agencies.

The major professional organization is the International Union of Nutritional Sciences (43). Other international groups are: Caribbean Food and Nutrition Institute (21); Commonwealth Bureau of Nutrition (22), which offers information services; Institute of Nutrition of Central America and Panama (24); NATO's Committee on the Challenges of Modern Society (26), which has a study in the field; the OAS Inter-American Children's Institute (29); and the International Organization of Consumers Unions (41), which has been interested in nutritional labelling of foods and regulation of nutritionally undesirable food products.

UNITED STATES:  The Agricultural Research Service of the U.S. Department of Agriculture (49) has a Human Nutrition Laboratory and a Nutrient Data Bank, among other nutrition-related activities.  The Office of Nutrition of the U.S. Agency for International Development (55) has broad concerns in this field, including testing and development of new sources of nutrition.  The Food and Nutrition Board of the National Academy of Sciences (57) provides advice to other U.S. agencies, particularly AID's Office of Nutrition.

U.S. non-governmental organizations especially concerned with nutrition include: Columbia University's Institute of Nutrition (69); Concern, Inc. (71); Council for Agricultural Science and Technology (73); the Earth Foods Center of the International Independence Institute (81); National Beef Boycott Center (85); Nutrition Foundation (90); and the UCLA Division of Population, Family, and International Health (98).

The League for International Food Education (83) is a nutrition information clearinghouse. The Society for Nutrition Education (94), in addition to its functions as a professional organization in the field, operates a National Nutrition Education Clearing House (95).

OTHER COUNTRIES:  Canadian National Committee for the International Union of Nutritional Sciences (108).  Other affiliates of the IUNS are listed among the entries on pages 113-124.

# ORGANIC AGRICULTURE

Groups that promote "organic" agriculture, which includes avoiding the use of pesticides and chemical fertilizers, are numerous.  Those listed in this book are: Acres, U.S.A. (58); Bio-Dynamic Farming and Gardening Association (65); the Agricultural Development Program of the Direct Relief Foundation (74), which promotes the "intensive method" of agriculture; National Food and Conservation Through Swine (FACTS) (89); and The Soil Association (123) in the U.K.  Environmental groups, including Friends of the Earth (78) and the Sierra Club (94) are also concerned.

# PEST CONTROL AND PESTICIDES

The following organizations have a special interest in controlling agricultural pests or pests, such as rodents, that consume food in storage; or the effects of pesticides on health and environment.  See also: Organic Agriculture.

The Food and Agriculture Organization of the United Nations (11-14) has a major concern in this field, especially through its various regional locust control and plant protection commissions.  It has a Committee on Experts on Pesticides in Agriculture and a Panel of Experts on Integrated Pest Control.

The United Nations Environment Programme (8) is interested in the long-term effects of pesticide use on the environment.  Other inter-governmental organizations involved are the Commonwealth Institute of Entomology (21); Commonwealth Mycological Institute (21); Commonwealth Institute of Biological Control (21); Commonwealth Bureau of Helminthology (21); Desert Locust Control Organization for Eastern Africa (22); European and Mediterranean Plant Protection Organization (23); Inter-American Committee for Crop Protection (24); Regional International Organization of Plant Protection and Animal Health (30); and International Institute of Tropical Agriculture (40), which has a Pesticides Residues Study.

Non-governmental organizations involved include: International Union for Conservation of Nature and Natural Resources (42); American Society of Agricultural Consultants (63); and Association of Applied Insect Ecologists (64).

The Agricultural Research Service of the U.S. Department of Agriculture (48) conducts studies on pest control and pesticides.

USER'S GUIDE - PLANT FOODS

# PLANT FOODS

The following organizations have general interests in food derived from plants:  Food and Agriculture Organization of the United Nations (11-14); IAEA/FAO Joint Division of Atomic Energy in Food and Agriculture (18); Commonwealth Bureau of Plant Breeding and Genetics (21); Caribbean Food Crops Society (33); European Union for the Grain, Oilseed and Fodder Trades and Derivatives (34); International Association of Cereal Chemistry (35); International Seed Testing Association (42); American Institute of Crop Ecology (62); American Society of Agronomy (63); Crop Science Society of America (74); National Grain and Feed Association (89); National Grain Trade Council (89); North American Export Grain Association (90); Protein Grain Products International (92); U.S. Feed Grains Council (97).

The International Center of Tropical Agriculture (35) conducts research and development on plant crops for the tropical lowlands of the Western Hemisphere.  The International Crops Research Institute for the Semi-Arid Tropics (37) focuses on crops for the semi-arid belt of South Asia, Africa, the Middle East, and South and Central America.  The International Institute of Tropical Agriculture (40) focuses on crops for the humid tropics, particularly in Africa.

The following organizations focus on particular crops:

Rice:  International Rice Commission (14); International Rice Research Institute (41); West Africa Rice Development Association (45); Rice Council for Market Development (93).

Wheat:  International Wheat Council (25); International Maize and Wheat Improvement Center (40); Great Plains Wheat, Inc. (79); Millers' National Federation (84); National Association of Wheat Growers (85); Western Wheat Associates (99); Canadian Wheat Board (105); Grains Marketing Office of the Canadian Department of Industry, Trade, and Commerce (106).

Corn (maize):  International Maize and Wheat Improvement Center (40); Latin American Corn Society (43); National Corn Growers Association (86).

Other crops: International Potato Center (41); International Seaweed Symposium (42); American Soybean Association (63); National Peanut Council (89); National Soybean Processors Association (89); Potato Association of America (92).

# PUBLIC OPINION

The following organizations are particularly concerned with marshaling public opinion in industrialized countries in support of measures to meet the world food problem.  Some of them are simply educational; others lobby for political action as well as conducting programs of public information.  See also: Religious and Ethical Questions.

INTERNATIONAL:  In the United Nations System, the Centre for Social and Economic Information (3) is responsible for mobilizing world opinion in support of the UN's development programs.  The Freedom from Hunger Campaign/Action for Development program of the Food and Agriculture Organization (12) works to enlarge public consciousness of world food problems.  UNESCO's Co-operative Action Program (16) links individuals with specific development projects in the Third World.

Non-governmental organizations involved include: Friends World Committee for Consultation (34); Oxfam (44); Pan American Development Foundation (44) and its Operation Niños; World Council of Churches (46); and World University Service (46).

UNITED STATES: The Action Center (58); Ad Hoc Jewish Committee on Hunger (58); Africare (58); American Freedom from Hunger Foundation (61); American Friends Service Committee (61); Boston Industrial Mission (65); Center for War/Peace Studies (67); Center of Concern (67); Foreign Policy Association (77); National Association for Foreign Student Affairs (85); CROP, the Community Hunger Appeal of Church World Service (87); National

Council of Churches Division of Education and Ministry (88); Network (90); New Directions (90); Overseas Development Council (91); Population Crisis Committee (92); Southern Baptist Convention Christian Life Commission (95); Union of American Hebrew Congregations (96); United Methodist Center for the Study of Power and Peace (96); United Nations Association of the U.S.A. (97); Campaign for Human Development and Office of International Justice and Peace of the U.S. Catholic Conference (97); United States Committee for UNICEF (97); Women, Food and Population (99); World Hunger Education/Action Together (WHEAT) (99); and World Without War Council (101).

The Center for Science in the Public Interest (66) sponsors the annual Food Day. The Arca Foundation (64) funds communications projects on world food problems.

CANADA: British Columbia Inter-Church Committee for World Development Education (108); Canadian UNICEF Committee (108); Canadian University Service Overseas (108); Development Education Center (109); Development Education Library Project (109); Interchurch Committee for World Development Education (109); Ontario Institute for Studies in Education (110); Regina Committee for World Development (110); Salvation Army (110); Ten Days for World Development (110); United Nations Association of Canada (110).

OTHER COUNTRIES:

Denmark: International Forum (115)
Netherlands: Gaast an Tafel (Guest at Your Table) (119)
Norway: Future in Our Hands (120)
Switzerland: Erklaerung von Bern (121)
United Kingdom: New Internationalist Publications (122); Third World First (123); World Development Movement (123)



# RELIGIOUS AND ETHICAL QUESTIONS

While many of the religious groups listed in this User's Guide under Relief and Development Agencies, and the groups listed under Alternate Diet, are motivated by religious or moral concern, the following organizations are particularly interested in the religious and ethical issues involved in the world food situation:

The World Council of Churches (46) works in this area mainly through its Commission on the Churches' Participation in Development. In the U.S., the Interreligious Task Force on U.S. Food Policy (81) links Protestant, Roman Catholic, and Jewish organizations; Bread for the World (65) is an effort of Protestant, Roman Catholic, and Orthodox denominations; the National Council of Churches' Commission on Faith and Order (88) links major Protestant groups; and the Synagogue Council of America (95) coordinates the work of Jewish religious organizations.

Other U.S. groups include: Ad Hoc Jewish Committee on Hunger (58); American Jewish Committee (62); Boston Industrial Mission (65); Center of Concern (67); Christian Reformed World Relief Committee (68); Council on Religion and International Affairs (73); Shakertown Pledge Group (94); and Union of American Hebrew Congregations (96).

# SOIL AND LAND USE

The following organizations are particularly concerned with soil conservation and preservation of prime agricultural lands:

United Nations Environment Programme (8); Commonwealth Bureau of Soils (21); International Geographical Union (39); International Society of Soil Science (42); International Union for Conservation of Nature and Natural Resources (42); American Society of Agronomy (63); Friends of the Earth (78); Sierra Club (94); The Soil Association (123) in the U.K. The Soil Conservation Service of the U.S. Department of Agriculture (50) has a training program for foreign nationals.

## STATISTICS

Many of the organizations listed in this book publish statistics; the following groups are among the principal sources of data on food, agriculture, and fisheries:

The Food and Agriculture Organization of the United Nations (11) is the major international source of statistics in the food field. Other UN agencies involved include the regional economic commissions (3-5), and the World Health Organization (17). UN publications are described on page 3.

The International Wheat Commission (26) issues statistics on the world wheat trade. The Organisation for Economic Co-operation and Development is the major source of data on development assistance; it also publishes statistics on agricultural trade.

In the U.S. Government, the Foreign Agricultural Service (51) in the Department of Agriculture is an important source of statistics on world agricultural production. The Statistical Reporting Service (52) in the same department trains foreign nationals in agricultural statistics as well as publishing figures on crops and livestock in the U.S. The National Marine Fisheries Service (53) in the Department of Commerce issues fisheries statistics.

## STORAGE

The following organizations are particularly concerned with the problems of storing crops and foods: Food and Agriculture Organization of the United Nations (11-14); International Institute of Refrigeration (25); International Commission on Microbiological Specifications for Foods (36); International Institute of Tropical Agriculture (40), which operates the FAO/ African Rural Storage Center; and the Agricultural Research Service (49) in the U.S. Department of Agriculture.

## TRADE AND ECONOMICS

The following organizations are especially concerned with economic aspects of the world food situation and international trade in food:

In the United Nations System, the key agencies involved with trade in foodstuffs are the UN Conference on Trade and Development (6) and the General Agreement on Tariffs and Trade (16). The Food and Agriculture Organization (11), especially through its Committee on Commodities, also has a major role.

The UN Economic and Social Council (3) and the UN regional economic commissions (3-5) study economic aspects of trade and development. The research program of the UN Development Program (15) focuses on economic questions of development.

The Commonwealth Bureau of Agricultural Economics (22) provides information services in the field. The European Economic Community (23) has a special trade relationship with some 60 "associated" developing countries. The Organisation for Economic Co-operation and Development has a major program of studies on trade and development economics.

Professional organizations involved include the European Scientific Association of Applied Economics (34) and the International Association of Agricultural Economists (35).

The International Federation of Agricultural Producers (37) represents the interests of producers, while the International Organization of Consumers Unions (41) represents the interests of consumers.

In the U.S. Department of Agriculture, the Foreign Agricultural Service (51) collects, analyzes, and distributes data on world agricultural trade. The Economic Research Service (51) conducts studies on agricultural trade both in the U.S. and globally.

Other groups concerned with food economics and trade include: Exploratory Project for Economic Alternatives (76); the Food Research Institute at Stanford University (95); the Giannini Foundation at the University of California (98); and a Canadian group, GATT-Fly (109).

# MAJOR WORLD REGIONS

Listed here are organizations that specialize in the problems of particular regions of the world.  Not included are organizations having worldwide interests or their regional offices (e.g., United Nations agencies; Catholic Relief Services).

See also the listings for "Other Countries" on pages 113-124.

AFRICA:  UN Economic Commission for Africa (5); Regional Commission on Animal Production and Health in Africa (11); Joint FAO/WHO Regional Food and Nutrition Commission for Africa (11); Indian Ocean Fishery Commission (11); FAO Fisheries Committee for the Eastern Central Atlantic (12); General Fisheries Council for the Mediterranean (14); Afro-Asian Rural Reconstruction Organization (20); Desert Locust Control Organization for Eastern Africa (22); East Africa Agricultural and Forestry Research Organization (22); East Africa Freshwater Fisheries Research Organization (22); East Africa Marine Fisheries Research Organization (22); European and Mediterranean Plant Protection Organization (23); International African Migratory Locust Organization (24); International Commission for the Southeast Atlantic Fisheries (25); Africa Committee for the Rehabilitation of the Southern Sudan (33); International Institute of Tropical Agriculture (40); International Laboratory for Research on Animal Diseases (40); International Livestock Center for Africa (40); Western Africa Rice Development Association (45); Africare (58); Near East Foundation (90).

ASIA:  UN Economic and Social Commission for Asia and the Pacific (3); UN Economic Commission for Western Asia (5); Commission for Controlling the Desert Locust in the Eastern Region of its Distribution Area in South West Asia (11); Plant Protection Committee for the South East Asia and Pacific Region (11); Regional Commission on Farm Management for Asia and the Far East (11); Indian Ocean Fishery Commission (11); Regional Commission on Agricultural Extension for Asia and the Far East (11); Indo-Pacific Fisheries Council (13); Afro-Asian Rural Reconstruction Organization (20); Asian Development Bank (20); Asian Development Center (20); International North Pacific Fisheries Commission (25); HEED Bangladesh (34); American Kor-Asian Foundation (62); Asia Foundation (64); Asian-American Free Labor Institute (64); Columban Fathers (69); Dooley Foundation (75); East-West Food Institute (75).

EUROPE:  UN Economic Commission for Europe (5); European Commission for the Control of Foot and Mouth Disease (11); European Commission on Agriculture (11); European Inland Fisheries Advisory Commission (11); General Fisheries Council for the Mediterranean (14); Council for Mutual Economic Assistance (22); European and Mediterranean Plant Protection Organization (23); European Communities (23-24); North Atlantic Treaty Organization (26); North-East Atlantic Fisheries Commission (26); European Scientific Association of Applied Economics (34); European Union for the Grain, Oilseed, and Fodder Trades and Derivatives (34).

LATIN AMERICA:  UN Economic Commission for Latin America (3); Caribbean Plant Protection Commission (11); Regional Fisheries Advisory Commission for the South West Atlantic (11); Caribbean Food and Nutrition Institute (21); Caribbean Development Bank (21); Institute of Nutrition of Central America and Panama (24); Inter-American Committee for Crop Protection (24); Inter-American Development Bank (24); Inter-American Tropical Tuna Commission (24); Organization of American States (28-29); Regional International Organization of Plant Protection and Animal Health (30); South West Atlantic Fisheries Advisory Commission (30); Caribbean Food Crops Society (33); Gulf and Caribbean Fisheries Institute (34); Inter-American Association of Agricultural Librarians and Documentalists (35); International Center of Tropical Agriculture (35); Latin American Corn Society (43); Pan American Development Foundation (44); Inter-American Foundation

(56); Accion International (58); Andean Foundation (64); Partners of the Americas (91); Latin American Working Group (109).

MIDDLE EAST: UN Economic Commission for Western Asia (5); UN Relief and Works Agency for Palestine Refugees in the Near East (9); Commission for Controlling the Desert Locust in the Near East (11); Animal Production and Health Commission in the Near East (11); Near East Plant Protection Commission (11); Near East Commission on Agricultural Planning (11); General Fisheries Council for the Mediterranean (14); Afro-Asian Rural Reconstruction Organization (20); European and Mediterranean Plant Protection Organization (23); League of Arab States (26); Organization of Arab Petroleum Exporting Countries (29); American Near East Refugee Aid (62); Iran Foundation (82); Near East Foundation (90).

OCEANIA: UN Economic and Social Commission for Asia and the Pacific (3); Plant Protection Committee for the South East Asia and Pacific Region (11); Indo-Pacific Fisheries Council (13); East-West Food Institute (75); Foundation for the Peoples of the South Pacific (78).

# Part 2.
# Intergovernmental Organizations

# A. THE UNITED NATIONS

The chart on the following page shows how the United Nations System is organized. The standard reference on UN activities is the Yearbook of the United Nations (which, however, is usually about two years out of date). UN documents are indexed in UNDEX: United Nations Documents Index. The UN Chronicle (11 times a year) reports on current activities within the organization and lists new documents and publications and forthcoming conferences and meetings.

Other UN periodicals include the Monthly Bulletin of Statistics, which has a section of food statistics; Commodity Trade Statistics (about 34 issues a year; Monthly List of Selected Articles; and Current Bibliographical Information (twice monthly).

For a checklist of UN books and periodicals and ordering information, write to United Nations Publications, LX 2300, New York, New York 10017; or Palais des Nations, 1211 Geneva 10, Switzerland.

UNITED NATIONS SECRETARIAT
New York, New York 10017

    +Centre for Economic and Social
     Information (CESI)
    Room 1061
    United Nations
    New York, New York 10017
                212-754-1234

CESI is responsible for mobilizing public opinion throughout the world in support of UN development programs. It publishes Development Forum, monthly, an excellent source of information on UN issues and activities related to food and development generally; and various booklets and briefing papers (list available).

CESI also has an office at the United Nations, Palais des Nations, Room C-511, 1211 Geneva 10, Switzerland (Telephone: 34-60-11).

ECONOMIC AND SOCIAL COUNCIL (ECOSOC)
United Nations
New York, New York 10017

ECOSOC, one of the major organs of the United Nations, has general responsibility for its economic and social activities. Its standing committees include: Committee on Natural Resources; Advisory Committee on the Application of Science and Technology to Development; and Committee for Development Planning.

Much of the United Nations' work in the economic and social field is done through five regional economic commissions, which are responsible to ECOSOC.

Regional economic commissions of the United Nations:

    +Economic and Social Commission for
     Asia and the Pacific (ESCAP)
    United Nations Building
    Rajdamnern Avenue
    Bangkok, Thailand         829161

    Formerly: Economic Commission for Asia and the Far East (ECAFE). Includes a Working Party on Economic Development and Planning.

    There is also a Joint ESCAP/FAO Agriculture Division (joint with the Food and Agriculture Organization of the United Nations), whose main function is to improve agricultural plans and policies of countries in the region and promote regional cooperation in agriculture.

    Pub.: Economic Bulletin for Asia and the Pacific, q. Statistical Yearbook for Asia and the Pacific. Monographs.

    +Economic Commission for Latin America
     (ECLA)
    Avenida Dag Hammarsjold, Vitacura
    Santiago, Chile

    Includes a Joint ECLA/FAO Agriculture Division, and the Latin American Centre for Economic and Social Documentation (CLADES).

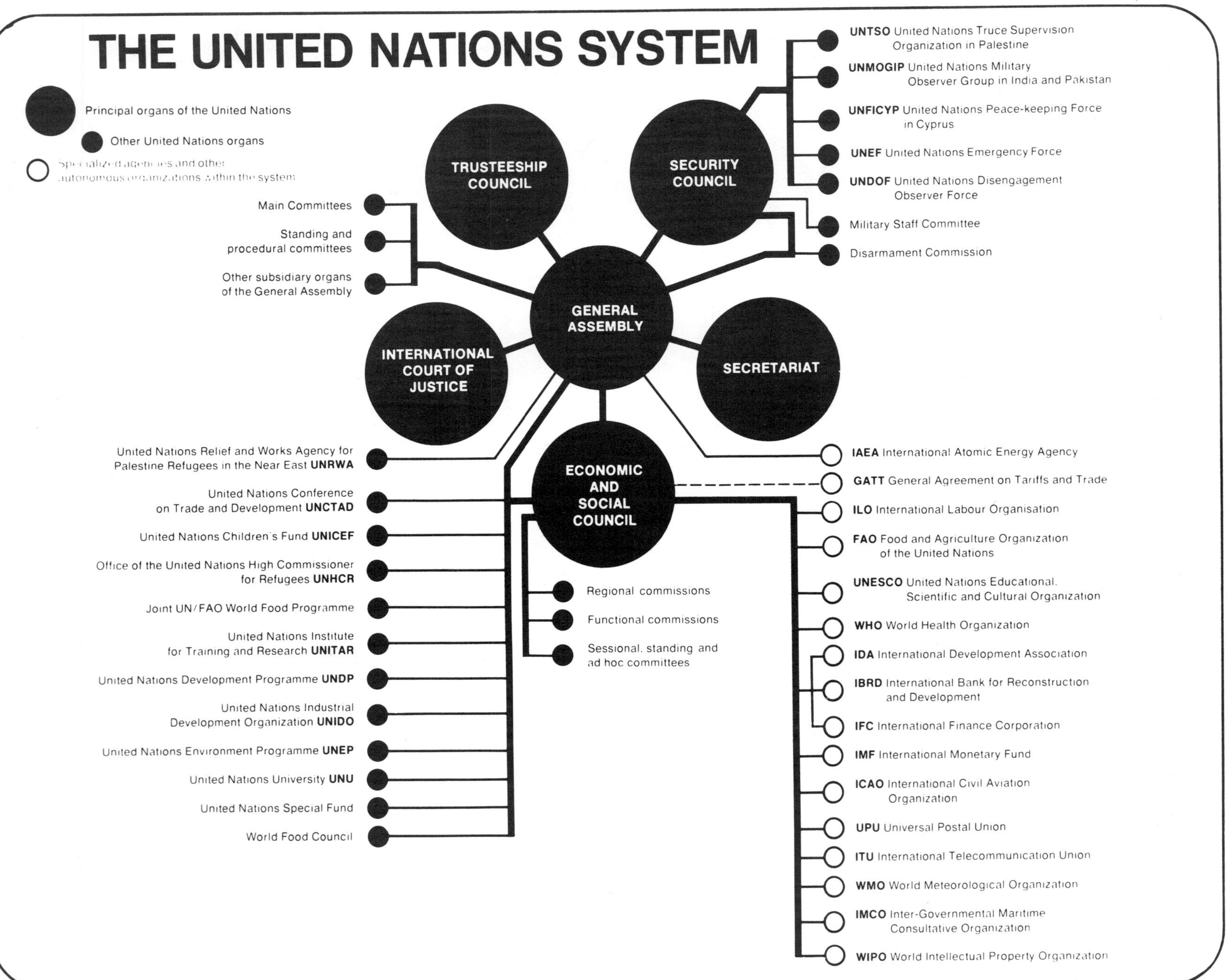

THE UNITED NATIONS SYSTEM

Principal organs of the United Nations
Other United Nations organs
Specialized agencies and other autonomous organizations within the system

TRUSTEESHIP COUNCIL
SECURITY COUNCIL
GENERAL ASSEMBLY
INTERNATIONAL COURT OF JUSTICE
SECRETARIAT
ECONOMIC AND SOCIAL COUNCIL

Main Committees
Standing and procedural committees
Other subsidiary organs of the General Assembly

UNTSO United Nations Truce Supervision Organization in Palestine
UNMOGIP United Nations Military Observer Group in India and Pakistan
UNFICYP United Nations Peace-keeping Force in Cyprus
UNEF United Nations Emergency Force
UNDOF United Nations Disengagement Observer Force
Military Staff Committee
Disarmament Commission

United Nations Relief and Works Agency for Palestine Refugees in the Near East UNRWA
United Nations Conference on Trade and Development UNCTAD
United Nations Children's Fund UNICEF
Office of the United Nations High Commissioner for Refugees UNHCR
Joint UN/FAO World Food Programme
United Nations Institute for Training and Research UNITAR
United Nations Development Programme UNDP
United Nations Industrial Development Organization UNIDO
United Nations Environment Programme UNEP
United Nations University UNU
United Nations Special Fund
World Food Council

Regional commissions
Functional commissions
Sessional, standing and ad hoc committees

IAEA International Atomic Energy Agency
GATT General Agreement on Tariffs and Trade
ILO International Labour Organisation
FAO Food and Agriculture Organization of the United Nations
UNESCO United Nations Educational, Scientific and Cultural Organization
WHO World Health Organization
IDA International Development Association
IBRD International Bank for Reconstruction and Development
IFC International Finance Corporation
IMF International Monetary Fund
ICAO International Civil Aviation Organization
UPU Universal Postal Union
ITU International Telecommunication Union
WMO World Meteorological Organization
IMCO Inter-Governmental Maritime Consultative Organization
WIPO World Intellectual Property Organization

Pub.: <u>Economic Survey of Latin America</u>,
annual.  Studies and reports.

+<u>Economic Commission for Africa</u> (ECA)
P.O. Box 3001
Addis Ababa, Ethiopia

+<u>Economic Commission for Western
  Asia</u> (ECWA)
P.O. Box 4656
Beirut, Lebanon

+<u>Economic Commission for Europe</u> (ECE)
Palais des Nations
1211 Geneva 10, Switzerland

Includes a <u>Committee on Agricultural
Problems</u>.

## WORLD FOOD COUNCIL
Via delle Terme di Caracalla
00100 Rome, Italy            5797

Est. 1975.  Reports to the General Assembly
of the UN through the Economic and Social
Council.  Consists of 36 member states.

The Council is charged with the responsibility
of implementing the resolutions of the World
Food Conference of 1974 (see page 19).
functions as a "coordinating mechanism to
provide overall, integrated and continuing
attention for the successful coordination and
follow-up of policies concerning food production, nutrition, food security, food trade and
food aid, as well as other related matters, by
all the agencies of the United Nations system."

Its main activities are: (1) to monitor the
world food situation in all its aspects, including what international organizations and
governments are doing to develop short-term
and long-term solutions to food problems; (2)
to look at the total food picture and determine
in its coordinating role whether the world food
strategy as a whole makes sense; (3) to identify
malfunction, gaps, and problem areas; and (4)
to make recommendations to the General
Assembly in order to use the political influence of the United Nations to bring about the
desired results.

+<u>World Food Council Liaison Office</u>
United Nations Headquarters
New York, New York 10017
                    212-754-1234, ext. 3388

## WORLD FOOD PROGRAMME (WFP)
Via delle Terme de Caracalla
00100 Rome, Italy            5797

Est. 1961, as a joint program of the United
Nations and FAO.  Supervised by an Intergovernmental Committee (IGC) composed of
representatives of member states, 12 of whom
are elected by ECOSOC, and 12 by the FAO
Council.

The purpose of WFP is to provide food aid,
that is, aid in the form of food, rather than
cash or technical assistance.  Food is supplied
as an incentive to development self-help
projects, as part wages in labor-intensive projects of many kinds, particularly in rural
development and in support of institutional
fedding projects where the emphasis is mainly
on enabling the beneficiaries to enjoy an
adequate and balanced diet.  The Programme
has also provided food aid in cases of natural
disasters and to refugees.

Countries submit requests for WFP assistance.
In scrutinizing a request, the staff considers
whether the proposed project is technically
and economically feasible, whether it is relevant to the country's development, whether the
local arrangements for carrying it out and
handling the food are adquate and, "often most
important, whether there is any danger that
the arrival of the food may have a harmful,
dampening effect on local food production or
the country's agricultural trade." WFP encourages presentation of projects which the recipient country can continue after food aid has
ceased.

Through the end of 1975, WFP had assisted
736 development projects in 101 countries at
a total cost of $2.2 billion, and had under-
taken 214 emergency operations in 90 countries at a cost of $207 million.

More than 100 countries have donated food,
cash, or services to the Programme.  Largest
donors, in order of size of contribution, have
been the United States, Canada, the European

Economic Community, Denmark, Netherlands, Sweden, Federal Republic of Germany, Norway, and United Kingdom.

Pub.: World Food Programme News, q. World Food Program: A Story of Multilateral Aid (revised periodically). Food Aid to Education and Training (1973). Food Aid and Employment (1973).

UNITED NATIONS DEVELOPMENT
  PROGRAMME (UNDP)
1 United Nations Plaza
New York, New York 10017     212-754-1234

Est. 1965. The major arm of the UN, and the world's largest channel, for international technical cooperation in development. Assistance is provided to developing countries in the form of experts, fellowships, equipment, and specialized technical services, as well as a limited amount of capital for pilot production facilities in industry and agriculture.

Agriculture, forestry, and fisheries is the largest single component of UNDP activity, representing about 30% of expenditures, or some $576 million in approved projects (late 1975), in some 100 countries.

UNDP is mainly a financing, overall programming, and monitoring organization. Most of the field work it supports is actually carried out by the other international agencies of the UN development system. These agencies include (in the field of food and agriculture): United Nations, FAO, UNESCO, WHO, World Bank, WMO, World Food Programme, UNICEF, and the Inter-American, African, and Asian Development Banks.

The decision on which agency will implement any given project is made by UNDP, in consultation with the government of the developing country concerned. Though a single agency is always in charge of a particular project, two or more often collaborate in providing the services required.

UNDP also directly implements a relatively small number of projects (amounting to some 5% of its budget).

UNDP allocations related to food during the period 1972 through 1976 were divided as follows: plant production, $40.5 million; animal production and health, $50.0 million; fisheries, $27.8 million; land and water use, $46.2 million; agricultural institutions and rural training, $68.3 million.

UNDP participates in the Consultative Group in International Agricultural Research and the Consultative Group on Food Production and Investment in Developing Countries (both World Bank-FAO-UNDP groups).

UNDP field operations are conducted through regional and country offices throughout the world.

Pub.: Commitment, q. Business Bulletin, mon. Action UNDP, bimon. (part of Development Forum, issued monthly by the UN Centre for Economic and Social Information). UNDP: Compendium of Approved Projects, annual. Various booklets, reports, leaflets, articles, speech reprints, and audio-visual materials (list available).

UNITED NATIONS CONFERENCE ON TRADE
  AND DEVELOPMENT (UNCTAD)
Palais des Nations
1211 Geneva 10, Switzerland     34-60-11

Est. 1964. Consists of a Conference, which normally meets every four years; the Trade and Development Board, which meets annually; various committees, including a Committee on Commodities; and a secretariat.

UNCTAD is the central UN body concerned with the relationship between trade and development and is the international focal point for a continuing debate leading to formulation of trade and development policies and negotiation of multilateral agreements in the field.

UNCTAD's activities are increasingly geared to meeting the objectives of the UN International Development Strategy for the Second Development Decade, which was adopted by the General Assembly in 1970. Concerns include adopting special trade measures in favor of the least developed countries; the economic duties and rights of states; and the impact of transnational business corporations on world trade and payments.

The fourth session of the Conference, held at Nairobi, Kenya in 1976, established an integrated program for commodities, including procedures to set "remunerative and just" prices for products produced by developing countries which take into account inflation, monetary changes, and the cost of manufactured imports.  The commodities involved include bananas, cocoa, coffee, meat, sugar, tea, and vegetable oils.

Pub.:  Proceedings and reports of conferences and meetings of committees.

UNITED NATIONS CHILDREN'S FUND
  (UNICEF)
New York, New York 10017

Est. 1946.  UNICEF provides aid to governments in their efforts to undertake long-range and far-reaching programs to benefit children and youth.  The emphasis is on extending basic services to children in under-served areas, including rural areas and urban slums. The Fund focuses on helping countries to devise a package of essential services for children in the interrelated fields of food and nutrition, health measures, family planning, basic education, and supporting services for women.

About 80% of UNICEF's program expenditures is for supplies and equipment.  The remainder is for training (including training in nutrition) and providing consulting services to governments.

The Fund's annual budget is about $90 million. Over 100 countries receive assistance.  Pub.: UNICEF News, q.  Pamphlets and reports.

UNICEF regional offices:

+UNICEF Regional Office
P.O. Box 2810
Lusaka, Zambia
    Covers Zambia, Botswana, Lesotho, Malawi, and Swaziland.

+UNICEF Regional Office
B.P. 2110
Brazzaville
    Covers Cameroon, Central African Empire, Chad, Congo, Gabon, and Zaire.

+UNICEF Regional Office for East Africa
P.O. Box 7047
Kampala, Uganda
    Covers Burundi, Comoro Islands, Kenya, Madagascar, Mauritius, Rwanda, Seychelles, Somalia, and Uganda.

+UNICEF Regional Office for Europe and North Africa
20, rue Pauline Borghese
Neuilly-sur-Seine, France

+UNICEF Regional Office
B P. 429
Dakar, Senegal
    Covers Gambia, Guinea, Mali, Mauritania, Senegal, and Sierra Leone.

+UNICEF Regional Office for Ghana and Nigeria
P.O. Box 1282
Lagos, Nigeria

+UNICEF Regional Office for West Africa
B.P. 4443
Abidjan Platea, Ivory Coast
    Covers Dahomey, Ivory Coast, Liberia, Niger, Togo, and Upper Volta.

+UNICEF Regional Office for East Asia and Pakistan
P.O. Box 2-154
Bangkok, Thailand

+UNICEF Regional Office for the Eastern Mediterranean
Beirut, Lebanon
    Covers Lebanon, Cyprus, Israel, Jordan, Saudi Arabia, and Syria.

+UNICEF Regional Office for the Philippines and the South Pacific
P.O. Box 883
Manila, Philippines

+UNICEF Regional Office for South
  Central Asia
UNICEF House, 11 Jorbagh
New Delhi 3, India

+UNICEF Regional Office
Calle 37, No. 8-43
Bogota, Colombia
  Covers Colombia, Ecuador, Guyana,
  Surinam, Venezuela, and the Caribbean
  Islands.

+UNICEF Regional Office
Avenida Javier Prado 705, San Isidro
Lima, Peru
  Covers Argentina, Bolivia, Chile,
  Paraguay, Peru, and Uruguay.

+UNICEF Regional Office
Apartado 525
Guatemala City, Guatemala
  Covers Central America and Panama.

+UNICEF Regional Office
Hamburgo 63, 7o Piso
Mexico 6, D.F., Mexico
  Covers Cuba, Dominican Republic,
  Haiti, and Mexico.

+UNICEF Office for Latin America
Casilla 13970
Santiago, Chile
  Covers all of Latin America.

UNITED NATIONS INSTITUTE FOR
  TRAINING AND RESEARCH (UNITAR)
801 United Nations Plaza
New York, New York 10017  212-754-1234

Est. 1963. The central body within the UN
system in the undertaking of research and
training. Special Project on the Future
focuses on major trends and developments
having implications for the future, including
those related to the food situation. Pub.:
Important for the Future, 5 times a year.
Chronicle, semiann. Reports.

UNITED NATIONS RESEARCH INSTITUTE
  FOR SOCIAL DEVELOPMENT (UNRISD)
Palais des Nations
1211 Geneva 10, Switzerland  34-60-11

Est. 1963. Conducts research into problems
and policies of social development during
different phases of economic growth. Major
projects have include a study of the social and
economic implications of large-scale introduction of high-yield food grains, and a study
of rural agricultural cooperatives as agents of
social change.

Pub.: Reports, including (for example):
Food and the New Agricultural Technology (1972).
The Green Revolution: An Economic Analysis
(1972). List available.

UNITED NATIONS ENVIRONMENT
  PROGRAMME (UNEP)
P.O. Box 30552
Nairobi, Kenya

Est. 1972. Basic purposes are to promote
international cooperation in the environmental
field; to review the world environmental situation to ensure that environmental problems of
wide international significance receive appropriate consideration by governments; and to
promote the acquisition, assessment, and
exchange of environmental knowledge.

A number of UNEP's program areas relate
directly or indirectly to the world food problem.
These include action-oriented projects on
range lands management in arid and semi-arid
regions; soil conservation; conservation of
genetic resources; safeguarding the life-
support systems of the oceans; promoting an
integrated approach to environment and development (the concept of "ecodevelopment") and
environmentally sound technologies; and
monitoring and analyzing climatic changes.

Projects are carried out by UNEP itself, by
other intergovernmental agencies, and by
national and international non-governmental
organizations.

UNEP served as the Secretariat for the United
Nations Conference on Desertification (Nairobi,
1977).

Projects funded by UNEP during its startup period, 1973-75, totaled $48.5 million.  Pub.: Uniterra, mon. newsletter.  Technical studies. Annual review.

Regional and liaison offices, UNEP:

+UNEP Liaison Office
United Nations Headquarters
P.O. Box 20
Grand Central Station
New York, New York 10017
                    212-754-8139

+UNEP Liaison Office
Palais des Nations
1211 Geneva 10, Switzerland    34-22-00

+UNEP Regional Office for the ECA Region
P.O. Box 30552
Nairobi, Kenya           33-39-30

+UNEP Regional Office for the ESCAP
 Region
United Nations Building, 10th Floor
Rajadamnern Avenue
Bangkok, Thailand           829615

+UNEP Regional Office for the ECLA
 Region
Edificio Naciones Unidas
Presidente Mazaryk 29
Apartado Postal 6-718
Mexico 5, D.F.           250-1555

+UNEP Regional Office for the ECWA
 Region
P.O. Box 814
Manama, State of Bahrain   8687

THE UNITED NATIONS UNIVERSITY (UNU)
15-1, Shibuya 2-Chome, Shibuya-ku
Tokyo 150, Japan           03-499-2811

Est. 1973.  "Not a traditional degree-granting university but a worldwide network of advanced study institutes devoted to research, post-graduate training, and dissemination of knowledge... There are many national and international organizations working on major world problems, and on specific areas of the physical and social sciences, and the humanities.  UNU will seek to stimulate and draw on all such existing activities and to coordinate the practical application of their results.  It will also establish new institutes for research and advanced training when existing programs do not meet important needs."

A World Hunger Programme is one of UNU's first three priority areas.  This program emphasizes human nutritional needs and their fulfillment; post-harvest food conservation; nutrition and food objectives in national development planning; and the agricultural production/food-nutrition interfaces.  The Programme is assisted by a World Hunger Programme Advisory Committee.

Three institutes have been chosen as the initial centers of the World Hunger Programme network.  These are the Institute of Nutrition of Central America and Panama (INCAP), in Guatemala; the Central Food Technological Research Institute (CFTRI) in Mysore, India; and the Nutrition Center of the Philippines (NCP).

Pub.: UNU Newsletter, bimon.

+United Nations University Liaison Office
United Nations, Room 3194
New York, New York 10017

UNITED NATIONS HIGH COMMISSIONER FOR
 REFUGEES (UNHCR)
Palais des Nations
1211 Geneva 10, Switzerland    34-60-11

Est. 1951.  Promotes and safeguards the interests of refugees.  Activities include providing emergency relief, including food aid from the World Food Programme.  In recent years, food aid has been given primarily to refugees in Africa.  Maintains regional and country offices throughout the world.

UNITED NATIONS RELIEF AND WORKS
 AGENCY FOR PALESTINE REFUGEES IN
 THE NEAR EAST (UNRWA)
United Nations
New York, New York 10017

Est. 1949.  Provides services, including food, to registered refugees of the 1948 Arab-Israeli conflict and, on a temporary and limited basis, to persons displaced as a result of the 1967 hostilities.  Budget for 1976 was $139 million.

<u>CONSULTATIVE GROUP ON FOOD
PRODUCTION AND INVESTMENT IN
DEVELOPING COUNTRIES</u> (CGFPI)
1818 H Street, N.W.
Washington, D.C. 20433      202-477-2041

Est. 1975. A joint group of the World Bank, FAO, and UNDP. Its main functions are to encourage larger external resource flows for food production in developing countries; to coordinate activities of donors; and to encourage more effective use of resources.

<u>CONSULTATIVE GROUP ON INTERNATIONAL
AGRICULTURAL RESEARCH</u> (CGIAR)
c/o World Bank
1818 H Street, N.W.
Washington, D.C. 20433

Est. 1973. A joint group of the World Bank, FAO, and UNDP, as well as donor governments; regional development banks; the Commission of the European Communities; the Ford, Kellogg, and Rockefeller Foundations; and the International Development Research Centre of Canada.

CGIAR coordinates support to, and the programs of, the several international institutes for agricultural research (listed elsewhere in this book), which include:

-- International Rice Research Institute (IRRI)

-- International Maize and Wheat Improvement Center (CIMMYT)

-- International Institute of Tropical Agriculture (IITA)

-- International Center of Tropical Agriculture (CIAT)

-- International Crops Institute for the Semi-Arid Tropics (ICRISAT)

-- International Potato Center (CIP)

-- International Fertilizer Center (IFC)

-- International Board for Plant Genetic Resources (IBPGR)

-- International Laboratory for Research on Animal Diseases (ILRAD)

-- International Livestock Center for Africa (ILCA)

<u>PROTEIN-CALORIE ADVISORY GROUP OF
THE UNITED NATIONS SYSTEM</u> (PAG)
866 United Nations Plaza, Room 606
New York, New York 10017

An interdisciplinary committee of internationally-recognized experts who advise the United Nations and its agencies on technical, economic, educational, social, and other aspects of global malnutrition problems and programs and new areas of activity needed to combat them.

Sponsored by FAO, WHO, UNICEF, World Bank, and the United Nations. Pub.: <u>PAG Bulletin</u>, q.

# B. SPECIALIZED AGENCIES OF THE UNITED NATIONS

<u>INTERNATIONAL FUND FOR AGRICULTURAL
DEVELOPMENT</u> (IFAD)
Via delle Terme di Caracalla
00100 Rome, Italy      5797

Est. 1977. The creation of IFAD was one of the most important accomplishments of the World Food Conference of 1974. With an initial operating fund of $1.07 billion, the Fund finances agricultural and related activities of existing development agencies, such as the World Bank, FAO, UNDP, and regional development banks. IFAD is particularly interested in projects that combine three objectives: raising food production on small farms; providing incomes for the landless; and reducing malnutrition by producing the kinds of foods that the poorest people normally consume and by improving food distribution systems.

The creation of IFAD greatly increased the amount of "highly concessional" funding available for food production projects in the developing countries. Funding will be in the form of donations or soft loans.

The unique features of the Fund are the sources of its money and how voting power is distributed.  Of its initial resources, $400 million was contributed by the Organization of Petroleum Exporting Countries (OPEC) and $676 million, by 18 developed countries.  The Fund's governing body, the Executive Board, consists of 6 representatives from developed countries, 6 from developing contributing (OPEC) countries, and 6 from developing recipient countries.

FOOD AND AGRICULTURE ORGANIZATION OF THE UNITED NATIONS (FAO)
Via delle Terme di Caracalla
00100 Rome, Italy                    5797

Est. 1945.  Governed by a Conference of all member states, which meets in odd-numbered years; and a 34-member Council.

FAO's broad purposes are to raise the levels of nutrition and standards of living of people in member states; secure improvements in the efficiency of production and distribution of all food and agricultural products; and better the conditions of rural populations.

Information, research, and advice
FAO is an international center of information on all aspects of agriculture, fisheries, forestry, and nutrition.  Statistics on production, trade, and consumption of hundreds of commodities are gathered from all over the world and published in statistical reviews and yearbooks, monographs, directories, and reporting services.

A wide range of research activities focus on problems affecting the world agricultural economy, on rural unemployment, on increasing the availability of protein foods, on raising agricultural productivity, on reduction of waste from pests and spoilage, and on prices for agricultural commodities.

Consultation
FAO facilitates international consultation on food and agriculture matters by means of a complex system of commissions, committees, working parties, and panels.

Major committees include: Committee on Commodity Problems, which reviews commodity problems of an international character affecting trade, distribution, consumption, and related matters and makes recommendations to the Council on policy issues; and which has a Subcommittee on Surplus Disposal and intergovernmental groups on various commodities, including rice, grains, oilseeds, and meat.  Committee on Fisheries (COFI), which reviews fisheries problems of an international character and promotes cooperation and consultation in fisheries on a global scale.  Committee on Agriculture, which reviews and makes recommendations on agricultural problems, particularly those relating to social, technical, economic, and institutional aspects of agricultural and rural development. Committee on World Food Security, which submits periodic reports to the Council on the state of world food stocks and demands in exporting and importing countries, reviews the basic food situation and actions taken by governments on world food security, and recommends measures to assure adequate cereal supplies.

FAO bodies set up under conventions and agreements include the International Rice Commission (see below); Indo-Pacific Fisheries Council (see below); General Fisheries Council for the Mediterranean (see below); European Commission for the Control of Foot and Mouth Disease; Commission for Controlling the Desert Locust in the Near East; Commission for Controlling the Desert Locust in the Eastern Region of its Distribution Area in South West Asia; and Plant Protection Committee for the South East Asia and Pacific Region.

Other FAO bodies concerned with basic food problems include: European Commission on Agriculture; Regional Commission on Animal Production and Health in Africa; Animal Production and Health Commission in the Near East; Regional Commission on Farm Management for Asia and the Far East; Joint FAO/WHO Regional Food and Nutrition Commission for Africa; Near East Plant Protection Commission; Caribbean Plant Protection Commission; Regional Fisheries Advisory Commission for the South West Atlantic (CARPAS); European Inland Fisheries Advisory Commission (EIFAC); Indian Ocean Fishery Commission; Near East Commission on Agricultural Planning; Regional Commission on Agricultural Extension for Asia and the Far East.

Various groups of experts have been set up
to advise FAO; those concerned with basic food
problems include: FAO/Fertilizer Industry
Advisory Committee of Experts; Joint FAO/
UNICEF Policy Committee; FAO/WHO Com-
mittee of Experts on Nutrition; FAO Desert
Locust Control Committee; FAO Committee
of Experts on Pesticides in Agriculture; FAO
Fisheries Committee for the Eastern Central
Atlantic; Advisory Committee of Experts on
Marine Resources and Research (ACMRR);
Panel of Experts on Animal Nutrition; Panel
of Experts on Integrated Pest Control.

In addition, FAO participates in the Consultative Group on International Agricultural Research and the Consultative Group on Food
Production and Investment in Developing
Countries, both joint World Bank-FAO-UNDP
groups listed separately in this book.

Technical and financial assistance
Through its regional offices and country staffs,
FAO provides a wide range of technical assistance and funds for development projects in
over 125 countries and territories.  UNDP
provides over half of the funding for these
field activities, which had a total aid allocation of $567.5 million in 1975.

Projects include training, applied research,
comprehensive development planning, and
demonstration activities in agriculture and
fisheries.

The FAO Investment Centre promotes investment in agriculture in developing countries
by identifying and preparing projects for financing by various international banks and funding
agencies, particularly the World Bank.

The FAO Industry Cooperative Programme
(ICP) promotes cooperation between world
business and UN agencies in agricultural development.

The World Food Programme, sponsored jointly
by FAO and the United Nations itself, is listed
separately in this book.

Secretariat
The FAO Secretariat includes a Development
Department (which includes the Investment
Centre and Industry Cooperation Programme);
Economic and Social Policy Department (with
divisions of Commodities and Trade; Human
Resources and Industries; Food Policy and
Nutrition; Policy Analysis; and Statistics);
Agriculture Department (with divisions of
Land and Water Development; Agricultural
Services; Plant Production and Protection;
Animal Production and Health; and a Joint
Division of Atomic Energy in Food and Agri-
culture with the International Atomic Energy
Agency); Fisheries Department (with divisions
of Fishery Resources; Fishery Economics and
Institutions; and Fishery Industries); Forestry
Department; and various administrative units.

Public education and publications
FAO's Freedom from Hunger Campaign/Action
for Development (FFHC/AD), carried out in
cooperation with over 100 non-governmental
organizations, aims to enlarge public consciousness of the extent and causes of world hunger
and poverty; it also raises funds for special
projects in developing countries through public
contributions.

FAO publishes a large number of periodicals,
monographs, meeting reports, manuals, maps,
official records, and reference materials.
A catalog, FAO Books in Print, is issued
annually.  A Bibliographic Catalogue (1976)
lists publications issued since 1945.  The
FAO Documentation Centre in Rome produces
a monthly Current Bibliography of FAO publications, and retrospective Special Indexes by
subject.

The International Information System for the
Agricultural Sciences and Technology (AGRIS),
part of FAO, publishes AGRINDEX, a monthly
bibliography of the latest agricultural literature, arranged by subject.

Other periodicals include: Ceres: FAO Review
on Development, bimon.  The State of Food
and Agriculture, ann.  FAO Plant Protection
Bulletin, bimon.  World Animal Review, q.
Animal Health Yearbook.  Monthly Bulletin of
Agricultural Economics and Statistics.  Production Yearbook.  Trade Yearbook.  FAO Commodity Review and Outlook, bienn.  World Grain

Trade Statistics: Exports by Source and Destination, ann.  Annual Fertilizer Review. Aquatic Sciences and Fisheries Abstracts, mon. Yearbook of Fishery Statistics.  Food and Nutrition: A Quarterly Review Devoted to World Development in Food Policies and Nutrition, q.  Food and Agricultural Legislation, q.

Selected series of publications:

World food situation: World Food Problems series (information booklets on such topics as rice, world agriculture, and pollution).  World Food Program Studies.  Freedom from Hunger Campaign Basic Studies series.

Agriculture: FAO Atomic Energy Series. Better Farming Series (instructional material for village-level extension work).  FAO Agricultural Studies series.  FAO Agricultural Development Papers.

Economics and statistics: FAO Commodity Policy Studies series.  FAO Marketing Guides series.  Commodity Bulletin Series.  Commodity Reports series (grain, rice, meat, etc.). Commodity Reference Series (statistics and bibliography).

Fisheries: FAO Fisheries Studies series. FAO Manuals in Fisheries Science.

Nutrition: FAO Nutritional Studies series (including surveys of maize, legumes, wheat, and dairy products in human nutrition).  FAO Nutrition Meetings Report Series.

Other: FAO Legislative Series.  Reports of FAO Conferences.

Selected monographs related to the world food crisis:

Food Aid: A Selective Annotated Bibliography on Food Utilization for Economic Development (1964).  International Directory of Agricultural Engineering Institutions (1973).  Guide to Extension Training (1966).  Fish in Nutrition (1962).  Atlas of the Living Resources of the Sea (1972).  The Fish Resources of the Ocean (1971).  Encouraging the Use of Protein-Rich Foods (1974).  Visual Aids in Nutrition Education: A Guide to Their Preparation and Use

(1971).  Human Nutrition in Tropical Africa (1965).  Nutrition in Relation to Agricultural Production (1971).  Grain Legumes in Africa (1966).

FAO regional offices:

+FAO Regional Office for Africa
P. O. Box 1628
Accra, Ghana

+FAO Regional Office for Asia and the
  Far East
Maliwan Mansion, Phra Atit Road
Bangkok, Thailand

+FAO Regional Office for Latin America
Casilla 10095
Santiago, Chile

+FAO Regional Office for the Near East
P. O. Box 2223
Cairo, Egypt

+FAO Liaison Office for North America
1776 F Street, N. W.
Washington, D. C. 20437     202-634-6215
    Pub.: Notes for North America, irreg.

+FAO Liaison Office for the United Nations
United Nations Headquarters, Room 2258
New York, New York 10017

See also: Regional economic commissions, listed under Economic and Social Council of the United Nations.

Major FAO commissions:

+Indo-Pacific Fisheries Council (IPFC)
Maliwan Mansion, Phra Atit Road
Bangkok, Thailand         817844

Est. 1948.  Concerned with the biological, environmental, scientific, and technical aspects of the problems of development and proper utilization of living aquatic resources of both marine and fresh waters in the Indian Ocean-West Pacific region. Advisory and coordinating body.  Pub.: Proceedings of conferences.  Classified Directory of Fisheries Technological Research Institutions and Programmes in the IPFC Region (1974).

+General Fisheries Council for the
  Mediterranean (GFCM)
Via delle Terme di Caracalla
00100 Rome, Italy                5797, ext. 616

Est. 1952.  Identifies fisheries problems
in the Mediterranean and contiguous waters
(including the Black Sea) and seeks solutions through coordinating and undertaking
research; exchange of information; and
training. Pub.: Proceedings of conferences; technical studies.

+International Rice Commission (IRC)
AGPC, FAO Headquarters
Via delle Terme de Caracalla
00100 Rome, Italy                5797, ext. 3639

Est. 1948.  Members are governments of
some 45 countries.  Promotes cooperative action by member countries in matters
relating to the production, conservation,
distribution, and consumption of rice,
except matters relating to international
trade.  Pub.: International Rice Commission Newsletter, semiann.

INTERNATIONAL BANK FOR RECONSTRUC-
TION AND DEVELOPMENT (IBRD) (The
World Bank)
1818 H Street, N.W.
Washington, D.C. 20433           202-393-6360

Est. 1944.  The IBRD and its affiliates, the
International Development Association (IDA)
and the International Finance Corporation
(IFC), are collectively known as the World
Bank Group.  Members are governments of
127 countries.

The purposes of the Bank are to assist in the
reconstruction and development of its member
countries by facilitating the investment of
capital for productive purposes; to make loans
for productive purposes out of its own funds
when private capital is not available on reaso-
nable terms; and to promote private foreign
investment by guarantees of and participation
in loans and investments made by private inves-
tors.

IDA was organized specifically to provide financing for development projects in less developed
countries on concessionary terms.  IFC makes

direct investments in projects that either
establish new businesses, or expand, modify,
or diversify existing businesses in the developing countries.

The Bank granted loans in fiscal year 1975
totaling $2.096 billion; at the end of the year,
it held loans in the amount of $22.322 billion.
IDA disbursements during the same year were
$1.0 billion; aggregate disbursements totaled
$4.953 billion at the end of the year.

Agriculture accounted for 32% of all of the
Bank's commitments in 1975.  More than half
of all Bank and IDA commitments for agriculture - involving nearly $1 billion - were for
rural development projects designed specifically
to increase the productivity of the rural poor.
Examples of such projects: Dairy development
projects in two states in India, where village
cattle owners will be organized into dairy
cooperatives which, in turn, will be grouped
into milk producers' unions; quality cross-
breeding, animal health improvement, and the
development of facilities for milk collection,
processing, and marketing are included.  A
series of projects in Nigeria to develop oil
palm estates involving 14,000 small landowners
that will produce palm oil for domestic use and
export and benefit some 100,000 people.

Other agricultural projects for which the World
Bank or IDA have granted loans involve research, agricultural credit, fisheries, area
development, and irrigation.

In addition, a number of projects outside the
Bank's agricultural sector relate to food problems: rural electrification, developing fertilizer
industries, and educational projects to increase
skills in rural areas.

Technical assistance is given to developing
countries in the course of planning, processing,
and monitoring its loans.  The Bank's Economic Development Institute (EDI) trains nationals
of developing countries in economic management and project analysis; the program includes
material on agriculture and rural development.

The Bank has organized a number of aid coordination mechanisms for countries and regions,
and participates in the Consultative Group on
International Agricultural Research and the

Consultative Group on Food Production and Investment in Developing Countries (both listed separately in this book).

The Bank's Research Program focuses on such topics as income distribution and employment, population, and rural and urban development.

In addition to regional departments, the Bank has an Agriculture and Rural Development Department and a Population and Nutrition Projects Department. Field operations are carried out through regional and country missions (see below). The Bank has loans outstanding to some 85 countries.

Pub.: Annual Report. Sector Policy Paper series, including Land Reform; Agricultural Credit; and Rural Development (all 1973). World Bank Paper series, including Rural Electrification (1975). World Bank Atlas: Population, Per Capita Product, and Growth Rates (1975). Quarterly financial statements.

World Bank offices:

+New York Office, World Bank
120 Broadway, 15th Floor
New York, New York 10005

+World Bank Office at the UN
United Nations Headquarters, Room 2245
New York, New York 10017

+World Bank European Office
66, avenue d'Iena
75116 Paris, France

+World Bank London Office
New Zealand House, 15th Floor
Haymarket
London SW1 Y4TE, England

+World Bank Tokyo Office
Kokusai Building
1-1 Marunouchi 3-Chome, Chiyoda-ku
Tokyo 100, Japan

+World Bank Regional Mission for
Eastern Africa
Extelcoms House, Haile Selassie Avenue
Nairobi, Kenya

+World Bank Regional Mission for Western
Africa
B.P. 1850
Abidjan, Ivory Coast

+World Bank Resident Mission
P.O. Box 211
Kabul, Afghanistan

+World Bank Resident Mission
G.P.O. Box 97
Dacca, Bangladesh

+World Bank Resident Mission
B.P. 1128
Yaounde, Cameroon

+World Bank Resident Mission
Edificio Aseguradora del Valle
Carrera 10, No. 24-55, Piso 17
Bogota D.E., Colombia

+World Bank Resident Mission
P.O. Box 5515
Addis Ababa, Ethiopia

+World Bank Resident Mission
P.O. Box M27
Accra, Ghana

+World Bank Resident Mission
P.O. Box 416
New Delhi 3, India

+World Bank Resident Staff
P.O. Box 324/JKT
Jakarta, Indonesia

+World Bank Resident Mission
P.O. Box 798
Kathmandu, Nepal

+World Bank Resident Mission
P.O. Box 127
Lagos, Nigeria

+World Bank Resident Mission
P.O. Box 1025
Islamabad, Pakistan

+World Bank Resident Mission
P.O. Box 2211
Khartoum, Sudan

+<u>World Bank Resident Mission</u>
P.O. Box 2054
Dar es Salaam, Tanzania

+<u>World Bank Resident Mission</u>
Udom Vidhya Building
956 Rama IV Road, Sala Daengh
Bangkok, Thailand

+<u>World Bank Resident Mission</u>
B.P. 622
Ouagadougou, Upper Volta

+<u>World Bank Resident Mission</u>
Centro Andres Bello
Avenida Andres Bello, 113-E
Caracas, Venezuela

+<u>World Bank Resident Mission</u>
B.P. 14816
Kinshasa 1, Zaire

+<u>World Bank Resident Mission</u>
P.O. Box 4410
Lusaka, Zambia

<u>GENERAL AGREEMENT ON TARIFFS AND
 TRADE</u> (GATT)
Palais des Nations
1211 Geneva 10, Switzerland      34-60-11

Est. 1948.  A multilateral treaty and and an
autonomous organization related to the United
Nations through the Economic and Social
Council.  Contracting parties account for over
4/5 of international trade.  The Agreement
itself and the body of case law developed by
the contracting parties constitute a general
code of conduct covering virtually the whole
field of commercial relations among the parties.
GATT is also a principal forum for working
out the terms of liberalization of trade.  Scope
includes food products.

Pub.: <u>International Trade</u>, ann.  <u>GATT Activi-
ties</u>, ann.  <u>GATT Studies in International
Trade</u> series.

<u>UNITED NATIONS EDUCATIONAL,
 SCIENTIFIC AND CULTURAL
 ORGANIZATION</u> (UNESCO)
Place de Fontenoy
75007 Paris, France              566-57-57

Est. 1945.  Activities include promoting
international cooperation in the natural and
social sciences by organizing meetings of
scientists, assisting activities of international
scientific organizations, and facilitating
exchange of scientific information.

UNESCO programs related to world food
problems include the <u>Man and the Biosphere
Programme</u> (MAB), whose objective is to
develop the scientific basis "for rational use
and conservation of the biosphere, and for
the improvement of the global relationship
between man and the environment." MAB's
focus is on non-oceanic ecosystems.  Its
projects have included studies of the impact
of agricultural activities on various kinds of
environments, such as tropical forest and
grassland.

In the field of marine science, UNESCO's
<u>Office of Oceanography</u> conducts its own
program, and also serves as secretariat for
the <u>Intergovernmental Oceanographic Commis-
sion</u> (IOC), which coordinates international
scientific investigation of the nature and
resources of the oceans.

The UNESCO <u>Ecological Programme</u> includes
such projects as an interagency project with
FAO and WMO in agricultural biometeorology.

The UNESCO <u>Co-operative Action Programme</u>
(Co-Action) permits individuals and members
of voluntary associations to participate in
funding projects in developing countries, many
of which relate to food.  National sponsoring
organizations issue blank checks in Unums
("Unesco Units of Money"), a means of facilitating the transfer of funds from one country
to another.  The donor selects a project of
his or her choice from a catalog, and then
makes it out and sends it directly to those
responsible for the chosen project (the checks
are not transferable).  Receipt is acknow-
ledged personally, usually with further details
on how the contribution will be used, and thus
communication is established between "Co-

Action Partners. "

UNESCO publications include: <u>UNESCO Chronicle</u>, mon.  <u>UNESCO Courier</u>, mon.  <u>Co-Action Newsletter</u>, ann.  <u>Impact of Science on Society</u>, q.  Monographs, bibliographies, etc.

<u>UNESCO regional science offices:</u>

+<u>UNESCO Field Science Office for Africa</u>
P.O. Box 30592
Nairobi, Kenya

+<u>UNESCO Field Science Office for Latin America</u>
P.O. Box 859
Montevideo, Uruguay

+<u>UNESCO Field Science Office for the Arab States</u>
8, Sh El Salamlik, Garden City
Cairo, Egypt

+<u>UNESCO Field Science Office for South Asia</u>
Unesco House, 40-B, Lodhi Estate
New Delhi 3, India

+<u>UNESCO Field Science Office for South East Asia</u>
Djalam Imam Bondjol 30, 273/DKJ
  Tromolpos
Jakarta, Indonesia

<u>WORLD HEALTH ORGANIZATION</u> (WHO)
1211 Geneva 27, Switzerland     34-60-61

Est. 1946.  Governed by the annual World Health Assembly and a 24-member Executive Board.  WHO's general objective is "the attainment of all peoples of the highest possible level of health."  Health is defined as "a state of complete physical, mental, and social well-being and not merely the absence of disease or infirmity."

Nutritional activities have been a part of WHO's health assistance programs in developing countries for many years.  In 1972, however, it was decided to strengthen the agency's nutrition element.

The nutrition program, part of the <u>Division of Family Health</u>, focuses focuses on five priority areas:

-- <u>National surveillance and monitoring</u> to identify populations needing immediate attention and, where possible, to predict any sudden deterioration of the nutritional situation so that preventive measures may be taken.  This activity takes the form of anthropometric surveys, national nutrition surveys, and setting up systems of nutritional surveillance through health centers in developing countries.

-- <u>National food and nutrition policy.</u>  WHO facilitates adoption of such policies through establishing guidelines, training, and sending interdisciplinary technical assistance teams.

-- <u>Nutrition and local health services.</u>  Governments are encouraged to integrate nutrition activities with their basic health services.

-- <u>Measures against specific deficiency diseases.</u>  Protein-calorie malnutrition, anemia, endemic goiter, and other diseases resulting from poor nutrition continue to be major health problems in almost all developing countries.  In collaboration with FAO and UNICEF, WHO has increased its assistance to countries in overcoming these problems with the help of new methods based on the use of unconventional sources of protein, peanut flour, cottonseed flour, and foods fortified with amino acids and vitamins.  WHO also supports research in the field.

-- <u>Training of professionals in nutrition.</u>

WHO has programs in nearly every developing country.  Its annual budget in 1974 was $211.5 million.  Field projects are carried out through regional offices (listed below).  There is an <u>Expert Committee on Nutrition</u>.

WHO publications include: <u>World Health</u>, bimon., a popular magazine.  <u>WHO Chronicle</u>, mon., containing information for health professionals.  <u>Bulletin of the World Health Organization</u>, 2 vols. per year, containing original scientific articles.  <u>International Digest of Health Legislation</u>, q.  <u>World Health Statistics Report</u>, mon.  <u>World Health Statistics Annual.</u>

Various series of technical reports are issued, as well as directories, bibliographies, and manuals.  WHO's publications catalog lists some 40 titles in nutrition.

WHO regional offices:

+WHO Regional Office for Africa
B.P. 6
Brazzaville, Congo

+WHO Regional Office for the Americas/ Pan American Sanitary Bureau
525 23rd Street, N.W.
Washington, D.C. 20037

+WHO Regional Office for the Eastern Mediterranean
P.O. Box 1517
Alexandria, Egypt

+WHO Regional Office for Europe
8 Schefigsvej
2100 Copenhagen Ø, Denmark

+WHO Regional Office for South-East Asia
World Health House, Indraprastha Estate
Ring Road
New Delhi 1, India

+WHO Regional Office for the Western Pacific
P.O. Box 2932
12115 Manila, Philippines

+WHO Liaison Office with the United Nations
United Nations
New York, New York 10017

INTERNATIONAL ATOMIC ENERGY AGENCY (IAEA)
P.O. Box 590
1011 Vienna, Austria          52-45-11

Est. 1957.  Governed by an annual General Conference of all member states (over 100), and a 25-member Board of Governors.

General purposes are "to seek to accelerate and enlarge the contribution of atomic energy to peace, health and prosperity throughout the world" and "to ensure that assistance provided by it...is not used in such a way as to further any military purpose."

In 1964, the IAEA and FAO combined forces in a Joint Division of Atomic Energy in Food and Agriculture.  This division works to develop high-protein strains and varieties of plants, to confer disease resistance characteristics on some crops, and to improve animal health.  It supports some 200 projects in member states.

Accomplishments of the division include producing higher-yielding, earlier-maturing, and stronger-stemmed rice plants; developing the sterile-insect release method of pest control; and determining optimum use of phosphate and nitrogen fertilizers.

Pub.: Atomic Energy Review, q.  Technical reports and proceedings of meetings, including titles on entomology, agronomy, food preservation, plant breeding, and animal science. Annual Report.  Publications Catalog, annual.

WORLD METEOROLOGICAL ORGANIZATION (WMO)
41, avenue Giuseppe- Motta
1211 Geneva 20, Switzerland    34-64-00

Est. 1947.  Governed by the World Meteorological Congress, composed of representatives of some 135 member governments, and held at least every four years; and an Executive Committee of 24.

General purposes are to facilitate worldwide cooperation in meteorology and further its application to aviation, shipping, water problems, agriculture, and other human activities.

WMO's main program areas are the World Weather Watch (WWW), research and training, the interaction of man and his environment, and technical cooperation.  WMO conducts the Global Atmospheric Research Program (GARP) jointly with the International Council of Scientific Unions; training and research under GARP focuses on enabling developing countries to participate more fully in international meteorological activities.

# WORLD FOOD CONFERENCE OF 1974

The World Food Conference, held in Rome, Italy in November 1974, was the third in a series of major United Nations Conferences which have become important means of focusing international attention on problems of a global nature, and of developing international policies and programs to meet those problems. The first in the series was the UN Conference on the Human Environment (Stockholm, 1972); the second was the World Population Conference (Bucharest, Romania, 1974).

The World Food Conference adopted a declaration and 22 resolutions laying the groundwork for an overall strategy to attack the world food problem.

The Universal Declaration on the Eradication of Hunger and Malnutrition states, among other things, that "Every man, woman and child has the inalienable right to be free from hunger and malnutrition in order to develop fully and maintain their physical and mental faculties... It is a fundamental responsibility of Governments to work together for higher food production and a more equitable and efficient distribution of food between countries and within countries."

Resolutions adopted by the Conference cover such topics as: objectives and strategies of food production; priorities for agricultural and rural development; fertilizers; food and agricultural research, extension, and training; policies and programs to improve nutrition; land capability assessment and establishing a World Soil Charter; scientific water management; population; women; pesticides; a global information and early warning system on food and agriculture; improved policy for food aid; international trade.

The main results of the World Food Conference were establishment of the UN International Fund for Agricultural Development (IFAD); the Consultative Group on Food Production and Investment in Developing Countries (CGFPI); a Committee on World Food Security within FAO; and the World Food Council. (Each of these new groups is listed separately in this book.)

The main strategy adopted by the Conference is to increase food production in the developing countries to at least 3.6% per year, and perhaps 4.0% per year, during the next decade. This depends on an increased flow of resources for food production from the developed to the developing countries. The goal is $5 billion per year.

Another proposal of the Conference was the International Undertaking on World Food Security (to be administered by FAO).

The Report of the World Food Conference, issued in 1975, is available from United Nations Publications, LX-2300, New York, New York 10017.

The Subcommittee on Foreign Agricultural Policy of the Committee on Agriculture and Forestry of the U.S. House of Representatives issued in 1975 a report, Hunger and Diplomacy: A Perspective on the U.S. Role at the World Food Conference.

Pan: Newspaper of the World Food Conference, published by ICVA with financial support from various non-governmental organizations, gave an independent view of the Conference proceedings.

WMO maintains a Committee on Agricultural Meteorology (CAgM). Its activities in this field include coordinating and regulating the application of meteorology to agriculture; developing means of using meteorological information and forecasts for protection of crops against insect pests and plant diseases; participating in international locust control efforts; and studies of the effects of weather modification.

A major interest has been climatic change and its effects on human activity, including agriculture. In a statement issued in 1976, WMO stated that "In view of the increasing importance of the inherent shorter-term variability of climate to many human activities, greater use should be made of existing knowledge of this variability in planning for economic and social development; for example, an assessment of the probability of occurence of rainfall within given ranges can provide an assessment of the viability of proposed agricultural or hydrological projects... Further research in climatic change is therefore of the greatest importance."

Pub.: WMO Bulletin, q. Technical reports, including studies in agricultural meteorology, for example: Drought and Agriculture (1975). Agricultural Meteorology (1972). An Introduction to Agrotopoclimatology (1974). Agrometeorology of the Wheat Crop (1974).

# C. OTHER INTERGOVERNMENTAL ORGANIZATIONS

AFRO-ASIAN RURAL RECONSTRUCTION ORGANIZATION (AARRO)
C-117/118, Defence Colony
New Delhi 110024, India

Est. 1962. General purposes are to develop understanding among member countries (some 24 in Africa and Asia) of each others' problems and explore collectively opportunities for coordination of efforts for promoting welfare and eradication of hunger and poverty among rural peoples in the two continents.

AARRO's work program for 1975-77 includes an integrated rural development project in the Sudan, Egypt, the Philippines, and South

Korea; and various regional seminars and training projects in rural development, emphasizing such topics as cooperatives, agricultural extension, and animal husbandry. Total budget for the three-year period is $235,900. Funding is provided by the more affluent members (e.g., Japan and Korea), International Cooperative Aloiance, and the League of Arab States, as well as other sources.

Maintains regional offices at Amman, Jordan; Addis Ababa, Ethiopia; Seoul, Korea; and Accra, Ghana. Pub.: Rural Reconstruction (journal), q. Conference proceedings and reports, for example: Comparative Study of Community Development Programmes in Afro-Asian Countries (1968). Directory of Professional Organizations of Farmers in Afro-Asian Countries (1968). Cooperative Movements in Afro-Asian Countries (1968).

ASIAN DEVELOPMENT BANK (ADB)
P.O. Box 789
Manila 2800, Philippines       80-72-51

Est. 1966. Members are some 35 governments of countries in Asia and Oceania, as well as in Europe and North America. An international development finance institution established for the purpose of lending funds, promoting investment, and providing technical assistance to developing member countries and, generally, for fostering economic growth and cooperation in the Asian region. Grants loans to agricultural projects. Pub.: Quarterly Review. Annual Report. Technical reports.

ASIAN DEVELOPMENT CENTER (ADC)
Philbanking Corp. Building, 11th Floor
Anda Circle, Port Area
Manila, Philippines       496024

Est. 1969. Affiliated with the Asian Parliamentarians' Union (APU). Serves legislative bodies of member countries of APU in their efforts to strengthen, intensify, and promote regional cooperation in economic and social development. Conducts studies and recommends policies and programs for regional cooperation in various fields, including agriculture. Pub.: Annual summary report.

## CARIBBEAN FOOD AND NUTRITION INSTITUTE (CFNI)
P.O. Box 140
Kingston 7, Jamaica          78338

Est. 1967.  Members are the 17 English-speaking countries of the Caribbean.  Works with and to augment existing national, international, and voluntary efforts in the region toward improvement of the food and nutrition situation.  Training (including a 1-year community nutrition course, and courses and workshops in food economics, food and nutrition policy, etc.); research (e.g., outpatient treatment of malnutrition; nutrition and working efficiency among sugar cane cutters); technical and advisory services (e.g., national food and nutrition surveys; seminars; technical group meetings).

Pub.: Cajanus, bimon.  Nutrient-Cost Tables, q.  Technical studies, manuals, etc., including: Protein Foods for the Caribbean. Human Resources Survey in Nutrition, Dietetics and Home Economics in the Caribbean.

+Trinidad Centre, Caribbean Food and Nutrition Institute
University of the West Indies Campus
St. Augustine, Trinidad      662-5510

## CARIBBEAN DEVELOPMENT BANK
P.O. Box 408
Bridgetown, Barbados          61152

Est. 1969.  Members are 17 countries in the Caribbean region, plus Canada and the U.K. Promotes economic growth and development of member countries by granting loans for various purposes, including agriculture.  Pub.: Annual Report.

## COLOMBO PLAN COUNCIL FOR TECHNICAL CO-OPERATION IN SOUTH AND SOUTH-EAST ASIA
Colombo Plan Bureau, P.O. Box 596
Colombo, Sri Lanka (Ceylon)      81813

Est. 1950.  The Colombo Plan was established by the British Commonwealth; subsequently, other Southeast Asian countries, Japan, and the U.S. joined.  Its purpose is to provide capital aid and technical assistance to developing member countries (all in Asia, except

Fiji) within a cooperative framework.  Aid has included grants and loans for agricultural projects and training and experts in agriculture. Pub.: Colombo Plan Newsletter, mon.  Annual Report.

## COMMONWEALTH AGRICULTURAL BUREAUX (CAB)
Farnham House, Farnham Royal
Slough SL2 3BN, England          Common 2281

A cooperative venture of the Commonwealth nations to provide a scientific information service for agricultural research workers. Members are the governments of the U.K., Canada, Australia, New Zealand, India, Pakistan, Sri Lanka, Ghana, Malaysia, Nigeria, Cyprus, Sierra Leone, Tanzania, Jamaica, Trinidad and Tobago, Uganda, Kenya, Malawi, Zambia, the Gambia, Guyana, Barbados, Rhodesia, and the dependent territories; Ireland is an associate member.

CAB's 4 institutes and 11 bureaus have as their main function providing abstracts of world literature covering the whole range of agriculture and related fields.  Their abstract journals circulate even more widely in non-Commonwealth than in Commonwealth countries.  In addition, the bureaus publish books, monographs, and pamphlets; provide reference services; arrange meetings; and have related functions.

In addition to the institutes and services listed separately below, CAB includes the following: Commonwealth Institute of Entomology; Commonwealth Mycological Institute; Commonwealth Institute of Biological Control; Commonwealth Bureau of Animal Breeding and Genetics; Commonwealth Bureau of Animal Health; Commonwealth Bureau of Animal Nutrition; Commonwealth Bureau of Dairy Science and Technology; Commonwealth Forestry Bureau; Commonwealth Bureau of Helminthology; Commonwealth Bureau of Horticulture and Plantation Crops; Commonwealth Bureau of Pastures and Field Crops; Commonwealth Bureau of Plant Breeding and Genetics; Commonwealth Bureau of Soils.

The International Food Information Service (IFIS), sponsored jointly by CAB, the Institute of Food Technologists, and German and Dutch organizations, publishes Food Science and

Technology Abstracts, mon. (covering 1300 journals), and Food Annotated Bibliographies, irreg. It also provides current awareness and computer search services.

The 2 CAB units most relevant to the world food crisis are:

+Commonwealth Bureau of Agricultural
   Economics
Dartington House, Little Clarendon Street
Oxford OX1 2HH          0865-59829

Est. 1966. Pub.: World Agricultural Economics and Rural Sociology Abstracts, mon. (each issue has over 6,000 abstracts). Annotated Bibliographies series (list available), including such titles as The Green Revolution (1973); Arid Land Agriculture (1974), and Oilseeds (1974).

+Commonwealth Bureau of Nutrition
c/o Rowett Research Institute
Bucksburn
Aberdeen AB2 9SB, Scotland

Pub.: Nutrition Abstracts and Reviews, mon. (covers human and animal nutrition "in the broadest sense").

COUNCIL FOR MUTUAL ECONOMIC
   ASSISTANCE (CMEA) (Comecon)
Kalinin Prospekt 56
Moscow G-205, U.S.S.R.          290-91-11

Est. 1949. Promotes economic cooperation among countries with centrally-planned economies: USSR, Bulgaria, Czechoslovakia, East Germany, Hungary, Poland, Romania, Cuba, and Mongolia, with Yugoslavia participating in some areas. Almost all aid from Comecon countries to the developing world has been bilateral. In 1973, however, they decided to set up a special fund equivalent to $1.3 billion to extend loans at low rates of interest to non-communist developing states. The fund is administered by the International Investment Bank in Moscow. Comecon also supports training of nationals of developing countries in Soviet and Eastern European institutions. Pub.: Annual Report. International Agricultural Review.

DESERT LOCUST CONTROL ORGANIZATION
   FOR EASTERN AFRICA (DLCO-EA)
P.O. Box 4255
Addis Ababa, Ethiopia

Est. 1962. Members are the governments of Ethiopia, Kenya, Somalia, Sudan, Tanzania, Uganda, and Djibouti. Promotes control of the desert locust in its region; coordinates and assists national action programs. Pub.: Desert Locust Situation Reports. Technical reports.

EAST AFRICAN AGRICULTURE AND
   FORESTRY RESEARCH ORGANIZATION
   (EAAFRO)
P.O. Box 30148
Nairobi, Kenya

Est. 1948. Members are the governments of Kenya, Tanzania, and Uganda. Conducts research in basic and applied agricultural fields; advises the 3 governments on agricultural research. Pub.: East African Agricultural and Forestry Journal, q. Record of Research, ann. Scientific papers.

EAST AFRICAN FRESHWATER FISHERIES
   RESEARCH ORGANIZATION (EAFFRO)
P.O. Box 343
Jinja, Uganda          20484

Est. 1946. Members are the governments of Kenya, Tanzania, and Uganda. Conducts research on the fish resources of East African inland lakes and other freshwater bodies; advises the 3 governments on freshwater fisheries exploitation. Pub.: African Journal of Tropical Hydrobiology and Fisheries. Annual Report.

EAST AFRICAN MARINE FISHERIES
   RESEARCH ORGANIZATION (EAMFRO)
P.O. Box 668
Zanzibar, Tanzania          2702

Est. 1951. Members are the governments of Kenya, Tanzania, and Uganda. Conducts research on the commercial marine fisheries of East Africa; advises the member governments on regulation and development of the resource. Pub.: Annual Report.

## EUROPEAN AND MEDITERRANEAN PLANT PROTECTION ORGANIZATION (EPPO)
1, rue LeNôtre
75016 Paris, France          870-77-94

Est. 1951.  Members are governments of countries in Europe and the Mediterranean region, including the USSR.  Promotes international cooperation in preventing the spread of pests and diseases of plants and plant products, including rodents; facilitates cooperation in research in the field.  Pub.: EPPO Bulletin, q.  EPPO Publications Series C, 3-4 times a year.  EPPO Newsletter, 3-4 times a year.

## EUROPEAN COMMUNITIES
Commission of the European Communities
200, rue de la Loi
1049 Brussels, Belgium          735-00-40

The European Communities are entities of 9 member countries: Belgium, Federal Republic of Germany, France, Italy, Luxembourg, Netherlands, Denmark, Ireland, and United Kingdom.  In law, there are 3 separate communities: European Coal and Steel Community (ECSC), est. 1951; European Economic Community (EEC), est. 1957; and European Atomic Energy Community (EURATOM), est. 1957.  They share the same institutions, which include the European Parliament, the Commission, and the Court of Justice.

The Communities' responsibilities are not restricted to the 9 member states.  In the founding Treaty of Rome, provision was made for a special associate relationship between the EEC and overseas territories linked to members of the original 6 EEC states (Belgium, West Germany, France, Italy, Luxembourg, and the Netherlands).  This included preferential trade relations with EEC countries, and access to EEC capital and aid.

As a result of Britain, Denmark, and Ireland joining the Community in 1973, and subsequent international agreements, there are now some 60 developing countries "associated" with the EEC.  The Community's objectives toward them, as stated in the Treaty of Rome, are to promote "the economic and social development and the furtherance of the interests and prosperity of the inhabitants of the associated countries in such a way as to lead them to such economic and social and cultural development as they expect."

The main instrument of the Communities' development aid policy is the European Development Fund (EDF), established in 1957.  The Fund gives non-repayable grants to the governments of the associated countries for various purposes, including agricultural development, but in 1974 44% of its disbursements (or $260 million) were for food aid.  In addition to their contributions to the EDF, most EEC countries also have significant aid programs of their own.

Pub.: Bulletin of the European Communities, mon.  Euroforum: Europe Day by Day.  Numerous studies, reports, and other publications.

In addition to maintaining offices in the member countries, the European Communities have the following information offices:

+European Communities Press and Information Office
Casilla 10093
Santiago 9, Chile          25-05-55

+European Communities Press and Information Office
Vassilisis Sofias 2
Athens, Greece          743-982

+European Communities Press and Information Office
Kowa 25 Building
8-7 Sanbancho, Chiyoda-ku
Tokyo 102, Japan          239-0441

+European Communities Press and Information Office
37-39, rue de Vermont
1202 Geneva, Switzerland   34-97-50

+European Communities Press and Information Office
Kavaklidere
13, Bogaz Sokak
Ankara, Turkey          27-61-45

+European Communities Press and
  Information Office
2100 M Street, N.W., Suite 707
Washington, D.C. 20037     202-872-8350

+European Communities Press and
  Information Office
277 Park Avenue
New York, New York 10017
                           212-371-3804

+European Communities Press and
  Information Office
Casilla 641
Montevideo, Uruguay        98-42-42

INSTITUTE OF NUTRITION OF CENTRAL
  AMERICA AND PANAMA (INCAP)
Apartado Postal 11-88
Guatemala, Guatemala       43765

Est. 1946.  Members are the governments of
Costa Rica, El Salvador, Guatemala, Honduras, Nicaragua, and Panama.  Research;
training; preparation of nutrition education
materials; technical assistance to projects
in member states.  Pub.: Annual report,
monographs, and documents.

INTER-AMERICAN COMMITTEE FOR CROP
  PROTECTION (CIPA)
Avenida Pueyrredon 1959, 13 piso A
Buenos Aires, Argentina    82-7077

Est. 1965. Promotes cooperation in combating
diseases affecting agriculture in member
countries (Argentina, Bolivia, Brazil, Chile,
Paraguay, and Uruguay).

INTER-AMERICAN DEVELOPMENT BANK
  (IDB)
808 17th Street, N.W.
Washington, D.C. 20577     202-393-4171

Est. 1959.  Members are the governments of
some 25 countries in the Western Hemisphere.
Works for the economic development of the
region by granting loans, about one-fifth of
which have been for agricultural projects.
Pub.: Annual Report.  Proceedings of annual
meetings.  Annual survey of socio-economic
progress in Latin America.

INTER-AMERICAN TROPICAL TUNA
  COMMISSION (IATTC)
c/o Scripps Institution of Oceanography
University of California
La Jolla, California 92037     714-453-2820

Est. 1949.  Members are the governments of
the USA, Costa Rica, Canada, France, Japan,
Mexico, Nicaragua, and Panama.  Purposes
are to study and conserve the tunas and tuna-
baitfishes of the eastern tropical Pacific.
Pub.: Annual Report.  Numerous technical
reports (list available).

INTERNATIONAL AFRICAN MIGRATORY
  LOCUST ORGANISATION (OICMA)
B.P. 136
Bamako, Mali

Est. 1955.  Members are the governments of
some 20 African countries.  Works to destroy
the African migratory locust in breeding areas;
research; surveys.  Pub.: Locusta, mon.
Annual report.

INTERNATIONAL COMMISSION FOR AGRICUL-
  TURAL AND FOODSTUFF INDUSTRIES (CIAA)
24, rue de Teheran
75008 Paris, France        282-2093

Est. 1934.  Members are the governments of
some 12 countries, mainly in Europe, but also
Madagascar, Tunisia, and Mexico.  Associate
members are national or international non-
governmental organizations concerned with the
field.  Main activities are congresses, symposia, and meetings on various topics, including
new protein sources (1968), use of enzymes
(1972), and "the use of natural or synthetic
additives in the feeding of mankind" (1972).
Pub.: Proceedings of conferences.

INTERNATIONAL COMMISSION FOR THE
  CONSERVATION OF ATLANTIC TUNAS
  (ICCAT)
Calle General Mola 17
75 Madrid, Spain           275-85-24

Est. 1969.  Members are the governments of
West African countries; Brazil; the U.S. and
Canada; Japan, Korea; and France, Portugal,
and Spain.  Works toward rational exploitation
of tunas and tuna-like species in the Atlantic to
maintain maximum sustainable catches.

Research; statistical work.  Pub.: Statistical Bulletin.  Biennial reports.

## INTERNATIONAL COMMISSION FOR THE NORTHWEST ATLANTIC FISHERIES
P.O. Box 638
Dartmouth, Nova Scotia B2Y 3Y9, Canada
902-469-9105

Est. 1950.  Members: governments of Bulgaria, Canada, Denmark, France, East Germany, West Germany, Iceland, Italy, Japan, Norway, Poland, Portugal, Romania, Spain, USSR, UK, and USA.  Investigation, protection, and conservation of the fisheries of the northwest Atlantic in order to make possible the maintenance of a maximum sustained catch.  Pub.: Annual Report.  Statistical Bulletin, ann.

## INTERNATIONAL COMMISSION FOR THE SOUTHEAST ATLANTIC FISHERIES
65 Paseo de la Habana
Madrid 16, Spain                458-87-66

Est. 1969.  Members are the governments of South Africa, Japan, Bulgaria, France, Poland, Portugal, Spain, and USSR.  Research and information exchange on the fishery resources of the region; advises member governments on exploitation.  Pub.: Technical reports.

## INTERNATIONAL INSTITUTE OF REFRIGERATION (IIR)
117, boulevard Malesherbes
75017 Paris, France             227-32-35

Est. 1920.  Members are the governments of some 50 countries.  Promotes research and information exchange on scientific, technical, and economic aspects of refrigeration, particularly in the field of food and agriculture.  Concerns include food freezing and applications in tropical countries.  Pub.: Technical Bulletin, bimon.  Proceedings of conferences and meetings.

## INTERNATIONAL INVESTMENT BANK (IIB)
17 Presnensky Val
Moscow D-22, U.S.S.R.

Est. 1970.  See: Council for Mutual Economic Assistance (Comecon).

## INTERNATIONAL NORTH PACIFIC FISHERIES COMMISSION (INPFC)
6640 Northwest Marine Drive
Vancouver, British Columbia V6T 1X2
604-228-1128

Est. 1952.  Members are the governments of Canada, Japan, and the U.S.  Works for the conservation of the fisheries resources of the North Pacific Ocean to ensure maximum sustained productivity.  Coordinates research by national institutions.  Pub.: Annual Report. Statistical Yearbook.  Bulletin, irreg.

## INTERNATIONAL SYSTEM OF SCIENTIFIC AND TECHNICAL INFORMATION IN AGRICULTURE AND FORESTRY
Slezskó 7
Prague 2, Czechoslovakia

Est. 1964.  Part of the Council for Mutual Economic Assistance (Comecon), which see. Promotes cooperation among Eastern European countries and the USSR in the field of scientific and technical information in agriculture and forestry.  Pub.: Bulletin (in Russian and German).

## INTERNATIONAL WHALING COMMISSION (IWC)
Great Westminster House, Room 276
Horseferry Road
London SW1P 2AE, England

Est. 1946.  Members are the governments of Argentina, Australia, Canada, Denmark, France, Iceland, Japan, Mexico, Norway, Panama, South Africa, Sweden, USSR, U.K., and USA.  Promotes "the conservation and rational utilization of the whale resources in the common interest."  Adopts rules for the harvesting of whales.  Pub.: Annual Report. Schedule (regulations).  Research papers.

## INTERNATIONAL WHEAT COUNCIL
Haymarket House, 28 Haymarket
London SW1Y 4SS, England        930-4128

Est. 1949.  Members are the governments of some 60 countries (exporting and importing) and the European Economic Community.  Has administered successive international wheat agreements since 1949.  The present agreement is the International Wheat Agreement, 1971, which consists of two separate legal instruments, the Wheat Trade Convention, 1971, and the Food Aid Convention, 1971. The latter is administered by a Food Aid Committee, which uses the services of the Council.

Objectives of the Agreement include furthering international cooperation on wheat problems; promoting expansion of international trade in wheat and wheat flour; contributing to the stability of the international wheat market; and providing a framework for negotiation of provisions relating to the prices of wheat and the rights and obligations of Council members in the wheat trade.

The Council continuously monitors wheat market conditions and conducts an annual review of the world wheat situation. Pub.: Wheat Market Report, mon. World Wheat Statistics, ann. Review of the World Wheat Situation, ann. Record of Operations, ann. Technical studies.

LEAGUE OF ARAB STATES (LAS) (Arab League)
Mahmud Road, Midan al Tahrir
Cairo, Egypt                              811960

Est. 1945. Members are the governments of 18 Arab countries in Africa and Asia. Among its activities is administering the Special Arab Fund for Africa (SAFA), a special oil relief fund initially funded at $200 million in 1974. Grants have been made to some 20 countries in Africa, with the largest amounts going to those most severely affected by food problems.

NORTH ATLANTIC TREATY
   ORGANIZATION (NATO)
1110 Brussels, Belgium            241-00-40

Est. 1949. Members are the governments of Canada, USA, Belgium, Denmark, France, Federal Republic of Germany, Greece, Iceland, Italy, Luxembourg, Netherlands, Norway, Portugal, Turkey, and United Kingdom. Among NATO's programs is the Committee on the Challenges of Modern Society (CCMS), which was directed in 1969 to examine "how to improve, in every practical way, the exchange of views and experience among the Allied countries in the task of

creating a better environment for their societies...and to consider specific problems of the human environment with the deliberate objective of stimulating action by member governments."

Studies carried out by CCMS are done on the "pilot country method" in which one country takes responsibility for a CCMS-approved project. The pilot country plans the study, pays for it, prepares necessary reports, and encourages implementation of its recommendations. Another country can become a "co-pilot" if it wishes to make a significant contribution to the study, and any other NATO member is welcome to participate.

CCMS has begun a study on "Nutrition and Health," the purpose of which is to identify means of changing people's dietary habits in the interest of health. Canada is the "pilot" country.

Pub.: NATO Review, bimon. CCMS papers.

NORTH-EAST ATLANTIC FISHERIES
   COMMISSION
Great Westminster House, Room 275
Horseferry Road
London SW1P 2AE, England

Est. 1959. Members are the governments of 14 European countries. Purpose is to ensure the conservation of the fish stocks of the Northeast Atlantic and adjacent waters.

ORGANISATION FOR ECONOMIC
   CO-OPERATION AND DEVELOPMENT
   (OECD)
Chateau de la Muette
2, rue Andre Pascal
75775 Paris, Cedex 16, France
                                   524-82-00

Est. 1961. Members are the governments of 24 developed countries: Australia, Austria, Belgium, Canada, Denmark, Finland, France, Federal Republic of Germany, Greece, Iceland, Ireland, Italy, Japan, Luxembourg, Netherlands, New Zealand, Norway, Portugal, Spain, Sweden, Switzerland, Turkey, United Kingdom, USA, and Yugoslavia (which has a special status).

General purposes of OECD are "to promote the highest sustainable economic growth and employment and a rising standard of living in the member countries" and "to contribute to the sound economic expansion of both member and non-member nations which are in the process of development."

OECD members are by far the most important suppliers of financial and technical aid to the developing countries, accounting for about 90% of total official and private flows from all sources (both bilateral and multilateral).

The OECD Development Assistance Committee (DAC) was established to secure an expansion of the volume of financial resources made available to the developing countries and to improve their quality. Members of DAC include the principal industrialized countries of OECD: Australia, Austria, Belgium, Canada, Denmark, Finland, France, West Germany, Italy, Japan, Netherlands, New Zealand, Norway, Portugal, Sweden, Switzerland, the UK, and the USA, as well as the European Economic Community (EEC).

Among the problems studied by DAC are: (1) ways to adapt aid to the requirements of the various sectors and to improve its distribution among the developing countries; (2) progress towards the unifying of aid, the adjustment of financial terms to the possibilities of various recipients, and the study of the debt problems of developing countries; (3) the role to be played by private flows, in particular, investment in promoting development; (4) better programming and management of aid; (5) improving statistics on resource transfers to developing countries.

One of the methods used by DAC is the Annual Aid Review, during which the aid efforts and policies of each of the member countries are intensively examined. The major product of this review is an annual report, Development Co-operation. DAC also maintains the OECD Development Centre (see below).

The OECD Committee for Agriculture and Committee for Fisheries are both served by the Directorate for Agriculture and Food. Their functions are: (1) to assess regularly the short-, medium-, and long-term outlook for demand and supply of food in the world, with particular emphasis on the policy implications of such outlook on the agricultural, trade, and aid policies of OECD countries; (2) to assess member countries' food and agriculture policies, including such aspects as price and incomes policies and commodity arrangements; (3) to assess developments in farm organization, food processing, and marketing; (4) to analyze the reciprocal relationships between the performance of the overall economy and the performance of agriculture; to analyze the food problems of the developing world and to determine the actions which the situation calls for, in particular, to review the aid contributions of DAC member countries for agricultural and food production in developing countries, and the food aid programs of DAC countries.

OECD publishes a large number of documents. OECD Observer, bimon., is a popular magazine. Other periodicals include: OECD Economic Outlook, semiann. OECD Financial Statistics, ann. with bimon. supplements. OECD Economic Surveys (one for each OECD country), ann. Main Economic Indicators, mon. Foreign Trade Statistics (various series). Liaison Bulletin Between Development Research and Training Institutes (including directories of institutes by region), irreg.

The most important publication of DAC is the annual Development Co-operation: Efforts and Policies of the Members of the Development Assistance Committee (which includes coverage of contributions of non-DAC countries, both in and out of OECD).

Series of publications in the development field include: Cost Benefit Analysis series. Development Assistance series. Technical Papers series. Series in the agriculture field include: Agricultural Policy Reports. Agricultural Products and Markets series. Review of Fisheries series.

OECD issues a Catalogue of Publications and a newsletter, Recent Publications. There are branch publications centers in Washington and Tokyo (see below).

+OECD Development Centre
94, rue Chardon-Lagache
75016 Paris, France

A "scientifically independent body" within
OECD, charged with innovation of ideas
and activities related to development
through research on economic policy
problems of developing countries and
experience through meetings.

+OECD Publications Center
1750 Pennsylvania Avenue, N.W.
Washington, D.C. 20006     202-298-8755

+OECD Publications Center
Akasaka Park Building
2-3-4 Akasaka, Minato-ku
Tokyo 107, Japan          03-586-2016

ORGANIZATION OF AMERICAN STATES
  (OAS)
Washington, D.C. 20006         202-393-8450

Est. 1890.  Members are the governments of
24 Western Hemisphere countries.  General
purposes are to strengthen peace and security
in the Americas and to promote economic,
social, and cultural development by cooperative
action.

The Inter-American Economic and Social
Council (IA-ECOSOC), parallel to ECOSOC in
the United Nations system, is concerned with
promoting economic and social development
in the Hemisphere; it is composed of representatives of all OAS member states, and meets
annually.

Major OAS subsidiary bodies concerned with
food problems are listed below.  OAS publishes
Americas, mon. popular magazine, an annual
Report of the Secretary General; Chronicle,
q.; and various conference and technical
documents.

  +Inter-American Committee for
    Agricultural Development (CIDA)
  1725 Eye Street, N.W.
  Washington, D.C. 20006     202-381-8537

  Eat. 1961.  Members represent the UN
  Economic Commission for Latin America
  (ECLA), the Food and Agriculture Organi-

zation of the UN (FAO), the Inter-American
Development Bank (IADB), OAS itself, and
the Inter-American Institute of Agricultural
Sciences (IICA).  Purposes are to fill in
gaps in information and identify bottlenecks
that obstruct agricultural development in
Latin America; advises governments on
agricultural development and agrarian
reform; conducts research.

Concerns include agricultural education,
research, and extension; farm credit;
maketing; and land tenure.  Pub.: Reports
of meetings; technical studies.

+Inter-American Institute of Agricultural
  Sciences (IICA)
Apartado 10281
San Jose, Costa Rica          22-20-22

Est. 1942.  IICA is the specialized agency
of the OAS for the agricultural sector.
Governing authority is a Board of Directors,
which meets annually.

General objectives are to assist the American countries to stimulate and promote
rural development and to support national
efforts to increase agricultural production
and productivity, especially of products that
offer competition in the world market or
improve the diet of the population; to
increase employment opportunities in
rural areas; and to increase participation
of the rural population in development
activities.

IICA's activities focus on analysis of rural
development and related information;
strengthening agricultural education institutions essential to disseminating knowledge
in the agricultural sciences, forestry,
sociology, economics, and home economics;
strengthening agricultural research institutions dedicated to increasing agricultural
production; support to various regional
integrative institutions; and strengthening
institutions concerned with rural reform
and agricultural policy and planning.

The Institute had a budget of $6.6 million
during its 1975 fiscal year.  Its funding
is contributed by OAS member states.

ORGANIZATION OF AMERICAN STATES

Examples of IICA projects:  Direct advisory services to new programs in university-level agricultural education in El Salvador.  Funding for agricultural research institutes in Brazil.  "Diagnostic studies" of national agricultural policies in various countries.  Advice to the government of the Dominican Republic on agricultural marketing.

Country and regional projects are carried out through regional offices (listed below) and country representatives.  IICA also maintains three specialized centers (listed below).

Pub.:  <u>El IICA en América</u>, q. (Spanish).  <u>Turrialba</u>, q. (scientific journal, Spanish).  <u>Desarrollo Rural en las Américas</u>, q. (technical journal, Spanish).  <u>Annual Report</u> (English and Spanish).  <u>Plan General</u> (bilingual).  Technical reports.

<u>IICA regional offices:</u>

> ++<u>IICA Regional Office for the Southern Zone</u>
> Casilla de Correos 1217
> Montevideo, Uruguay

> ++<u>IICA Regional Office for the Northern Zone</u>
> Apartado 1815
> Guatemala, Guatemala

> ++<u>IICA Regional Office for the Andean Zone</u>
> Apartado 11185
> Lima, Peru

> ++<u>Office of the Director of Institutional Relations</u>
> Inter-American Institute of Agricultural Sciences
> 1735 Eye Street, Room 725
> Washington, D.C. 20006

<u>IICA centers:</u>

> ++<u>Inter-American Center for Agricultural Documentation and Information</u> (IICA-CIDIA)
> Apartado 74
> Turrialba, Costa Rica

<u>IICA centers, contin.:</u>

> ++<u>Tropical Center for Training and Research</u> (IICA-CTEI)
> Apartado 74
> Turrialba, Costa Rica

> ++<u>Inter-American Center for Rural Development and Agrarian Reform</u> (IICA-CIRA)
> Apartado Aereo 14592
> Bogota, Colombia

+<u>Inter-American Children's Institute</u> (IIN) (IACI)
Avenida 8 de Octubre 2904
Montevideo, Uruguay          4-47-30

Est. 1919.  Governed by the Pan-American Child Congress.  A center of research, information, and social work on all matters relating to the life and welfare of the child in the Americas.  The Institute's <u>Health Section</u> is concerned with child nutrition. Projects have included, for example, a national seminar on child and family nutrition in Haiti; surveys of child nutrition in various countries.  Maintains close liaison with UNICEF.  Pub.:  <u>Boletin</u>, q. (Spanish).  <u>Report of the Director General</u>, ann. (English and Spanish).  Research papers and bibliographies (list available; almost all are in Spanish).

ORGANIZATION OF ARAB PETROLEUM EXPORTING COUNTRIES (OAPEC)
c/o Arab Fund for Economic and Social Development
P.O. Box 21923
Kuwait City, Kuwait          431870

Not to be confused with OPEC (see next entry), this group of Arab oil countries set up in 1974 a Special Account for emergency assistance to non-oil producing Arab countries.  Initial funding was $160 million (1974-76).  Major recipient has been the Sudan; other countries receiving aid include Mauritania, Morocco, Somalia, Arab Republic of Yemen, and People's Democratic Republic of Yemen.  The Special Account is administered by the Arab Fund at the address above.

ORGANIZATION OF THE PETROLEUM
  EXPORTING COUNTRIES (OPEC)
Dr. Karl Lueger-Ring 10
1010 Vienna, Austria         63-97-80

Est. 1960. Members are the governments of
Algeria, Libya, Venezuela, Abu Dhabi (United
Arab Emirates), Indonesia, Iran, Iraq, Kuwait,
Qatar, Saudia Arabia, and Nigeria. General
aims are the unification of oil policies of
member countries and determining the best
means of safeguarding their interests. The
OPEC Special Fund has contributed $400
million toward setting up the UN International
Fund for Agricultural Development (IFAD).

REGIONAL INTERNATIONAL ORGANIZATION
  OF PLANT PROTECTION AND ANIMAL
  HEALTH (OIRSA)
Apartado Postal 1654
San Salvador, El Salvador

Est. 1953. Members are governments of the
Central American countries and Panama.
Holds meetings to coordinate national programs
of research, prevention, and control of plant
and animal diseases.

SOUTH WEST ATLANTIC FISHERIES
  ADVISORY COMMISSION (SWAFAC)
  (CARPAS)
c/o SUDEPE
Edificio de Pesca, 3 andar
XV de Novembro
Rio de Janeiro, Brazil        27-6897

Est. 1962. Members are the governments of
Argentina, Brazil, and Uruguay. Pub.:
Bulletin and technical papers.

# Part 3.
# International
# Non-Governmental
# Organizations

Note: An "international non-governmental organization," for the purpose of listing in this part of the directory, must have a substantial membership in more than one country.  While many other groups have extensive international programs (e.g., the Ford Foundation), they are listed in the national organizations parts of this book if their memberships or management boards are essentially national in character.

## AFRICA COMMITTEE FOR THE REHABILITATION OF SOUTHERN SUDAN (ACROSS)
c/o Medical Assistance Programs
P.O. Box 50
Wheaton, Illinois 60187

Est. 1972.  Coalition of 9 Protestant missionary groups in the U.S., West Germany, Australia, and Sweden.  Operates community development, including agricultural, projects in the southern Sudan.  Filmstrip.

## BROTHERS TO ALL MEN (BAM)
9, rue de Savoie
75006 Paris, France                      033-05-71

Est. 1965.  Sponsors a volunteer service program for young men who work on development, including agricultural and fishing, projects in Bangladesh, Brazil, Ecuador, India, Peru, Upper Volta, and other developing countries.  Members are in 10 European countries.  Pub.: Newsletter.

## CARIBBEAN FOOD CROPS SOCIETY
P.O. Box H
Rio Piedras, Puerto Rico 00928    809-766-2331

Est. 1963.  Purpose is to "advance Caribbean food production and distribution in all their aspects to the end of improving levels of nutrition and standards of living." Information exchange; consultant services; coordination of, and development of joint, research and development projects.  Members are individuals in 25 countries in the Caribbean region.  Pub.: Newsletter; annual proceedings.

## CARITAS INTERNATIONALIS: INTERNATIONAL CONFEDERATION OF CATHOLIC CHARITIES
16, Piazza S. Calisto
00153 Rome, Italy                  (06) 6984597

Est. 1951.  An international confederation of Roman Catholic organizations engaged in charitable and social action in some 100 countries (U.S. members are the National Catholic Charities Congress and Catholic Relief Services-U.S.C.C.) Aims are to stimulate and aid the national Caritas groups; to study the causes of and propose solutions to the problems arising from poverty in the world; to foster foundation of national Catholic charities where none exists; and to stimulate and coordinate relief and emergency aid.

Commissions include: Social Studies and Formation; Development and Social Services; Mutual Aid Fund; and Emergency Aid.  Sponsors distribution of food in some countries; gifts of vegetable seeds; nutrition education and agricultural "micro-realisations" in Africa.

Regional Commissions in Africa/Middle East; Asia/Oceania; Europe; Latin America.  Delegations in Geneva, New York, Paris, Rome, and Strasbourg.  Pub.: Intercaritas, q.

## THE CLUB OF ROME
Via Giorgione 163
00147 Rome, Italy

Est. 1968.  Seeks to identify on a global basis the economic, political, natural, and social problems confronting man, and to develop methodology for their solution.  The relationships among food, population, and other resources have been a major interest.  Pub.: World Dynamics.  The Limits to Growth. Mankind at the Turning Point: The Second Report to the Club of Rome.

DAIRY SOCIETY INTERNATIONAL (DSI)
3008 McKinley Street, N.W.
Washington, D.C. 20015          202-363-3359

Est. 1946.  Purpose is "to enhance human
health and economic progress by encouraging
the development and extension of all phases of
the dairy industry throughout the world, and by
developing world markets for existing supplies
of milk."  Activities include market development; exchange of technical information and
promotional materials between the U.S. dairy
industry and groups in other countries; utilization research; assistance to voluntary development agencies (including Project HOPE); international exchange of dairy personnel; and technical assistance to nationals of developing countries.  Members are individuals in 50 countries.

Pub.: Market Frontier News, bimon.  Dairy
Situation Review.  Handbooks on dairy techniques, conference proceedings, and booklets.

EUROPEAN SCIENTIFIC ASSOCIATION OF
  APPLIED ECONOMICS (ASEPELT)
c/o Centre d'Econometrie, Universite de
  Geneve
6, rue de Saussure
1204 Geneva, Switzerland

Est. 1961.  Promotes original research in
applied economics.  Projects have included
a study, Europe's Future Food and Agriculture
(1971).  Other pub. include European Economic
Review, q.

EUROPEAN UNION FOR THE GRAIN, OILSEED,
  AND FODDER TRADES AND DERIVATIVES
248, Bourse de Commerce
75001 Paris, France

Est. 1953.  Functions are to facilitate and develop international trade in grain, oilseeds, and
feedstuffs, and their derivatives, on behalf of
the European industry.

FRIENDS WORLD COMMITTEE FOR
  CONSULTATION (FWCC)
Right Sharing of World Resources (RSWR)
1506 Race Street
Philadelphia, Pennsylvania 19102     215-563-0757

Committee est. 1937.  FWCC is the international organization of the Religious Society of
Friends (Quakers).  Right Sharing of World
Resources, originally known as the One Percent
More Fund, is a program of the FWCC Section
of the Americas, in cooperation with other
regional sections and the FWCC.  Established
in 1970, RSWR is directed mainly toward
Friends in affluent countries.  It raises funds
for the support of projects in developing
countries, emphasizing indigenous self-help
projects, experimental approaches, and projects with Quaker input.  Projects have included
fisheries and agricultural development activities.  Funding amounts to about $30,000 per
year.

RSWR also conducts an educational effort in the
U.S. and Canada, which provides literature
and action suggestions on development issues
to Friends, who are "encouraged to simplify
their personal lives, release resources to
share internationally (including the possibility
of personal service abroad), inform themselves
and others about the issues, and work on changing international structures for greater social
justice and economic equality."

Pub.: Friends World News, 3 times a year.
Right Sharing News, bimon.

GULF AND CARIBBEAN FISHERIES
  INSTITUTE (GCFI)
10 Rickenbacker Causeway
Miami, Florida 33149          305-350-7533

Est. 1948.  Promotes fisheries research and
exchange of information on the fisheries of the
Caribbean and the Gulf of Mexico; assists Caribbean countries in developing their fisheries.
Members are fishermen, fishery scientists,
and administrators in countries in the region.
Pub.: Proceedings, ann.

HEED BANGLADESH (HEED)
c/o Medical Assistance Programs
P.O. Box 50
Wheaton, Illinois 60187

Est. 1972.  H.E.E.D. means "Health, Education, and Economic Development."  A coalition
of six Protestant missionary groups in Britain,
West Germany, and the U.S.  Projects in Bangladesh have included agricultural extension.

INTER-AMERICAN ASSOCIATION OF
  AGRICULTURAL LIBRARIANS AND
  DOCUMENTALISTS (AIBDA)
c/o IICA-CIDIA
Turrialba, Costa Rica

Est. 1953.  Liaison center for agricultural
librarians in Latin America.  Promotes information exchange; helps develop agricultural
libraries in the region.  Members are librarians and associations in Latin American and
other countries.  Pub.: Boletin Informativo,
bimon. newsletter.  Bibliografia Agricola
Latino-americana, q.  Proceedings and technical reports.

INTERNATIONAL ASSOCIATION FOR
  CEREAL CHEMISTRY (ICC)
Schmidgasse 3-7
2320 Schwechat, Austria

Est. 1958.  Purposes are to study problems of
technical research in cereal and flour chemistry and allied fields.  Maintains a Committee
for Liaison with International Organizations.
Members are professional associations or institutes in some 40 countries.

INTERNATIONAL ASSOCIATION OF
  AGRICULTURAL ECONOMISTS (IAALD)
Dartington House
Little Clarendon Street
Oxford OX1 2HP, England          52921

Est. 1929.  Objectives are to "foster the application of the science of agricultural economics
in the improvement of the economic and social
conditions of rural people and their associated
communities; to advance knowledge of agricultural processes and the economic organization
of agriculture; and to facilitate communication
and exchange of information."  Holds a conference every three years.  Members are professionals in agricultural economics in some
85 countries.  Pub.: International Journal of
Agrarian Affairs, irreg.  Conference proceedings.

INTERNATIONAL BOARD FOR PLANT
  GENETIC RESOURCES (IBPGR)
c/o FAO, Via delle Terme di Caracalla
00100 Rome, Italy

An outgrowth of recommendations made by the
UN Conference on the Human Environment,
the Board is sponsored by the Consultative
Group on International Agricultural Research.
It is a clearinghouse for the collection and
exchange of genetic resources in agriculture,
coordinates cataloging efforts of various
national and international gene banks, and
certifies that the exchange of genetic materials
is disease-free.  It also works to preserve
genetic resources in danger of extinction.

INTERNATIONAL CATHOLIC CHILD BUREAU
  (ICCB)
65, rue de Lausanne
1202 Geneva, Switzerland          022-31-32-48

Est. 1948.  Forum for exchange of information;
advocate for the child in international debates.
Nutrition is among its concerns.  Pub.:
L'Enfance dans le Monde (English and French),
3 times a year.

INTERNATIONAL CENTER OF TROPICAL
  AGRICULTURE (CIAT)
Apartado Aereo 6713
Cali, Colombia

Est. 1968.  Focuses on improving agricultural
production in the lowland tropics of the Western
Hemisphere.  Programs concentrate on cassava
(manioc), field beans, maize, rice, beef
cattle, and swine.  A small-farms systems
team, cutting across the lines of the crop and
livestock programs, analyzes small-farm
dynamics and the factors that influence farmers'
decisions.

CIAT also conducts 12-month courses for
agricultural specialists; workshops and conferences; and an outreach program involving
direct consultation with governments and agricultural agencies.

Part of the network of institutes sponsored by
the Consultative Group on International Agricultural Research.

INTERNATIONAL COMMISSION ON
  MICROBIOLOGICAL SPECIFICATIONS
  FOR FOODS (ICMSF)
c/o D.S. Clark, National Research Council
100 Sussex Drive
Ottawa, Ontario K1A 0R6, Canada
                              613-992-3687

Est. 1962, by the International Association of
Microbiological Societies (IAMS). Primarily
a scientific advisory body concerned with
microorganisms in food. Proposes specifications for microbiological quality of food and
seeks to foster safe movement of foods in
international commerce by dealing with problems caused by differences in standards and
methods of analysis among nations. Pub.:
technical papers (list available).

   +Balkan and Danubian Subcommission,
    ICMSF
   c/o Prof H.J. Takacs
   Institute of Food Hygiene
   University of Veterinary Sciences
   P.O. Box 2
   1400 Budapest, Hungary

   +Latin American Subcommission, ICMSF
   c/o Dra. J. Gomez Ruiz
   Central University of Venezuela
   Apartado 50259
   Caracas, Venezuela

   +Middle East-North African Subcommis-
    sion, ICMSF
   c/o Prof. Refat Hablas
   Bacteriological Department, Faculty of
    Medicine, Al-Azhar University
   El Houssein Hospital
   Cairo, Egypt

INTERNATIONAL CONFEDERATION OF
  CATHOLIC CHARITIES
See: Caritas Internationalis

INTERNATIONAL CO-OPERATIVE
  ALLIANCE (ICA)
11 Upper Grosvenor Street
London WIX 9PA, England        499-5991

Est. 1895. Goals are to promote cooperative
principles and methods throughout the world
and to protect the international cooperative
movement. Information exchange; research;

training; collection of statistics. Maintains a
program of technical assistance to cooperative
organizations, including agricultural and fisheries cooperatives, in the developing countries,
through the ICA Development Fund. Pub.:
International Co-operation. Review of International Co-operation, bimon. Agricultural
Bulletin, mon. Film Bulletin. Various reports and special studies.

INTERNATIONAL COUNCIL OF SCIENTIFIC
  UNIONS (ICSU)
51, boulevard de Montmorency
75016 Paris, France          (01) 5277702

Est. 1919. An association of scientific unions,
academies, national research councils, and
related scientific and governmental institutions.
Coordinates and facilitates activities among
these groups in the natural sciences. Maintains a Committee on Science and Technology
in Developing Countries.

ICSU's work includes encouraging international
scientific activity in various aspects of biology,
the nutritional sciences, and water quality
related to global food problems. Pub.: ICSU
Bulletin, q. ICSU Yearbook.

INTERNATIONAL COUNCIL OF VOLUNTARY
  AGENCIES (ICVA)
7, avenue de la Paix
1202 Geneva, Switzerland        33-20-25

Est. 1962. The international confederation of
citizens' voluntary associations - extra-govern-
mental, non-commercial organizations -
engaged in worldwide developmental, social,
and humanitarian action. Provides a forum
for exchange of views and information; serves
as an instrument for the development, improvement, and growth of such agencies and their
activities, and as a means of publicizing the
problems to which the agencies address themselves. Maintains a Commission on Social and
Economic Development and a Commission on
Emergency Aid. Pub.: ICVA News, q.

## INTERNATIONAL CROPS RESEARCH INSTITUTE FOR THE SEMI-ARID TROPICS (ICRISAT)

1-11-256 Begumpet
Hyderabad, Andhra Pradesh 500016
India                                     72091

Est. 1972. Focuses on improvement of crops in the semi-arid tropics, "a wide belt across parts of South Asia, India, Africa, the Middle East, and in parts of South and Central America from northern Argentina and northeast Brazil to Mexico." In these regions, food production is limited mainly by the erratic nature of the rains.

ICRISAT has three main objectives: (1) to serve as a world center to improve the genetic potential for grain yield and the nutritional quality of sorghum, pearl millet, pigeon pea, and chick pea; (2) developing farm systems which will help to increase and stabilize agricultultural production through better use of natural and human resources; and (3) assisting national and regional research programs through cooperation and support of training, meetings, and extension activities.

Part of the network of institutes sponsored by the Consultative Group on International Agricultural Research. Pub.: At ICRISAT, q. Annual report.

## INTERNATIONAL DAIRY FEDERATION (IDF)

41, square Vergote
1040 Brussels, Belgium                    7339888

Est. 1903. Purpose is "to promote through international cooperation the solution of scientific, technical, and economic problems in the international dairy field." Members are national dairy committees in 30 countries. Commissions: Production of Milk; Technology; Economics; Legislation; Micobiology; Chemistry; Science. Pub.: IDF Bulletin, ann. IDF News, irreg. Technical reports (catalog available).

## INTERNATIONAL FEDERATION OF AGRICULTURAL PRODUCERS (IFAP)

1, rue de Hauteville
75010 Paris, France                       824-40-35

Est. 1946. Composed of farmers' associations in 44 countries, IFAP is the "international professional arm of its member organizations." Functions are: (1) to act as a forum in which world farm leaders can meet and exchange views; (2) to keep members informed of matters, especially international, of interest to them as farmer organizations; (3) to act as the spokesman and representative of farmers in all international, and especially intergovernmental, forums.

Maintains a Standing Committee on Agricultural Co-operation; Standing Committee on Agriculture in Developing Countries; International Dairy Committee; Standing Group on Grains; IFAP Meat Intelligence Service.

Holds a general conference about every 18 months. Concerns have included agricultural production in developing countries, agrarian reform, cooperatives, fertilizer supplies, research, extension, training, nutrition, financing agricultural development assistance, food security, food aid policy, and international agricultural trade.

About half of the member associations are in developing countries. The U.S. is represented by the National Council of Farmer Cooperatives and the National Farmers Union; Canada is represented by the Canadian Federation of Agriculture.

Pub.: IFAP News, mon. World Agriculture, q. Farming for Development, q. IFAP Handbook (includes descriptions of member associations). Conference reports.

Regional offices, IFAP:

+International Federation of Agricultural Producers
North American Representative
P.O. Box 28316
Washington, D.C. 20005

+International Federation of Agricultural
  Producers
c/o Chambre d'Agriculture, de l'Elevage
  et des Forets
B. P. 287
Yaounde, Cameroon

+International Federation of Agricultural
  Producers
c/o Farmers' Forum, India
1-A Nizamuddin-West
New Delhi 110013, India

+International Federation of Agricultural
  Producers
c/o Union Nigerienne de Credit et de
  Cooperation
B. P. 296
Niamey, Niger

+International Federation of Agricultural
  Producers
c/o Union Nationale des Agriculteurs
6, avenue Habib Thameur
Tunis, Tunisia

+International Federation of Agricultural
  Producers
c/o Farmers' Federation of Ghana
P. O. Box 7129
Accra, Ghana

+International Federation of Agricultural
  Producers
c/o Kenya National Farmers' Union
P. O. Box 1225
Nakuru, Kenya

+International Federation of Agricultural
  Producers
c/o Union of Turkish Chambers of Agric.
Izmir Cad. 24, Yaprak Apt. Kat 4-5
Yenisehir-Ankara, Turkey

+International Federation of Agricultural
  Producers
c/o Commercial Farmers' Bureau of
  Zambia
P. O. Box 395
Lusaka, Zambia

+International Federation of Agricultural
  Producers
Liaison Office with FAO
Via Yser 14
00198 Rome, Italy          86-12-41

INTERNATIONAL FEDERATION OF
  INSTITUTES FOR ADVANCED STUDY (IFIAS)
The Nobel House
Sturegatan 14, Box 5344
102 46 Stockholm, Sweden

Est. 1972, under the auspices of the Nobel and
Rockefeller Foundations.  Members are some
20 institutes of advanced study in 16 countries.
IFIAS "is an experiment in contacts, coordination and cooperation across geographical
and disciplinary boundaries."  Projects focus
on global problems and issues "that lie ahead
of those which have already penetrated official
consciousness.  By presenting careful and
responsible analyses of policy alternatives for
the world's future, IFIAS may serve as an
adviser and forewarner."

Projects related to the world food situation
have included:  "Impact of Climate Change on
the Character and Quality of Human Life"
(involving 8 institutes in 6 countries); "Options
for Regions Faced with Water Shortage" (proposed by the Weizmann Institute of Science,
Israel); "Interaction of Health, Nutrition and
Education on Human Growth and Development;"
and "Loss of Productive Soil."

Pub.:  Reports of workshops (list available).
Catalog of projects.

INTERNATIONAL FERTILIZER
  DEVELOPMENT CENTER (IFDC)
402 First Federal Building
Florence, Alabama 35630

Est. 1974.  Uses facilities at the U. S. National
Fertilizer Development Center, est. 1933.
Develops and promotes the use of new and
improved fertilizers in tropical and sub-
tropical agriculture; studies and assists in
solving marketing problems; training and
information services.  Part of the network of
institutes sponsored by the Consultative Group
on International Agricultural Research.

INTERNATIONAL FOOD POLICY RESEARCH
  INSTITUTE (IFPRI)
1776 Massachusetts Avenue, N.W.
Washington, D.C. 20036          202-833-1821

Est. 1975. Conducts research on selected policy problems affecting the production, consumption, availability, and equitable distribution of food in the world. Particular emphasis is directed to needs of low-income countries, and especially the needs of vulnerable groups within those countries.

IFPRI has four broad program areas: (1) an analysis of world food trends and the basic factors underlying them; (2) policies which influence the rate of technological change, investment, and resource productivity and thus, the food production potential in developing countries; (3) policies which affect the total availability and distribution of food between and within countries; (4) policies which affect the trade and concessionary food aid flows of significance to developing countries.

The Institute will also make periodic evaluations of the world food situation, including policy changes at the national and international levels which would affect the availability of food to developing countries. It will not generate new statistics, but will concentrate on analyzing material available from numerous national and international organizations.

IFPRI was formed in response to a recommendation of the Technical Advisory Committee of the Consultative Group on International Agricultural Research. It is governed by an international board of trustees and supported by grants from the International Development Research Centre (Canada), the Ford Foundation, and the Rockefeller Foundation.

Pub.: Food Policy Reports, semiann.

INTERNATIONAL GEOGRAPHICAL UNION
  (IGU)
c/o Department of Geography
University of Chicago
Chicago, Illinois 60637          312-753-3926

Est. 1922. Composed of national professional organizations or committees in some 70 countries. Promotes the study of geographical problems; encourages international cooperation in research. Study commissions include: World Land-Use Survey; Regional Aspects of Development; Agricultural Typology. Working Group on Desertification. Pub.: IGU Bulletin, semi-ann. Reports and reference materials.

INTERNATIONAL INSTITUTE FOR
  ENVIRONMENT AND DEVELOPMENT (IIED)
27 Mortimer Street
London W1A 4QW, England          01-580-7656

Est. 1971. Research and educational organization concerned with global implications of environment, development, and resource use. Sponsored a Rome Forum on World Food Problems just before the 1974 World Food Conference. The Forum issued a declaration calling for various measures, including detailed priorities for investment in ecologically sound farming.

  +North American Office, IIED
  1525 New Hampshire Avenue, N.W.
  Washington, D.C. 20036     202-462-0900

INTERNATIONAL INSTITUTE OF PROTEIN
  FOOD TECHNOLOGY (IIPFT)
Meals for Millions Foundation
1800 Olympic Boulevard
Santa Monica, California 90406

A training program sponsored by the Meals for Millions Foundation.

INTERNATIONAL INSTITUTE OF TROPICAL
  AGRICULTURE (IITA)
P. M. B. 5320
Ibadan, Nigeria

Est. 1967.  Conducts research in all areas of food production in the humid tropics, with special emphasis on grain legumes (cowpea, lima beans, soybeans, pigeon peas, etc. ); root and tuber crops (cassava, yam, sweet potatoes, and cocoyam); and cereals (maize and rice).  Develops production systems to replace traditional shifting and natural-fallow cultivation and enable farmers to maintain good yields of high-quality crops.  Distributes improved plant materials and diseeminates knowledge of improved farming practices to other research centers and to national food production programs throughout the tropics. Training of students, scientists, and technicians.  Workshops, symposia, and seminars.

Other projects at IITA include a Genetic Resources Conservation Project (in cooperation with the International Board for Plant Genetic Resources) to collect and conserve genetic resources of African food legumes and roots and tubers.  The FAO/African Rural Storage Center focuses on improving methods of drying and storing maize in Africa south of the Sahara.  The Pesticides Residues Study (in cooperation with the Center for Overseas Pest Research (COPR) focuses on changes in soil fertility due to pesticide use.

Library and Documentation Center includes the International Grain Legume Information Centre.  IITA is supported by the Ford Foundation, the Rockefeller Foundation, the Canadian International Development Agency, the U.K. Overseas Development Ministry, AID, the World Bank, the UN Environment Programme, and the governments of Nigeria, West Germany, Belgium, the Netherlands, and Iran, under the auspices of the Consultative Group on International Agricultural Research.

Pub.: IITA Letter, q.  Tropical Grain Legume Bulletin.  Technical and educational publications.

INTERNATIONAL LABORATORY FOR
  RESEARCH ON ANIMAL DISEASES (ILRAD)
P. O. Box 47543
Nairobi, Kenya                    592246

Est. 1973.  Focuses on two diseases of cattle that affect some 30 African countries: trypanosomiasis (carried by the tsetse fly), and East Coast fever (carried by ticks).  Conducts basic and applied research; tests results; information exchange with other groups.  Part of the network of institutes sponsored by the Consultative Group on International Agricultural Research.  Pub.: Annual Report on Research in Progress.

INTERNATIONAL LIVESTOCK CENTER
  FOR AFRICA (ILCA)
P. O. Box 5689
Addis Ababa, Ethiopia

Est. 1974.  Purpose is to "assist national efforts which aim to effect a change in the production and marketing systems in tropical Africa so as to increase the total yield and output of livestock products and improve the quality of life of the people of this region." Conducts interdisciplinary research; training of animal scientists.  Seminars; conferences; in-service courses.  Provides consultative, documentary, and statistical services to national, regional, and international organizations dealing with improvement of animal production in Africa.  Part of the network of institutes sponsored by the Consultative Group on International Agricultural Research.

INTERNATIONAL MAIZE AND WHEAT
  IMPROVEMENT CENTER (CIMMYT)
Londres 40
Mexico 6. D. F., Mexico

Est. 1966.  Conducts a major program of research and training in wheat and maize, including evaluation of genetic resources; beeding and testing of new grain varieties; agronomic research; biochemical and nutritional analysis of grain protein; assistance with production programs and consultation on agricultural policies; war on plant diseases and pests; training of specialists; exchange of scientific information; and development of new educational techniques and materials.

Operations are worldwide; consultation is provided annually to some 60 countries of Asia, Africa, and Latin America.  Part of the network of institutes sponsored by the Consultative Group on International Agricultural Research.  Pub.: Technical reports.

## INTERNATIONAL ORGANIZATION OF CONSUMERS UNIONS (IOCU)
9 Emmastraat
The Hague, Netherlands          070-834904

Est. 1960.  The world center for consumer affairs, linking the activities of consumer organizations in some 45 countries.  Among its concerns has been nutritional labeling and date marking of foods.

At the World Food Conference, IOCU put forth a number of recommendations on behalf of the consumer movement, including "far greater supervision" of commodity exchanges and better control of speculation; long-term contracts and international arrangements to make world food prices less volatile; development of a code of ethics for international trade in food, backed by a "Food Interpol;" and discouragement or even banning of the sale or excessive promotion in poorer countries of high-cost and nutritionally undesirable food products.

Pub.: _International Consumer_, irreg. magazine. _Consumer Review_, q.  _IOCU Newsletter_, 10 times a year.  _Asia-Pacific Consumer_, q. Reports and reference materials (list available).

## INTERNATIONAL POTASH INSTITUTE
SZB Building
3048 Worblaufen-Bern, Switzerland
          58-53-73

Est. 1952.  Collection and development of scientific information on soil fertilization and fertilizers, particularly potash.  Sends technical missions; provides scientific and technical assistance to all interested organizations. Pub.: _Revue de la Potasse_ (in four languages).

## INTERNATIONAL POTATO CENTER (CIP)
Apartado 5969
Lima, Peru          350842

Est. 1971.  Works to improve potatoes and potato growing in developing countries and to extend the potato's range of adaptation to new territory, including the lowland tropics.  Collects genetic material; develops breeding techniques; conducts research on disease control. Exchange of scientific information; training of specialists.  Activities are worldwide.  Part of the network of institutes sponsored by the Consultative Group on International Agricultural Research.  Pub.: Technical reports and conference proceedings.

## INTERNATIONAL RESEARCH CENTRE ON RURAL COOPERATIVE COMMUNITIES (CIRCOM)
P.O. Box 7020
Tel Aviv, Israel          263614

## INTERNATIONAL RICE RESEARCH INSTITUTE (IRRI)
P.O. Box 933
Manila, Philippines          88-48-69

Est. 1960.  Conducts research in genetic evaluation and utilization of rice; control and management of rice pests; irrigation water management; soil and crop management for rice; post-harvest management; constraints on rice production; increasing rice yield potential; cropping systems; machinery development and management; and related areas.  Resident training program for scientists and extension workers.

IRRI's program focuses on Asia, with about a third of its staff attached to "outreach" projects in Bangladesh, Egypt, India, Indonesia, the Philippines, Sri Lanka, and Thailand.  Part of the network of institutes sponsored by the Consultative Group on International Agricultural Research.

Pub.: _International Rice Research Newsletter_, bimon.  _IRRI Reporter_, q.  Annual Report. Research Highlights, ann.  Technical reports; symposia; reference materials; slides.  List of publications available.

INTERNATIONAL SEAWEED SYMPOSIUM
c/o Norwegian Institute of Seaweed Research
7034 Trondheim-NTH, Norway

Est. 1952.  Holds periodic symposia on the study and uses of seaweeds.  Pub.: Proceedings.

INTERNATIONAL SEED TESTING
  ASSOCIATION (ISTA)
P.O. Box 68
1432 Aas-NLH, Norway          941060

Est. 1924.  Members are representatives of official seed testing stations on some 55 countries, as well as laboratories and individual members.  Purpose is to protect agriculture against the sowing of inferior seed by developing, adopting, and publishing standard procedures for evaluating seeds moving in international trade and by promoting research in all areas of seed science and technology.  Pub.: Seed Science and Technology, q.  ISTA News Bulletin, q.  Technical publications (list available).

INTERNATIONAL SOCIETY OF
  BIOMETEOROLOGY (ISB)
Hofbrouckerlaan 54
Oegstgeest, Leiden, Netherlands

Est. 1956.  Professional organization of specialists in biometeorology (the study of the relationships between plant and animal life and weather and climate) working in agriculture, entomology, and other fields.  Pub.: International Journal of Biometeorology.

INTERNATIONAL SOCIETY OF SOIL
  SCIENCE (ISSS)
c/o Food and Agriculture Organization of the
  United Nations
Via delle Terme di Caracalla
00153 Rome, Italy          5797

Est. 1924.  Professional organization of soil scientists and national soil science societies in some 70 countries.  Promotes the application of soil science for agricultural development, with special reference to food production.  Maintains commissions on: Soil Physics; Soil Chemistry; Soil Biology; Soil Fertility and Plant Nutrition; Soil Genesis, Classification, and Cartography; Soil Technology; Soil Mine-

ralogy.  Pub.: Bulletin of the International Society of Soil Science, semiann.

INTERNATIONAL UNION FOR CONSERVATION
  OF NATURE AND NATURAL RESOURCES
  (IUCN)
1110 Morges, Switzerland          021-71-44-01

Est. 1948.  An independent international organization composed of national governments, governmental agencies, private organizations, and international groups.  Main purpose is to "promote or support action that will insure the conservation of nature and natural resources on a world-wide basis, not only for their intrinsic cultural or scientific values but also for the long-term economic and social welfare of mankind.  The Union considers that conservation is best defined as the rational management of the earth's resources to achieve the highest sustainable quality of living for mankind."

IUCN has had an active interest in promoting the idea of conservation as an integral part of development, including agricultural development programs.  Another major focus has been protection of the marine environment, "vital for the survival and productivity of food and commercial species as well as of rare and threatened ones."  Several of its current projects relate to problems of desertification.  Pub.: IUCN Bulletin, bimon.  Yearbook.  Ecological Principles for Economic Development (1973).  Technical reports, proceedings of meetings, and reference publications (list available).

  +IUCN Representative at the United Nations
  c/o Sierra Club
  800 Second Avenue
  New York, New York 10017

INTERNATIONAL UNION OF FOOD SCIENCE
  AND TECHNOLOGY (IUFoST)
c/o Swedish Institute for Food Preservation
  Research
400 21 Goteborg, Sweden

Est. 1970.  Members are national food science organizations of 32 countries.  Holds periodic international congresses, and symposia on specialized topics, often in cooperation with other organizations.  Topics have included, for example, the impact of food processing on nutrition; rice by-products utilization; and changes in proteins in frozen and dried foods.

IUFoST maintains a Committee on Technical Assistance to Developing Countries, which serves aid agencies as a source of resource personnel and advice. Pub.: IUFoST Newsletter, semi-ann. Papers, proceedings, and reviews.

INTERNATIONAL UNION OF NUTRITIONAL
  SCIENCES (IUNS)
c/o Institute of Clinical Nutrition
Sahlgren's Hospital
413 45 Gothenburg, Sweden

Est. 1946. Members are nutrition societies or institutes in some 40 countries. Promotes international cooperation in the science of nutrition and its applications. Holds periodic international congresses. Commissions include: Human Development, with Special Reference to the Pre-School Child; Diseases of Special Nutritional Importance; Nutrition Education and Training. Pub.: IUNS Newsletter. Commission and committee reports; miscellaneous publications (list available).

INTERNATIONAL VEGETARIAN UNION (IVU)
"Braidjule," 120 Knockan Road
Broughshane, near Ballymena
Northern Ireland BT43 7LE, U.K.
              Broughshane 202

Est. 1908. Promotes vegetarianism worldwide. Holds a World Vegetarian Congress every two years.

INTERNATIONAL VETERINARY ASSOCIATION
  FOR ANIMAL PRODUCTION (IVAAP)
c/o Faculdad de Veterinaria, Ciudad
  Universitaria, Madrid 3, Spain   2439459

Est. 1951. Promotes international exchange of information on animal production. Members are national associations and individuals in 27 countries. Pub.: Zootechnia, bimon. Reports of congresses.

INTERNATIONAL VOLUNTARY SERVICES
  (IVS)
1555 Connecticut Avenue, N.W.
Washington, D.C. 20036       202-387-5533

Est. 1953. "An apolitical, nonsectarian organization, with a multinational corps of technicians, staff, and directors." Provides volunteer technicians in the areas of agricultural development, nutrition, and cooperative development in 9 countries in Asia, Latin America, and the South Pacific. Funds are derived from a variety of sources, including corporations, foundations, individual donors, and governments (including the U.S. and West Germany). Pub.: IVS Reports, bimon.

INTERNATIONAL WORKING GROUP ON
  SOILLESS CULTURE (IWOSC)
c/o Ing. A.A. Steiner
P.O. Box 52
Wageningen, Netherlands

Est. 1955. Purposes are to extend the knowledge and uses of hydroponics worldwide, and to facilitate exchange of information among workers in the field. Pub.: Congress proceedings.

LATIN AMERICAN CORN SOCIETY/Sociedad
  Latinoamericano de Maiz (SLM)
c/o CIMMYT, Londres 40
Mexico, D.F., Mexico

LUTHERAN WORLD FEDERATION (LWF)
Department of World Service
150, route de Ferney
1211 Geneva 20, Switzerland     022-33-34-00

LWF est. 1947. Lutheran World Service (LWS), a part of LWF's Department of World Service, provides emergency relief assistance, operates agricultural rehabilitation and development projects, and gives support to similar activities carried out by churches in developing countries. Support has been given to some 45 countries in Africa, Asia, and Latin America. Pub.: Reports on projects.

    +Lutheran World Service
    P.O. Box 19178
    Jerusalem

+Lutheran World Service
3, Hungerford Street
Calcutta 700 017, India

+Lutheran World Service
Rangpur Dinajpur Rehabilitation Service
P.O. Box 618, Ramna
Dacca-2, Bangladesh          31-78-72

OXFAM
274 Banbury Road
Oxford OX2 7D2, England        0865 56777

Est. 1942.  An international relief and development agency functioning mostly on a funding,
rather than an operational basis.  It supports
other groups working in some 80 countries,
with programs including food production,
irrigation, food storage, soil and water conservation, nutrition, and food relief.  The
total budget in 1974-75 was about Ł3.25 million, of which 2% went for feeding projects and
16% went to agricultural projects.  Pub.:
Oxfam News, bimon.  Booklets and information sheets (list available).  National groups
in the U.K., Belgium, Australia, and the U.S.

+Oxfam New Delhi Office
D238 Defence Colony
New Delhi 110024, India

+Oxfam Bangladesh Office
Road 21, House 646, Dhanmondi "R/A,"
Dacca, Bangladesh

+Oxfam Indonesia Office
P.O. Box 103
Bogor, Indonesia

+Oxfam Malawi Office
P.O. Box 1363
Blantyre, Malawi

+Oxfam Ethiopia Office
P.O. Box 2333
Addis Ababa, Ethiopia

+Oxfam Upper Volta Office
B.P. 489
Ouagadougou, Upper Volta

+Oxfam Lome Office
B.P. 1251
Lome, Togo

+Oxfam Brazil Office
Caixa Postal 2283
Recife, Pernambuco, Brazil

+Oxfam Peru Office
Daniel Carrion 239C, Miraflores
Lima, Peru

+Oxfam Caribbean Office
c/o CADEC
P.O. Box 616
Bridgetown, Barbados

+Oxfam Zaire Office
B.P. 10362
Kinshasa 1, Zaire

PAN AMERICAN DEVELOPMENT
 FOUNDATION (PADF)
1725 I Street, N.W., Room 909
Washington, D.C. 20006        202-381-8651

Est. 1962.  A "special purpose foundation"
organized through the initiative of "leading
citizens of Latin America and the United States,
and the General Secretariat of the Organization
of American States."  Its purpose is to "assist
the lowest income people in Latin America to
raise their living standards by participating
in the socio-economic progress of their societies.  In carrying out this objective, the
Foundation encourages the involvement of the
local private sector, particularly the business
community, and stimulates the adoption of new
approaches to financing the lowest income
groups by national and international organizations."

PADF is also a service foundation, providing
financial services (grants, loans, and guarantees), technical services (technical assistance,
studies, and research), and material services
(equipment, tools, and machinery).  Operations
are funded by income derived from interest on
its loan program, investments, fees, and contributions from the OAS, U.S. corporations,
and individuals.

Through PADF, credit is made available to
poor people for such projects as a fishing boat,
a tractor, or land.  Agricultural and fishing
equipment is also provided through the PADF
Tools for Freedom program (TFF).  Operation
Niños raises funds from the U.S. public to

support projects to help school-age children in Latin America, including free lunch programs. Some $1 million has also been raised from the U.S. private sector for projects of the OAS Inter-American Institute of Agricultural Sciences.

In fiscal year 1975, PADF had total expenses of about $700,000. As of mid-1975, it had outstanding loans to national development foundations of some $743,000. Pub.: ACTION, q. Audiovisual materials (catalog available).

THE SALVATION ARMY
101 Queen Victoria Street
London EC4P 4EP, England          236-5222

Est. 1865. An evangelical and social welfare organization whose programs include financial, material, and personnel assistance to community agricultural schools, agricultural colonies, training centers for youth and small farmers, and farms. Operates in Kenya, Rhodesia, Argentina, Chile, Jamaica, Bangladesh, India, and Pakistan. Pub.: The War Cry, weekly.

SOCIETY FOR INTERNATIONAL
  DEVELOPMENT (SID)
1346 Connecticut Avenue, N.W.
Washington, D.C. 20036          202-296-3810

Est. 1957. Professional society of persons concerned with economic and social development in modernizing societies. Forum for exchange of ideas, information, and experience. Chapters in some 36 countries (8 in the U.S.). Maintains an Agricultural and Rural Development Section (see below). Holds world and regional conferences.

Pub.: International Development Review, q.
Survey of International Development, bimon.
Proceedings of conferences; directories and guides; other publications (list available).

  +European Office
Society for International Development
94, rue Chardon-Lagache
75775 Paris, Cedex 16, France

  +Agricultural and Rural Development
    Section
Society for International Development
c/o Simon Williams, Coordinacion Rural
Mineria 145, Edif. C., 1er Piso
Mexico 18, D.F., Mexico

  +Development Reference Service
Society for International Development
49, rue de la Glacière
75013 Paris, France

Clearinghouse for inquiries on social and economic development from official and semi-official agencies in developing countries.

TRANSNATIONAL NETWORK FOR
  APPROPRIATE/ALTERNATIVE
  TECHNOLOGIES (TRANET)
7410 Vernon Square Drive
Alexandria, Virginia 22306

Est. 1976. Network of individuals and centers concerned with promoting appropriate technology (also known as "intermediate," "soft," or "alternative" technology), methods that are "low cost, easily maintained, protect the environment, are resource conserving, and fit into established cultural patterns." Examples include simple farm machinery, windmill crop driers, hand pumps, and "soft" pest control techniques. Plans a directory and newsletter.

WEST AFRICA RICE DEVELOPMENT
  ASSOCIATION (WARDA)
P.O. Box 1019
Monrovia, Liberia

Promotes development and use of new strains of rice and methods of rice production in 14 countries of West Africa. Associated with the network of institutes sponsored by the Consultative Group on International Agricultural Research.

WORLD ASSOCIATION FOR ANIMAL
  PRODUCTION (WAAP)
Corso Trieste 67
00198 Rome, Italy          860-785

Est. 1965. Members are national animal production societies in 9 countries. Holds a world conference every 3-5 years to discuss scientific, technical, and educational problems related to animal production.

WORLD ASSOCIATION FOR THE STRUGGLE
  AGAINST HUNGER (ASCOFAM)
163-165, avenue Charles de Gaulle
9220 Neuilly-sur-Seine, France

Est. 1957. Purpose is to promote and organize efforts to combat hunger in all parts of the world.

WORLD COUNCIL OF CHURCHES (WCC)
150, route de Ferney
1211 Geneva 20, Switzerland      33-34-00

Est. 1948. Organization of churches in over 90 countries representing the major Protestant and Orthodox denominations. Promotes cooperation and facilitates common action by the churches.

The WCC Commission on Inter-Church Aid, Refugee and World Service (CICARWS) works to find support for development and relief projects initiated at the local level by member churches, church-related groups, and secular bodies. The Commission itself is responsible for several centrally-organized programs, including scholarships and leadership development, aid to refugees in Africa and the Middle East, and special Sahel and Sudan aid programs (both of which include agricultural components).

Its other main function is to provide a channel for church requests for development funds, people, and material aid for less developed countries and present them to sister churches that have resources to respond. Many of these requests (listed annually in the WCC's Service Programme and List of Projects) relate to food problems. In 1974, a total of 200 projects ($8 million) was funded in Africa; 148 ($10.7 million) in Asia; 179 ($1.6 million) in Europe; 106 ($2.3 million) in Latin America; 24 ($236,000) in the Middle East; and 28 ($544,000) in Oceania.

The related Ecumenical Church Loan Fund (ECLOF) grants "soft" loans to church and church-related projects. In 1974, 57 loans totaling $708,000 were made.

CICARWS has also held workshops on hunger problems, and in 1974 commissioned a study on "The World Food Crisis." In addition to the list of projects mentioned above, the Commission publishes an annual report, Ministries of Service. The complete report of the 1974 study, World of Hunger, by J. Power and A.-M. Holenstein, has been published by Temple Smith, London.

Another WCC commission, the Commission on the Churches' Participation in Development (CCPD) was set up in 1970 to stimulate reflection and experimental action aimed at justice, self-reliance, growth, and participatory development. It has issued a packet of informational materials, "Betting on the Weak: Some Experiences in People's Participation in Development" (1976), and publishes a CCPD Network Letter periodically, which alerts its readers to activities and publications in the general field of development.

Other WCC publications include: The Ecumenical Review, q. Risk, q. Study Encounter, q. Ecumenical Press Service, biweekly. Inter-Church Aid Newsletter, mon. International Review of Missions, q.

WORLD UNIVERSITY SERVICE (WUS)
20 W. 40th Street
New York, New York 10018      212-LO3-1736

Est. 1920. Members are national committees or groups in some 60 countries. Sponsors action-oriented programs that emphasize the role of the university in society and in the solution of political, economic, and social problems, including those of development. Conducts a Campus Global Hunger Awareness Program (lectures, seminars, resource persons); raises funds on campuses for WUS-sponsored hunger-relief projects conducted by local WUS committees in developing countries. Pub.: Newsletter, bimon. Pamphlets.

WORLD'S POULTRY SCIENCE ASSOCIATION
  (WPSA)
c/o Rupert Coles
Treramleon, Bidnija, Malta

Est. 1912. Promotes exchange of information among those concerned with all branches of the poultry industry. Pub.: Journal, q.

# Part 4.
# United States
# Organizations

# A. UNITED STATES GOVERNMENT

Note: U.S. Government entries are divided as follows: Congress; Executive Office of the President; executive departments; independent agencies of the Federal Government.

Congress:

OFFICE OF TECHNOLOGY ASSESSMENT
 (OTA)
119 D Street, N.E.
Washington, D.C. 20510          202-224-8711

Est. 1972 to assist Congress to anticipate and plan for, the consequences of uses of techology. National food policy is one of the seven broad program areas in which the Office concentrates its efforts.

CONGRESSIONAL COMMITTEES
Several Senate and House committees consider legislation and oversee the implementation of enacted laws relating to domestic and international food matters. These include the Senate committees on Agriculture and Forestry, Commerce, Foreign Relations, and Government Operations, and the Select Committee on Nutrition and Human Needs; and the House committees on Agriculture, Government Operations, International Relations, Interstate and Foreign Commerce, Merchant Marine and Fisheries, and Science and Technology. For listings of hearings, reports, and other documents issued by congressional committees, consult the publications of Congressional Information Service or other standard references.

Executive Office of the President:

BOARD FOR INTERNATIONAL FOOD AND
 AGRICULTURAL DEVELOPMENT
Executive Office of the President
Washington, D.C. 20500

Est. by the International Development and Food Assistance Act of 1975 to encourage research into the production, distribution, storage, marketing, and consumption of agricultural products. Makes policies and establishes criteria for grants to U.S. universities for such research, and maintains a roster of institutions with research capability in the field.

DEVELOPMENT COORDINATION COMMITTEE
c/o Administrator, USAID
Washington, D.C. 20523

Est. in 1975 by executive order. Advises the President on coordination of foreign policies and programs affecting the development of developing countries, including programs of bilateral and multilateral assistance. Members represent 12 federal agencies; chairman is the Administrator of the Agency for International Development.

Executive departments:

DEPARTMENT OF AGRICULTURE (USDA)
Washington, D.C. 20250

+Agricultural Research Service (ARS)
Washington, D.C. 20250          202-447-3656

The chief research agency of the Department of Agriculture, with an annual budget of about $263 million, and a total staff of 9,500, including some 2,800 scientists and engineers. ARS has 155 laboratories, field stations, and work sites in 46 states, 3 territories, and 9 foreign countries. Projects extend from improving farm practices to human nutrition. Major work areas include: plant sciences; animal and veterinary research; agricultural engineering; entomology; soil and water conservation; utilization research and development; marketing and transportation; human nutrition; and consumer economics.

One of ARS' top priorities is to improve farm production to meet increasing domestic and world food needs. Processing and distribution technology, and nutrition, are also major interests.

The ARS International Programs Division administers foreign research grants and contracts under Public Law 480 and related legislation, and coordinates other USDA activities in international economic, technical, and cooperative assistance. Grants are made to foreign governments and scientific organizations for research on developing new and extended uses of U.S. agricultural products, and for conducting farm, human nutrition, and animal nutrition

Department of Agriculture, Agricultural
Research Service, contin.

studies.  The Division also provides agricultural advisors to developing countries
through the Agency for International Development, monitors foreign trainee programs in biological research related to
agriculture, and acts as liaison for the
Animal and  Plant Health Inspection Service (APHIS) of USDA for international
requests for assistance in inspection for
agricultural diseases and pests.

ARS maintains a Nutrient Data Bank, and
also has a Human Nutrition Laboratory
(at 2420 Second Avenue N., Grand Forks,
North Dakota 58201).  These programs are
concerned with determining the nutrient
composition of food and nutritional gaps in
diets.

Pub.: Agricultural Research, mon. magazine.  Technical reports, research progress reports, public information booklets.

+Cooperative State Research Service
  (CSRS)
Washington, D.C. 20250     202-447-4348

CSRS administers federal grant funds for
research in agriculture, rural development, and related fields, primarily
through agricultural experiment stations
and other institutions related to state
governments in the U.S.  Among its responsibilities is monitoring programs
offered to foreign trainees in the state
land-grant colleges and universities under
USDA funding.

+Extension Service (ES)
Washington, D.C. 20250     202-447-3691

ES provides agricultural information and
advisory services to agricultural communities in the U.S.  Its Office of International Extension provides advisors to foreign
governments to assist in developing extension services.  The Office also plans,
monitors, and evaluates USDA's extension
training program for foreign nationals.

+National Agricultural Library
Food and Nutrition Information and
  Educational Materials Center
10301 Baltimore Boulevard
Beltsville, Maryland 20705

                           301-344-3750

Facilities of the Library, including this
special center on food and nutrition, are
available to those who have a serious
interest in the topics it covers.  The
Library is the largest agricultural library
in the U.S. Pub.: Bibliography of Agriculture.  National Agricultural Library Catalog.

+Soil Conservation Service (SCS)
Washington, D.C. 20250     202-447-4263

SCS administers national soil and water
conservation programs, watershed protection, and related activities, all in cooperation with farmers and landowners.  Its
Foreign Programs Office plans and monitors on-the-job and academic training in
cooperation with USDA's Economic Research Service and the Food and Agriculture
Organization of the UN.

+Commodity Credit Corporation (CCC)
Washington, D.C. 20250     202-447-7583

CCC determines the availability of U.S.
agricultural commodities for sale to
foreign governments and, in the case of
certain sales, is authorized under Public
Law 480 to provide the funding for such
transactions.

+Federal Crop Insurance Corporation
  (FCIC)
Washington, D.C. 20250     202-447-3325

FCIC administers the national crop insurance program in the U.S.  It has also
provided practical training for foreign
nationals in the administration of such
programs, and supplies U.S. advisors to
foreign governments to assist in developing
crop insurance programs.

+Foreign Agricultural Service (FAS)
Washington, D.C. 20250     202-447-6725

The main responsibility of FAS is to develop, maintain, and expand foreign markets for the U.S. agricultural producer. It seeks to enhance the American farmer's position in the world market by providing up-to-date information on world agricultural production and trade prospects, thus enabling the farmer to plan his production; providing support to trade associations and state agriculture departments in their export promotion efforts; and providing representation at international negotiations that effect the U.S. farmer's position.

The focus of FAS is on commercial aspects of world agricultural trade. It believes that this trade "is an important element in the solution of long-term world food problems. We consider the reliability of the American farmer in...the world market a significant force in planning for the future."

FAS' export promotion work is assisted by some 40 trade associations (those concerned with basic world food commodities are listed elsewhere in this book - see the subject index).

FAS administers the system of agricultural attaches in U.S. embassies, and assists in the development of U.S. international trade policy for agricultural commodities, including sale of U.S. agricultural commodities under Public Law 480.

The Representation and Foreign Visitors Staff of FAS conducts information programs on American agriculture for high-level foreign officials.

The world agricultural commodity information collected by FAS has become "the basic system of agricultural commodity information for the world...and is the source most used by other governments."

Pub.: Foreign Agriculture, weekly magazine. Foreign Agriculture Circular series. FAS Special Reports series. Publications lists available.

+Agricultural Marketing Service (AMS)
Washington, D.C. 20250     202-447-6235

AMS is the regulatory agency which inspects and grades agricultural products. It administers a foreign visitors program and recruits inspection specialists upon request for AID, the USDA Economic Research Service, and FAO to serve overseas.

+Food and Nutrition Service (FNS)
Washington, D.C. 20250     202-447-8138

Administers federal food assistance programs in the United States, including the Food Stamp Program, National School Lunch Program, School Breakfast Program, Summer Food Service Program for Children, Child Care Food Program, and Special Milk Program, as well as related nonfood assistance.

+Farmers Home Administration (FmHA)
Washington, D.C. 20250     202-447-3660

Provides loans to farmers who are unable to get credit from other sources. FmHA's International Development Office assists foreign governments in developing systems of credit for farmers through training and consultant services which are funded by AID or FAO.

+Rural Electrification Administration (REA)
Washington, D.C. 20250     202-447-3361

REA has provided selected foreign officials with field training in the establishment and development of rural electric distribution systems.

+Economic Research Service (ERS)
Washington, D.C. 20250     202-447-8038

ERS carries out a national program of economic research and analysis, statistical programs, and other work relating to the production and marketing of farm commodities. The Service deals with the entire agriculture sector and centers around the more aggregative issues cutting across commodity lines. It focuses on

Department of Agriculture, Economic
Research Service, contin.

worldwide, as well as domestic, supply
and demand conditions, and the impact of
U.S. and foreign policies on world farm
trade.

ERS' Foreign Development Division is
responsible for coordinating all of the
foreign technical assistance and economic
development activities of the Department
of Agriculture. Through the Division's
International Training Office, USDA provides training programs for over 2,000
foreign trainees per year in agricultural
administration, policy, and economics;
agricultural education; agricultural engineering; home economics; agronomy, horticulture, conservation and development
of agricultural and forest resources; animal husbandry; and extension methods.
These programs are sponsored by AID,
FAO, and other international organizations.

The Division's Technical Assistance Office
recruits agricultural specialists to serve
as advisors to foreign governments and
international organizations, drawing on the
whole range of USDA agencies and resources.

The Division's International Organization
Affairs Office coordinates USDA's relations with FAO, the World Bank, OECD,
and other intergovernmental bodies.
The Reports and Technical Inquiries Staff
performs information retrieval services
in the field of agricultural technology relating to developing countries; it draws on
USDA documents, the National Agricultural
Library, and other agencies, research
centers, university libraries, and resources.

Pub.: Farm Index, mon. Agricultural
Economics Research, q. Series of periodic reports analyzing the economic situation of U.S. agriculture. Research reports.

+Farmer Cooperative Service (FCS)
Washington, D.C. 20250     202-447-8672

FCS provides research, education, and
technical assistance in the organization
and operation of agricultural cooperatives
in the U.S. Its International Training
Office, in cooperation with AID and ERS,
provides training in the U.S. for foreign
nationals, and advisory services to foreign
governments, in the development and management of cooperatives.

+Statistical Reporting Service (SRS)
Washington, D.C. 20250     202-447-5455

SRS prepares estimates and reports of
production, supply, price, and other
items relating to U.S. crops and livestock.
(A list of its reports, the Crop Reporting
Board Catalog, is issued annually.)

SRS' International Programs Office provides technical assistance to foreign governments in agricultural data collection and
analysis to serve as a basis of economic
planning for development. The Office also
conducts courses for foreign trainees in
the U.S.

DEPARTMENT OF COMMERCE
Washington, D.C. 20230

+National Oceanic and
Atmospheric Administration
(NOAA)

++Environmental Data Service (EDS)
3300 Whitehaven Street, N.W.
Washington, D.C. 20852
202-343-6226

Acquires, stores, and disseminates
worldwide data on various natural
phenomena, including climate and
weather. Meteorological data are
used by the State and Agriculture
Departments and other agencies to
examine the potential effects of drought
and other climatic fluctuations on national and global food supplies. EDS
has joined with USDA and NASA in a
Large Area Crop Inventory Experiment (LACIE) to determine whether

Department of Commerce, NOAA, Environmental Data Service, contin.

satellite crop-monitoring and meteorological observations can be used with environmental data products to make timely and accurate estimates of future crop production worldwide. EDS maintains a Center for Climatic and Environmental Assessment. Access to data is facilitated by a one-stop information referral service called ENDEX/OASIS (Environmental Data Index/Oceanic and Atmospheric Scientific Information System). Pub.: Environmental Data Service, mon. magazine.

++National Marine Fisheries
  Service (NMFS)
Washington, D.C. 20235
     202-634-7281

NMFS has an integrated program of research and services related to the protection and rational use of living marine resources for their aesthetic, economic, and recreational value.

Its Marine Resources Monitoring, Assessment, and Prediction program (MARMAP) provides systematic assessments of the principal fish and shellfish stocks, both domestic and worldwide, of interest to the U.S. The Service also conducts basic biological studies to provide information necessary for management of the fisheries; studies of ecological factors influencing the production of marine organisms; and research in aquaculture designed to make commercial production of selected species economically feasible.

The NMFS Office of Resource Utilization conducts economic and marketing research, works with industry to increase fish supplies from domestic resources, collects and disseminates information on the U.S. commercial fishing industry, and conducts research on fishery products.

Department of Commerce, NOAA, National Marine Fisheries Service, contin.

The Office of International Fisheries participates in international negotiations on fisheries issues and in implementation of U.S. international fisheries policy. Its International Fisheries Analysis Division collects, analyzes, and disseminates information on foreign activities in the field. The Language Services Division is a national clearinghouse for translated literature on fisheries and related areas (about 27,000 translations are distributed annually).

Pub.: Current Fisheries Statistics, various series. Data Report, irreg. Fishery Bulletin, q. Fishery Facts series. Fishery Market Development Series. Marine Fisheries Abstracts, mon. Marine Fisheries Review, mon. Market News, various series. Current Economic Analysis (3 subseries for food, industrial, and shellfish. Statistical Digest, ann.

++Office of Sea Grant
Washington, D.C. 20852
     202-967-3854

Provides support for U.S. institutions engaged in comprehensive marine research, education, and advisory programs; individual projects in marine research and development; and training of personnel in the field. Projects of Sea Grant institutions include development of new uses and sources of food from the sea. The National Aquaculture Information System (NAIS) is a joint EDS-Office of Sea Grant project. Pub.: Sea Grant 70s, mon. (issued by Texas A&M Sea Grant Program, College Station, Texas 77843); includes listings of new Sea Grant publications.

Department of Commerce, NOAA, contin.

### ++Office of International Affairs
NOAA
Washington, D.C. 20852

301-496-8635

Coordinates NOAA's foreign programs, which include training of foreign nationals in facilities of the National Marine Fisheries Service, under sponsorship of AID and FAO.

### +National Technical Information Service (NTIS)
Washington, D.C. 22161    703-451-3322

NTIS is the central point in the U.S. for the public sale of federal government-funded research and development reports and other analyses prepared by federal agencies, their contractors, or grantees. A weekly newsletter, Agriculture and Food, contains abstracts and ordering information for new publications in those fields. Also available is NTISearch, published computer searches for documents in such specialized fields as "Fish Protein Concentrates," "Synthetic Foods," and "Aquaculture." List available.

Under agreement with AID, NTIS also transfers relevant scientific and technical information to developing countries, helps organize similar services in those countries, and provides orientation programs for foreign officials in the U.S.

### DEPARTMENT OF STATE
Office of Food Policy and Programs (OFP)
Washington, D.C. 20520    202-632-3090

The Office of Food Policy and Programs is responsible for formulating U.S. foreign policy on world food matters and coordinating the State Department's activities relating to food aid and commercial sales of foodstuffs. The Office is divided into two divisions:

The Food for Freedom Division (OFP/FFD) develops the Department's position on the eligibility of countries to receive food aid and coordinates allocation of available resources. It develops and coordinates the Department's

position on the terms of food aid agreements and on self-help criteria and the performance of recipient countries in light of these criteria. It participates in development of marketing requirements, export limitations, and offset purchase requirements. The Division also conducts consultations on U.S. food aid programs with countries having food export trade with recipient countries; coordinates food aid policy from the point of view of overall international economic policy; and coordinates the Department's participation in the Inter-Agency Staff Committee on Food Aid and the FAO Subcommittee on Surplus Disposal.

The Food Policy Division (OFP/FPD) develops and coordinates the Department's position on the foreign policy aspects of domestic farm legislation, international trade policy in temperate agricultural products, and on proposals to promote exports and protect domestic agricultural and livestock production from import competition. It also represents or advises the U.S. representative in international organizations concerned with food policy, such as the FAO, other UN bodies, OECD, the International Wheat Council, and appropriate GATT commodity groups; advises on export expansion programs for U.S. agricultural products; and exerts Department of State leadership in follow-up activity from the World Food Conference.

Pub.: Some basic U.S. food policies are outlined in "Crisis in Food," Special Report no. 19, available from the Department's Office of Media Services.

### DEPARTMENT OF STATE
Agency for International Development (AID)
Washington, D.C. 20523

AID's food and nutrition programs fall into three broad categories: food relief; agricultural and fisheries development; and research.

### Food relief
The Food for Peace Program, authorized by Public Law 480, is directed by AID's Office of Food for Peace (202-632-8572). Food for Peace is directed principally toward responding to disaster and emergency feeding requirements; continuation of mother-child feeding, school feeding, and Food for Work projects; and sales to needy countries facing the greatest food

deficits.  Food for Peace programs are of two types.  Title I is a sales program administered by the Department of Agriculture in collaboration with AID, allowing purchase of farm products in the U.S. commercial market. Title I sales, made through long-term loans at concessional rates, are about 75% of the total P.L. 480 program.  The absolute need for food is the most important consideration.

Title I programs coordinate with development loans and technical assistance projects.  Commodities are sold in the recipient country for local currency; these receipts are used primarily to increase and improve local agricultural production.  Currently, most Title I aid goes to countries in South Asia, and to Haiti, Chile, Honduras, Tanzania, and Guinea.

Title II of P.L. 480 is a donation program administered by AID, providing food to needy people, particularly children, through U.S. voluntary agencies, the World Food Program, and bilaterally to governments of developing countries.  USDA buys the food in the U.S. commercial market.  AID usually pays ocean freight to the point of entry.  Except for emergency programs, Title II donations are used for project assistance of two kinds: short-term immediate-impact Food for Work projects (in which commodities are used as part payment of wages for community development projects); and long-term, extended-impact child nutrition projects.

In fiscal year 1976, all Food for Peace programs provided some 6 million tons of food grains and grain products valued at $1.2 billion.  Some $160 million was also spent for ocean transportation.

Development assistance
AID's development assistance programs in food and nutrition are coordinated by the Bureau for Technical Assistance and its Office of Agriculture (202-632-3339) and Office of Nutrition (202-632-3959).  Food and nutrition activities amounted to 40% of AID's budget for fiscal year 1978, or $587.0 million.

Goals are to increase food production, improve nutrition, and enhance the quality of life for the rural poor in developing countries. AID's strategy is to help the poor and under-

nourished grow more of their own food; develop appropriate market incentives for small farmers to produce more; strengthen institutions and agribusinesses that provide supporting services to family farms; assist in development of supporting infrastructure; promote national strategies for improving nutrition among the poor; and support agricultural research.

About one-fifth of the current AID food and nutrition program goes for development and diffusion of improved technologies for small producers.  Substantial aid is given to the international agriculture research centers within the framework of the Consultative Group on International Agricultural Research. Funding is also given to projects at U.S. universities and other institutions to develop improved technologies in such areas as crop, livestock, and fish production, fertilizer use, production and use of appropriate mechanical implements, resource assessment, and energy production.  Support also goes to research programs in developing countries, with special emphasis on adapting research efforts to the needs of small producers.

About one-tenth of the budget is devoted to activities which address the policy and institutional factors that broadly influence access to improved technologies and the impact of rural change.  These include, for example, support for land tenure reform, development of cooperatives, strengthening of governmental administration, and settlement of new lands.

Some 40% of the AID food and nutrition budget supports the expansion of rural physical infrastructure and related institutions, including land and water development, secondary and rural roads, and rural electrification.

Another third of the budget supports projects to provide small producers with better access to inputs, finance, and markets.  Examples: financing and technical assistance to small-scale rural enterprises to expand the market for small-farmer crops and generate rural employment; expansion of grain storage facilities to reduce post-harvest losses.

AID's nutrition program focuses on continued testing and development of low-cost nutritious foods; assessment of alternative nutrition interventions; assistance to governments for nutrition surveys; and planning and initiation of research on the impact of varying degrees of malnutrition. AID also supports efforts to motivate responsible groups to seek explicit nutrition goals as part of the development process; to formulate national, regional, and local plans, policies, and strategies to achieve specific nutrition objectives; and to develop programs and delivery systems to produce trained people to staff the institutions responsible for these tasks.

Research
As part of its food and nutrition program, AID sponsors a wide variety of research projects at institutions in the U.S. and abroad, emphasizing higher-yielding crop varieties, with higher nutrient levels; more efficient systems for using soil and water; better fertilizers and cheaper means of using nitrogen for assimilation by plants; and improved livestock systems, particularly in parts of Africa and Latin America where animals forage and do not compete with humans for grain consumption.

Contributions to international organizations
AID also contributes substantial funds to various intergovernmental organizations concerned with the world food problem. It administers the $200 million initial U.S. contribution to the International Fund for Agricultural Development (IFAD). Other grants have been provided to the UN Development Programme, UNICEF, FAO, UNEP, and OAS.

AID bilateral programs are carried out through USAID missions in the countries concerned. Food and nutrition projects are assisted in some 18 countries in Africa, 8 in Asia, 16 in Latin America, and 4 in the Near East.

Pub.: AID publishes Front Line, a biweekly internal newsletter; AID Research and Development Abstracts, q.; and War on Hunger, mon., a magazine focused on food and population programs. "Food & Nutrition," a booklet issued annually, describes the Agency's food program. Some 75 research reports and other publications on agricultural topics are listed in the Catalog of Selected AID Publications (1974). AID Research, 19- , issued irregularly, includes reviews of agricultural and nutrition projects funded by the Agency. A Summary of Ongoing

Research and Technical Assistance Projects in Agriculture was issued in 1975. The Office of Private and Voluntary Cooperation issues a compendium of reports of voluntary agencies involved in overseas relief and development, Voluntary Foreign Aid Programs. AID's Office of Public Affairs provides the above and various other publications, including pamphlets on specific problems, as well as films and speaker services.

Independent agencies of the
federal government:

ACTION
806 Connecticut Avenue, N.W.
Washington, D.C. 20525          202-393-3111

The Peace Corps, part of ACTION, administers a U.S. volunteer service program in developing countries, providing trained manpower to fill specific needs, including those related to food, nutrition, and rural development. The Peace Corps has some 7,000 volunteers in 68 countries.

FARM CREDIT ADMINISTRATION (FCA)
Washington, D.C. 20578          202-755-2170

FCA is responsible for supervision, examination, and coordination of the borrower-owned banks and associations that comprise the cooperative Farm Credit System in the U.S. The FCA's Foreign Training Office plans and monitors training of foreign nationals in administration of agricultural credit, including screening of loan applications, determining credit worthiness, bookkeeping, and regulation of credit systems. FCA also recruits short-term advisors from U.S. institutions to work with foreign governments in setting up agricultural credit systems. Coordinates with USDA, AID, and FAO.

INTER-AMERICAN FOUNDATION (IAF)
1515 Wilson Boulevard
Roslyn, Virginia 22209          703-841-3800

An independent federal government corporation that provides financial support for private, community-level, sel-help efforts to solve basic social and economic problems in Latin America and the Caribbean. IAF has provided aid to some 350 projects in 27 countries, including credit and production cooperatives and agriculture extension services.

NATIONAL ACADEMY OF SCIENCES/
NATIONAL RESEARCH COUNCIL(NAS/NRC)
2101 Constitution Avenue, N.W.
Washington, D.C. 20418          202-393-8100

A private, not-for-profit organization chartered by the Congress to advise the federal government on scientific matters of importance to the public welfare.  The following NAS units are directly concerned with food matters:

+Board on Agriculture and Renewable Resources (BARR)
National Academy of Sciences
Washington, D.C. 20418     202-389-6761

Responsible for public science and technology problems in agriculture and renewable resources, including plant and animals sciences, agrichemicals, soils and hydrology, agriclimatology, utilization and management of products, agricultural lands, and fisheries. Also responsible for world food and population issues and rural development.

Recent studies have included enhancement of food production for the U.S., African agricultural research capabilities, agricultural production efficiency, nutrition and production of fish, genetic improvement of seed protein, and alternative sources of protein for animal production.  Pub.: various reports (list available).

+Food and Nutrition Board
National Academy of Sciences
Washington, D.C. 20418     202-389-6366

Maintains various committees on aspects of food and nutrition, including a Committee on International Nutrition Programs, which advises AID's Office of Nutrition. Pub.: various reports (list available).

+Board on Science and Technology for International Development
National Academy of Sciences
Washington, D.C. 20418     202-389-6521

Includes a Panel on Promising Technologies in Arid-Land Water Development, which has issued a report, More Water for Arid Lands (1974).

In addition to the reports of its various boards and committees, NAS publishes News Report, 10 times a year; and monthly Proceedings. A list of Academy publications is available from the Printing and Publishing Office.

NATIONAL SCIENCE FOUNDATION (NSF)
Washington, D.C. 20550          202-655-4000

NSF supports basic and applied research in the sciences, and research aimed at formulating science policy.  Several of its programs relate to world food problems, including, for example, research on regulation of pest populations and global weather.  The Division of International Programs encourages and supports U.S. scientific participation in international science programs and activities, and provides travel and teaching grants for U.S. scientists and engineers to apply their experience to specific development problems abroad under the Scientists and Engineers in Economic Development (SEED) program.  Pub.: NSF Bulletin, mon.  Mosaic, bimon. magazine. Guide to Programs, ann.

# B. OTHER ORGANIZATIONS

Note: Even though a number of organizations listed in this section have extensive international programs (e.g., Agricultural Cooperative Development International), they are listed as national, rather than international, organizations if their memberships or management boards are essentially national in character.

THE ACADEMY FOR CONTEMPORARY
  PROBLEMS
1501 Neil Avenue
Columbus, Ohio 43201          614-421-7700

Est. 1971.  The policy research and conference center for six organizations: Council of State Governments, International City Management Association, National Association of Counties, National Conference of State Legislatures, National League of Cities, and U.S. Conference of Mayors.  Projects have included a major conference (1975), "Toward a National Food Policy."  Pub.: The Policy Reporter, q.  Conference proceedings.

ACCION INTERNATIONAL
10-C Mt. Auburn Street
Cambridge, Massachusetts 02138
                              617-492-4930

Works to establish autonomous national community action programs in Latin America, providing launching capital and technical assistance for an initial period.  Provides credit and technical assistance to small business entrepreneurs, including food production projects.

ACRES U.S.A.
10227 E. 61st Street
Raytown, Missouri 64133          816-737-0064

Promotes eco-agriculture: "To be economical, agriculture has to be ecological."  Pub.: Acres U.S.A., mon. newspaper; The Case for Eco-Agriculture (by Charles Walters, Jr.).

THE ACTION CENTER
1028 Connecticut Avenue, N.W., Suite 302
Washington, D.C. 20036          202-466-3726

Works to mobilize young people, particularly college students, to act on the issues of food, population, social justice, and development. Formerly called the Food Action Center; based at the National Student Association and sponsored by the Institute for World Order.  Pub.: Newsletter, mon.

AD HOC JEWISH COMMITTEE ON HUNGER
808 West End Avenue, Suite 1004
New York, New York 10025

Works to increase awareness in the Jewish community about the world food situation; encourages Jews to act individually by reducing their consumption of meat, fertilizer, and

other scarce resources and by reducing waste; and works to mobilize the Jewish community to take political action to reorder U.S. priorities in light of the world situation.  Pub.: Pamphlets.

AFRICARE
1424 Sixteenth Street, N.W.
Washington, D.C. 20036          202-462-3614

Est. 1972.  Dedicated to improving the quality of life in rural Africa, especially in the areas of water resource development, agriculture and food production, and rural health services. Works currently in the drought region of the Sahel in Mauritania, Mali, Senegal, Niger, Upper Volta, Chad, Ethiopia, and the Gambia.

Several projects are focused on food production, e.g., irrigation projects in Niger and Ethiopia; farmer cooperatives in Senegal and the Gambia; and vegetable farming in Upper Volta.

Although Africare has provided relief assistance to these countries, including purchase of food for local emergencies and refugees, most of its activities have been in water resource development, food production, and integrated development planning.

A special mission is to create an awareness among black Americans of the needs, problems, and potentialities of the people of Africa. About 65% of individual contributions to its work are from American blacks. Chapters in some 20 cities. Pub.: Africare Newsletter, q.

AGRIBUSINESS ACCOUNTABILITY PROJECT
1000 Wisconsin Avenue, N.W.
Washington, D.C. 20007　　　202-338-6331

Est. 1970, by the Center for Community Change and the Center for Corporate Responsibility as a research group to report on the effect of agribusiness corporations (large firms involved in food growing and manufacturing) on consumers and on the environment. Currently developing an alternative national food policy.

Pub.: Hard Tomatoes, Hard Times: The Failure of the Land Grant College Complex (1972). The Great American Grain Robbery and Other Stories (1972). Who's Minding the Co-op? (1974). The Fields Have Turned Brown: Four Essays on World Hunger (1975). Publications list available.

AGRICULTURAL COOPERATIVE
　DEVELOPMENT INTERNATIONAL (ACDI)
1430 K Street, N.W.
Washington, D.C. 20005　　　202-638-4661

Est. 1968. An educational, consulting, and technical organization created by leading cooperatives in the U.S. to organize and provide technical assistance to cooperatives and governments of developing countries in promoting cooperatives.

The major part of ACDI's activity is supported by grants from the U.S. Agency for International Development. Member coops also contribute funds and services.

ACDI advises coops and governments in agricultural marketing, supply, credit; carries out feasibility studies for specific coop ventures; and arranges formal and on-the-job training in coop theory and practice.

Major recent projects have focused on Guatemala (organization and credit); Honduras (management and accounting training); Kenya (farmer credit); Paraguay (strengthening cooperative programs); the Philippines (farmer institutional development); and Tanzania (credit, grain storage, financial management, and marketing).

Members of ACDI are 24 regional farm supply and marketing agricultural coops, six national organizations, one international coop, one regional consumer coop, two insurance coops, six district farm credit banks, and the Central Bank for Cooperatives.

Pub.: News of Cooperative Development, bimon.

AGRICULTURAL DEVELOPMENT COUNCIL
620 Fifth Avenue
New York, New York 10020

Est. 1953, by John D. Rockefeller III to support teaching and research activities related to the problems of agricultural development. Main focus is on agricultural economics, rural sociology, and extension education in Asia. Graduate fellowships; pilot research projects; sponsorship of Asian projects to enable social scientists to work on common problems; grants in related fields.

Pub.: Newsletter, q. ADC Papers, irreg.

AGRICULTURAL MISSIONS
See: National Council of Churches

AGRICULTURAL MISSIONS FOUNDATION,
　LTD.
P.O. Box 388
Yazoo City, Mississippi 39194　601-842-4615

Est. 1970. Supports agricultural missionaries in less developed countries. Supplies and equipment have also been sent. The 1976 budget was $130,000, mainly in $1,000 to $4,600 grants to projects in South America and Africa. Grants are used for such purposes as seed and fertilizer, dairy goats, and trucks.
Pub.: Agricultural Missions Newsletter, mon.

AGRISERVICES FOUNDATION
3699 E. Sierra Avenue
Clovis, California 93612          209-299-2263

Est. 1964.  Programs include an annual
International Stockmen's School and study tours
of such places as Guatemala and the People's
Republic of China.

Pub.: Beef Cattle Science Handbook, annual.
Dairy Science Handbook, annual.  Stud Mana-
ger's Handbook, annual.

AMERICAN BAPTIST CHURCHES IN THE
  U.S.A.
Board of International Ministries
Valley Forge, Pennsylvania 19481
                              215-768-2000

Provides personnel and funds to agricultural
extension programs, community development
leadership training, vocational agriculture and
nutrition training in schools and local communities; introduces new crops, seeds, farming
methods, tools, livestock, and fish culture;
operates demonstration farms and experimental
plots at its missions in Zaire, Burma, the
Philippines, Haiti, India, and Thailand.

AMERICAN CHEMICAL SOCIETY (ACS)
1155 Sixteenth Street, N.W.
Washington, D.C. 20036          202-872-4600

Est. 1876.  The main national association of
chemists.  Publications include the Journal
of Agricultural and Food Chemistry, bimon.

AMERICAN CORN MILLERS FEDERATION
1030 15th Street, N.W.
Washington, D.C. 20005          202-296-5488

Est. 1918.  Organization of manufacturers of
dry corn meal.  Promotes CSM, a blended food
product made of precooked corn meal, toasted
soy flour, powdered milk, and vitamins and
minerals, and designed to meet the needs of
growing children, especially in developing
countries.

AMERICAN COUNCIL OF VOLUNTARY
  AGENCIES IN FOREIGN SERVICE, INC.
200 Park Avenue South
New York, New York 10003     212-777-8210

Est. 1943.  Members are some 40 U.S.-based
voluntary agencies engaged in programs of
active service overseas.  Provides a means
of consultation, coordination, and planning to
assure maximum effective use of contributions
by the American people for overseas aid.  Since
1955, the Council has operated the Technical
Assistance Information Clearing House (TAICH),
a center of information on the socio-economic
development programs abroad of U.S. nonprofit organizations.  Through publications and
an inquiry service, TAICH makes available to
organizations, the U.S. Government, researchers, and other users, information about
development assistance with particular reference
to the resources and concerns of the private,
voluntary, nonprofit sector.

TAICH publications include: TAICH News, q.
U.S. Non-Profit Organizations in Development
Assistance Abroad, 1971, contains profile
descriptions of over 400 groups and their development programs in 124 countries.  A Country
Reports series updates the information in the
1971 directory.  A Profile Reports series
(6 have been issued through January 1977)
provides information on organizations not included in the 1971 directory.

Other titles include: A Listing of U.S. Non-
Profit Organizations in Food Production and
Agricultural Assistance Abroad (1974).
A TAICH Bibliography on Development Assistance (1975).  Bibliography of Materials Integrated into the TAICH Information System on
Case Studies and Program Planning, Management and Evaluation (1976).  The library issues
a biweekly annotated Acquisitions List.

AMERICAN DRY MILK INSTITUTE (ADMI)
130 N. Franklin Street
Chicago, Illinois 60606              312-782-4888

Est. 1925. Group of some 125 manufacturers
of nonfat dry milk and other dry milk products.
Promotes market expansion, including exports.
Has developed grades for products.

AMERICAN ENTERPRISE INSTITUTE FOR
  PUBLIC POLICY RESEARCH (AEI)
1150 17th Street, N.W.
Washington, D.C. 20036               202-296-5616

Est. 1943. Business-oriented research and
educational organization with broad interests.
Food-related publications have included: Food
Stamps and Nutrition (1975), World Food Problems and Prospects (1975), and Food Safety
Regulation (1974). Also publishes Memorandum,
a newsletter.

AMERICAN FISH FARMERS FEDERATION
  (AFFF)
P.O. Box 191
Lonoke, Arkansas 72086               501-676-6519

Est. 1965. National organization of the fish
farming industry. Pub.: American Fish Farmer, mon.

AMERICAN FISHERIES SOCIETY (AFS)
5410 Grosvenor Lane
Bethesda, Maryland 20014             301-897-8616

Est. 1870. Professional organization of those
concerned with fishery science and practice and
conservation, development, and wise use of
fisheries. Works for improved fisheries management, fish culture, and mariculture. Its
"North American Fisheries Policy" includes a
section on food fisheries. Pub.: Transactions
of the American Fisheries Society, bimon.
bulletin. Other serial, monograph, and special
publications (list available).

AMERICAN FREEDOM FROM HUNGER
  FOUNDATION (AFFHF)
1625 Eye Street, N.W., Suite 719
Washington, D.C. 20006               202-254-3487

Est. 1961. Committed "to reducing world
hunger through community education and community action." Also a citizen support group
for the Food and Agriculture Organization of the
UN. Seeks to arouse public awareness of the
causes of hunger and malnutrition, both in the
U.S. and abroad.

AFFHF has raised funds for projects of over 100
private U.S. organizations working with poor
people overseas. Its Walk for Development
Program has generated more than $12 million
for self-help development projects for the poor
in the U.S. Holds public education meetings in
the U.S.; provides technical consultation on
rural development abroad; produces educational
materials; sponsors the annual National Week of
Concern for World Hunger. Local chapters.

Pub.: Bulletin, mon. Packets on "World
Hunger Issue" (1964) and "Hunger and Develop-
ment" (1972); "Religious Hunger Packet" (1974).
Population and Development (1972). Guide to
Films About Development (1976). Hunger
Action Handbook (1976).

AMERICAN FRIENDS SERVICE COMMITTEE
  (AFSC)
160 N. 15th Street
Philadelphia, Pennsylvania 19102
                                     215-563-9372

Est. 1917. A social welfare organization related to the Religious Society of Friends (Quakers).
Among its activities is a World Hunger Project,
designed to "develop an informed public engaged
in an ongoing effort to effect the policies necessary to end the world hunger problem." Main
activities are leadership development sessions
and issue briefings in various parts of the
country, and developing and disseminating
policy-oriented publications and slide shows.

In addition, AFSC carries on an extensive rural development program in Asia, Africa, and Latin America, where it organizes farmer cooperatives and credit unions, carries out food production and general agricultural projects, and provides assistance to national health and welfare agencies.

Pub.: Quaker Service Bulletin, q. Relay/Act, newsletter of the World Hunger Project. Packets; simulation game; slide show; papers on specific issues.

AMERICAN INSTITUTE FOR FREE LABOR DEVELOPMENT (AIFLD)
1925 K Street, N.W.
Washington, D.C. 20006          202-659-6300

Est. 1960. Organized by the American Federation of Labor-Congress of Industrial Organizations; governed   by a board composed of AFL-CIO officials, Latin American leaders, and U.S. public figures. Dedicated to development of "free and democratic trade unions in the Americas." Among its programs are courses and seminars for rural workers and agrarian unions in Latin America; support for community development projects and cooperatives for agricultural credit and marketing of fish; and funding for agrarian union development.

AMERICAN INSTITUTE OF CROP ECOLOGY
809 Dale Drive
Silver Spring, Maryland 20910   301-589-4185

Est. 1947. Independent nonprofit research organization supported by U.S. Government contracts. Projects include studies of plant-climate relationships and crop geography.

AMERICAN JEWISH COMMITTEE (AJC)
165 E. 56th Street
New York, New York 10022     212-751-4000

Est. 1906. Major human rights and inter-group relations agency of the organized Jewish community in the U.S. World hunger has been among its concerns; it gave testimony before the Ad Hoc Senate Committee on World Hunger and has issued a statement on "The Poorest Among Us."

Pub.: Commentary, mon.

AMERICAN JEWISH JOINT DISTRIBUTION COMMITTEE (JDC)
60 E. 42nd Street, Room 1915
New York, New York 10017     212-687-6200

Est. 1914. Maintains welfare programs for needy Jews in some 25 countries, including feeding programs. Also known as: Joint Distribution Committee. Pub.: annual reports on activities.

AMERICAN KOR-ASIAN FOUNDATION
345 E. 46th Street
New York, New York 10017     212-697-1960

Provides assistance for land reclamation and poultry projects; demonstration farm; courses in agriculture; scholarships. Operates in South Korea.

AMERICAN NEAR EAST REFUGEE AID (ANERA)
900 Woodward Building
733 15th Street, N.W.
Washington, D.C. 20005     202-347-2558

Est. 1968. An American voluntary organization working to increase opportunities for Palestinian refugees and other needy individuals in the Arab world. Many of the institutions it supports provide food to participants in their programs. Pub.: Newsletter, bimon.

AMERICAN ORT FEDERATION (ORT)
817 Broadway
New York, New York 10003     212-677-4400

Est. 1922. ORT is an acronym for Organization for Rehabilitation through Training. A Jewish agency with some 100,000 members, the American ORT Federation provides various kinds of assistance to developing countries, including aid related to food problems. For example, training has been given to agromechanics in the Ivory Coast; to veterinary laboratory technicians in Mali; and to those involved with food preservation through cold storage in Chile. Pub.: ORT Bulletin, three times a year.

## AMERICAN SEED RESEARCH FOUNDATION (ASRF)

1030 15th Street, N.W., Suite 964
Washington, D.C. 20005          202-223-4080

Est. 1959. Organization of breeders, producers, and distributors of seeds. Supports research on seeds. Pub.: Search, q.

## AMERICAN SHEEP PRODUCERS COUNCIL (ASPC)

200 Clayton Street
Denver, Colorado 80206          303-399-8130

Est. 1955. Voluntary industry organization for promotion of lamb and wool, and recognized by the U.S. Department of Agriculture as the industry's self-help organization. The Council's "Blueprint for Expansion" is a program to reverse "the long decline in sheep production in the U.S. It acknowledges the irony of the present situation - that at a time when the world is rapidly growing short of food and fiber, an industry that can provide both products is at its lowest point since the Civil War." Pub.: American Lamb and Wool Promotion News, mon.

## AMERICAN SOCIETY OF AGRICULTURAL CONSULTANTS (ASAC)

c/o Bob Garey
Association Building, 9th & Minnesota
Hastings, Nebraska 68501          402-462-5515

Est. 1963. Organization of independent consultants in various specialized fields providing services to agribusiness throughout the world. Referral services for business. Committees include: Ecological Concerns; International Consulting; and Pesticides. Pub.: Newsletter, quarterly.

## AMERICAN SOCIETY OF AGRONOMY (ASA)

677 S. Segoe Road
Madison, Wisconsin 53711          606-274-1212

Est. 1907. Professional society of some 7,500 agronomists (those who work in the applied plant and soil sciences) and related fields. Maintains an International Agronomy Committee.

Pub.: Crops and Soils Magazine, 9 times a year. Agronomy Journal, bimon. Agronomy News, bimon. Journal of Agronomic Education, semiann. Journal of Environmental Quality, q. Other technical serials and monographs.

## AMERICAN SOYBEAN ASSOCIATION (ASA)

Hudson, Iowa 50643          319-988-3294

Est. 1920. National organization of some 17,000 producers of soybeans and soybean products. Promotes products in the U.S. and abroad. Pub.: Soybean Profits, 32 times a year.

ASA is a market development cooperator with the U.S. Department of Agriculture. It maintains the following overseas market development offices:

+American Soybean Association
Prinz Eugen-Strasse 14
1040 Vienna, Austria          65-74-12

+American Soybean Association
Centre International Rogier
Passage no. 6, Salle no. 2501
Brussels, Belgium          02-217-20-75

+American Soybean Association
P.O. Box 3512
Taipei, Republic of China    782-110

+American Soybean Association
Pelzerstrasse 13
2 Hamburg 1, West Germany
                              040-33-05-16

+American Soybean Association
Akasaka Yomo Building, 4th Floor
12-21, 3-chome
Akasaka, Minato-ku
Tokyo, Japan          585-5826

+American Soybean Association
Latin American Office
Rio Sena no. 26, Desp. 1
Cuahutemoc,
Mexico 5, D.F., Mexico     905-535-0659

AMERICAN VEGAN SOCIETY
P.O. Box H
Malaga, New Jersey 08328          609-694-2887

Est. 1960.  Promotes total vegetarianism for humane and personal health reasons, and also because a "considerable amount of people presently lacking a sufficient quantity of food could be fed by using plant foods directly rather than using them second hand through animals."  Pub.: Ahimsa, bimon. newspaper. Pamphlets.

AMERICAN VEGETARIAN UNION (AVU)
P.O. Box 68
Duncannon, Pennsylvania 17020
                                  717-834-4504

Est. 1949.  Promotes a vegetarian philosophy of non-violence through a diet excluding fish, flesh, or fowl.  Works with the International Vegetarian Union (which see) to develop foods "for the relief of famine by humane methods." Pub.: American Better Health, bimon.  American Vegetarian Hygienist, bimon.  Pamphlets.

ANDEAN FOUNDATION
810 18th Street, N.W.
Washington, D.C. 20006          202-347-4199

Est. 1965.  Promotes economic and social development in the Andean region of South America.  Projects have included assistance to agriculture in the highlands of Peru.

THE ARCA FOUNDATION
100 E. 85th Street
New York, New York 10028       212-861-8300

Est. 1952.  Formed to "help promote the well-being of mankind throughout the world," Arca has made grants totaling more than $6.8 million.  At present, the Foundation is concentrating its attention on population problems and on cooperative efforts in the areas of population, food, and nutrition that emphasize effective communication of the critical issues. Recent funding for food-related activities has included support for the National Food Day program organized by the Center for Science in the Public Interest, the Agricultural Accountability Project of the Center for Community Change, and campus study and action programs on the world hunger crisis and domestic food problems of the United States National Student Association.

THE ASIA FOUNDATION
P.O. Box 3223
San Francisco, California 94119
                                  415-982-4640

Est. 1954.  Projects in Asian countries related to food and nutrition include cattle feeding, fish farming, improving farming techniques, agricultural research, and technical assistance to improve water distribution.

ASIAN-AMERICAN FREE LABOR INSTITUTE
  (AAFLI)
815 Sixteenth Street, N.W., Room 406
Washington, D.C. 20006          202-737-3000

Organized by the American Federation of Labor-Congress of Industrial Organizations.  Among its activities are providing training, advice, and financial support for the organization of cooperatives in Asia among small farmers for production, credit, and marketing; providing assistance for establishing fishermen-owned marketing cooperatives.

ASSOCIATION OF APPLIED INSECT
  ECOLOGISTS
10202 Cowan Heights Drive
Santa Ana, California 92705      714-838-1550

Est. 1966.  Small society of professional agricultural pest management consultants who promote "integrated pest management," which emphasizes methods of pest control other than chemicals, such as cultural methods, genetic changes, biological control, pest-specific diseases and hormones, and pest sterilization. Pesticides are also used, but only when needed. Pub.: Newsletter, mon.

ASSOCIATION OF U.S. UNIVERSITY
  DIRECTORS OF INTERNATIONAL
  AGRICULTURAL PROGRAMS
c/o International Programs in Agriculture
Purdue University
Lafayette, Indiana 47907         317-494-8753

Est. 1964.  A group which promotes communication among directors of university-based international agricultural programs in the U.S.  Pub.: Report of annual meeting.

## BAPTIST WORLD RELIEF
1628 16th Street, N.W.
Washington, D.C. 20009          202-265-5027

Raises and disseminates funds for various overseas relief and development projects, including
provision of seeds, irrigation, and an agricultural school.

## BATTELLE MEMORIAL INSTITUTE
505 King Avenue
Columbus, Ohio 43201            614-299-3151

Est. 1929.  A major non-profit, public-
purpose research organization that conducts
scientific studies on a contract basis for
firms and governmental agencies in a wide
variety of fields.

Recent Battelle research related to the food
problem has included studies on improved land
use, hydroponic farming, protein substitutes,
economic aspects of food processing and distribution, and future pesticide needs.  Examples
of projects: experimental harvesting and
analysis of sargassum marine algae as a possible food; looking into ways of speeding up
development of  vegetable-protein meat substitutes that are acceptable to more people.
Pub.: Research Futures, q.

## BIO-DYNAMIC FARMING AND GARDENING
   ASSOCIATION (BDFGA)
c/o Michael Scully
1019 S. Sixth Street
Springfield, Illinois 62704

Est.: 1937.  Promotes "bio-dynamic farming,"
a form of organic farming that stresses resto-
ration of organic matter to the soil; use of
special materials to engender plant and soil
activity; and other methods of farming.  Pub.:
Bio-Dynamics, q.

## BIOLOGISTS' GROUP ON GLOBAL FOOD
   PROBLEMS
c/o Prof. Walter H. Shank
4057 Udal Street
San Diego, California 92107

## BOSTON INDUSTRIAL MISSION (BIM)
56 Boylston Street
Boston, Massachusetts 02138     617-491-6350

An ecumenical group working on "critical
social and ethical problems related to the impact of science and technology on society and
individuals." Engages in both action and reflection.  Regarding the world food situation, BIM
has collected, prepared, and distributed educational materials "beyond the repetition of slo-
gans." It plans to continue this activity, emphasizing social analysis, theological reflection, and experiments in new life styles, as
well as cooperating with other groups in political activity.

BIM works primarily through the structure of
the Protestant churches.  Pub.: Vectors, q.

## BREAD FOR THE WORLD
235 E. 49th Street
New York, New York 10017        212-751-3925

Est. 1974.  A "Christian citizens' movement
on hunger and poverty," embracing church
leaders from the Protestant, Roman Catholic,
and Othodox faiths in its board of directors.
Main purpose is to "enlist ordinary citizens to
contact their members of Congress and other
government leaders regarding U.S. policy
matters that vitally affect hungry people."
Concerns include hunger and poverty in the
U.S.  Sees its role as promoting the interests
of "citizen-advocates for the world's poor."

Pub.: Pamphlets, e.g., "An Alternative Diet
for People Concerned about Hunger."

## CALIFORNIA FOOD POLICY COALITION
944 Market Street, 4th Floor
San Francisco, California 94102
                                415-433-6317

## CARE
See: Cooperative for American Relief
   Everywhere

CATHOLIC RELIEF SERVICES - U.S.C.C.,
INC.
1011 First Avenue
New York, New York 10022        212-838-4700

"Official overseas relief and development
agency of the [Roman] Catholic hierarchy of
the U.S." 1976 budget was $256 million.
Operated as part of the U.S. Catholic Conference.  Board of Trustees consists of 25
bishops, archbishops, and a Cardinal.

Supports efforts to increase food production in
underdeveloped countries, with priority on
nutritious foods for consumption at the small
farmer-village level, through technical assistance to and/or provision of: cultural training
through schools, rural centers, radio, and
printed media; demonstration projects; improved agricultural technology (seeds, tools,
fertilizer, and methods), agricultural equipment and draft animals, with emphasis on appropriate technology; promotion of rural organization through cooperatives, 4-H, etc.;
water projects such as construction of wells,
pumps, small dams, windmills, and irrigation
systems; credit programs; and funds to assist
small or new efforts, such as purchase of
land; use of small animals; cattle breeding
and raising, especially for milk; crop storage
and food preservation; nutrition education;
construction of access roads to market centers;
and related activities.

Major food-related programs are in Morocco,
Jordan, Egypt, Tunisia, India, Bangladesh,
the Philippines, Indonesia, Chad, Mali, Mauritania, Niger, Senegal, Upper Volta, Ghana,
Tanzania, Rwanda, Ethiopia, Guatemala, Dominican Republic, Honduras, El Salvador, Haiti,
Bolivia, Chile, Colombia, Peru, and Ecuador.

Field operations for all regions are directed
from the New York office, except for CRS
Region 1, Europe, Near and Middle East, and
North Africa:

> +Catholic Relief Services-U.S.C.C.
> Via Boezio 21
> 00192 Rome, Italy

CENTER FOR COMMUNITY CHANGE (CCC)
1000 Wisconsin Avenue, N.W.
Washington, D.C. 20007        202-333-0176

Est. 1968.  Provides technical assistance to
domestic minority groups in housing, economic
development, communications, and general
revenue sharing.  Pub.: Monitor, bimon.

Hunger and Development Program is an effort
to "devise and/or execute domestic and international rural assistance programs and imple-
mentations; management and feasibility studies; educational seminars on hunger and
development issues; and educational programs
for organizations with local constituencies on
hunger and development." Offers public speakers, fund raising and financial reporting
assistance, and evaluations of self-help projects. Pub.: Newsletter, irreg.

CENTER FOR SCIENCE IN THE PUBLIC
INTEREST (CSPI)
1757 S Street, N.W.
Washington, D.C. 20009        202-332-4250

Est. 1971.  "Initiated to people-oriented technology and to establish the legitimacy of advocacy science in the public interest." Food
Project is the sponsor and clearinghouse for
Food Day, an annual day of education and action
on food issues; monitors the food industry and
related governmental agencies.

Food Day Symbol

Food Project concerns include the food business,
nutrition, world hunger, and hunger in the U.S.
Issues two lists of the "Terrible Ten," the first of
"policymakers presiding over the demise of our
food supply;" the second, of ten foods that are
undesirable for reasons of nutrition or politics.
Issues of special interest have included chemical
additives in food and alcoholic beverages, excessive sugar in processed foods, infant feeding,
dietary fiber, and analysis of the nutritional
value of common foods.

Pub.: Nutrition Action, monthly magazine.
Bread Line, newsletter for Food Day. CSPI
Newsletter, q. 99 Ways to a Simpler Life-
style (1976). Nutrition Scoreboard (rev. 1975).
From the Ground Up: Building a Grassroots
Food Policy (1976). Food for People, Not for
Profit (1975, an anthology). Food: Where
Nutrition, Politics, and Culture Meet (1976).
Creative Food Experiences for Children (1974).
Various pamphlets and posters. Publications
list available.

CENTER FOR WAR/PEACE STUDIES
218 E. 18th Street
New York, New York 10003     212-475-0850

Est. 1966. Quaker-related organization that
provides experts and advice on programs and
materials to educational institutions, the mass
media, and voluntary organizations on war-
peace problems, including hunger. Pub.:
Intercom, q. Teaching materials and bibliographies.

CENTER OF CONCERN
3700 13th Street, N.E.
Washington, D.C. 20017     202-635-2757

Est. 1971. Purpose is to promote social
justice in the world community, both at the
decisionmaking level and with the general
public. It believes that "a prerequisite to
global dignity is the assurance that every
individual has access to nutrition and shelter,
basic education, and minimum health services,
and that every person should be guaranteed
participation in the decisions affecting his or
her life opportunities."

Current major project is titled Policy and
Value Questions in a New International Economic Order. Food is addressed as a global
issue of social justice within the context of
the NIEO. Lectures, workshops, commissioned
writings. Pub.: Center Focus, bimon.

CHICAGO GREY PANTHERS
Hunger-Food Stamp Committee
c/o Beverly Williams, Eighth Day Center
22 E. Van Buren Street
Chicago, Illinois 60602

CHRISTIAN CHILDREN'S FUND, INC. (CCF)
P.O. Box 26511
Richmond, Virginia 23261     804-644-4654

Est. 1938. Provides supplementary aid to
children and families through programs assisting homes, day care centers, and Family
Helper Projects. CCF income is generated
through a sponsorship program in which sponsors are assigned a child and contribute $15.00
per month. The annual budget is about $30
million. More than 1,000 projects are supported
in over 40 countries.

Services include providing food to homeless
children in group-care facilities; supplemental
funds for children who live with their parents
or relatives, for various purposes including
food; noontime meals for children attending
elementary or secondary schools; and funds
for meals in affiliated day care centers. Pub.:
CCF World News, q.

Programs are administered through 15 field
offices:

+Christian Children's Fund
Casilla de Correo Central 1923
Buenos Aires, Argentina    31-3577

+Christian Children's Fund
Caixa Postal 1223
60000 Fortaleza, Ceara
Brazil     26-3549

+Christian Children's Fund
Caixa Postal 2548
30000 Belo Horizonte, Minas Gerais
Brazil     0312-442-5655

+Christian Children's Fund
Apartado 699
Guatemala, Guatemala    60-645

+Christian Children's Fund
Apartado Postal 13-576
Mexico 13, D.F.
Mexico     672-3439

+Christian Children's Fund
21 Chatham Road
Kowloon, Hong Kong  K-667271

+Christian Children's Fund
P.O. Box 5054
Bangalore 560001, Karnataka,
India  52157

+Christian Children's Fund
New Delhi Sub-Office
P.O. Box 4229
B-84 Greater Kailash
New Delhi 110048, India  618502

+Christian Children's Fund
P.O. Box 364
Jakarta, Indonesia  71185

+Christian Children's Fund
I.P.O. Box 1278
Seoul, Korea  24-3121

+Christian Children's Fund
P.O. Box 486, M.C.C.
Makati, Rizal D-708
Philippines  58-04-95

+Christian Children's Fund
P.O. Box 205
Taichung, Taiwan 400
Republic of China

+Christian Children's Fund
P.O. Box 11-1062
Bangkok, Thailand  515586

+Christian Children's Fund
P.O. Box 14038
Nairobi (Westlands), Kenya
  60728

+Christian Children's Fund
Box 117, Route 2
Park Hill, Oklahoma 74451
  918-456-8917
 Office for projects in the U.S., Puerto
 Rico, Haiti, and Jamaica.

CHRISTIAN CHURCH (DISCIPLES OF CHRIST)
Division of Overseas Ministries
222 S. Downey Avenue
Indianapolis, Indiana 46219  317-353-1491

Supports an agricultural institute; water development; experimental work in agriculture;
and a cattle-raising project. Programs are
in Zaire, Paraguay, and India.

CHRISTIAN NATIONAL'S EVANGELISM
 COMMISSION, INC.
1470 N. Fourth Street
San Jose, California 95112  408-298-0965

Supports practical and technical training in
agriculture; community farms projects, including poultry, cattle, vegetable crops; and
development of experimental farm projects to
increase production. Works in Brazil, the
Philippines, Ivory Coast, Liberia, and Nigeria.

CHRISTIAN REFORMED WORLD RELIEF
 COMMITTEE (CRWRC)
2850 Kalamazoo Avenue
Grand Rapids, Michigan 49508 616-241-1691

Est. 1962. With a total budget for foreign
programs of about $1.3 million, CRWRC
concentrates its assistance on six countries.
Food-related projects include agricultural
aid to Mexico, the Philippines, Bangladesh,
and Nigeria, where agriculturists work with
poor farmers to teach them better care of
their land, the value of fertilizers, the benefits
of new crops or hybrid strains of their traditional crops, and the care and raising of small
animals.

Child-feeding and nutrition education projects
are supported in Honduras and the Philippines.
CRWRC also promotes study, reflection, and
political action on hunger issues within the
membership of the Christian Reformed Church.
Pub.: CRWRC Newsletter, 3 times a year.
Pamphlets, including "Ideas for Churches and
Other Groups in Response to World Food
Needs."

CHURCH OF THE BRETHREN GENERAL
  BOARD
World Ministries Commission
1451 Dundee Avenue
Elgin, Illinois 60120            312-742-5100

Missionary activities in Nigeria, Ecuador, and
India include agricultural training, demonstra-
tions in animal husbandry, and extension work.

CHURCH OF GOD, INC.
Missionary Board
1303 E. Fifth Street
Anderson, Indiana 46011          317-642-0258

Provides support to local churches in Kenya,
Bangladesh, and India for agricultural training
and self-help programs.

CHURCH WOMEN UNITED (CWU)
475 Riverside Drive, Room 812
New York, New York 10027         212-870-3048

Est. 1941.  Major national movement "through
which Protestant, Roman Catholic, and Orthodox women express the ecumenical dimensions
of their faith." Hunger Fund, set up in 1974,
provides assistance to projects designed to
alleviate hunger and prevent the lasting harm of
hunger.  Examples of projects: milk for a
nursery in Viet-Nam, food ditribution to American Indians, feeding programs for children
and nutrition training for mothers in Haiti,
and drought relief for Ethiopia.  Most projects
are operated by such agencies as Church
World Service, UNICEF, and various churches.
Pub.: The Church Woman, 10 times a year.

CHURCH WORLD SERVICE
See: National Council of Churches

CITIZENS' COMMISSION ON SCIENCE, LAW
  AND THE FOOD SUPPLY
1230 York Avenue
New York, New York 10021         212-360-1797

Est. 1973.  Conducting a "major study of the
scientific, legal, and social factors involved
in decisionmaking relative to the safety,
availability, and nutritional values of the
world's food supply." Aim is to design guidelines for legal and regulatory processes that
will afford maximum public benefits and
minimal risks within the varied social, cultural,
and economic patterns of society.

COLUMBAN FATHERS
St. Columban's Foreign Mission Society
St. Columban's, Nebraska 68056
                                 402-291-1920

Missionary activities in Fiji, the Philippines,
and South Korea include technical assistance to
agriculture, including helping to set up credit
unions.

COLUMBIA UNIVERSITY
Institute of Human Nutrition
701 W. 168th Street
New York, New York 10032         212-694-6991

Est. 1948.  Part of the Faculty of Medicine.
Training of scholars and researchers in the
field; augmenting the training of physicians
interested in emphasizing nutrition in their
professions.  Divisions: Growth and Development; Nutrition and Metabolism; Community
Nutrition.  Center for Nutrition, Genetics,
and Human Development opened in 1976.
Research projects have included a survey of
the nutritional status of a poor urban community,
a study of the value of government-assisted
nutrition programs in the U.S., and a study of
community nutrition education.

COMMITTEE FOR ECONOMIC DEVELOPMENT
  (CED)
477 Madison Avenue
New York, New York 10022         212-688-2063

Est. 1942.  Non-partisan group of businessmen
and scholars who conduct research and formulate policy recommendations on economics,
government, and social and educational issues.
Has issued a statement, "A New U.S. Farm
Policy for Changing World Food Needs."

COMMITTEE ON THE WORLD FOOD CRISIS
1315 Sixteenth Street, N.W.
Washington, D.C. 20036          202-232-2650

Est. 1965.  Set up as an umbrella organization
of groups and individuals concerned with the
world food problem to focus support for programs, policies, and measures that would
assure that the U.S. makes its contribution to
solving the world's food and population problems.
Has sponsored conferences.  No longer active,
but may be reactivated.


COMMUNITY DEVELOPMENT FOUNDATION
  (CDF)/ SAVE THE CHILDREN FEDERATION
  (SCF)
Westport, Connecticut 06880

Est. 1932.  Affiliated organizations with a
combined annual budget of about $7 million.
Seeks to advance the wellbeing of children,
families, and communities by providing grants
or interest-free loans for self-help projects and
scholarship aid.  The "multi-purpose impact
program" combines community development
with aid to the entire child population of an
impact area. Projects in some 15 countries.

In the area of food, CDF/SCF's main interest is
in long-range anti-hunger projects focused on
increased agricultural production through use
of improved seeds and fertilizer, better technology, and related assistance.  Construction
maintenance of health clinics in developing
countries, with emphasis on nutrition counseling,
is also a priority.  Pub.: World Reporter, ann.

Projects are operated through 4 domestic and
11 foreign field offices:

    +Save the Children Federation
    American Indian Program
    123 Yale Boulevard, S.E.
    Albuquerque, New Mexico 87106
                        505-247-0279

    +Save the Children Federation
    Appalachian and Rural South Programs
    P.O. Box 319
    Berea, Kentucky 40403      606-986-3901

+Save the Children Federation
Chicano Program
P.O. Box 8
Canones, New Mexico 87516
                        505-638-5463

+Save the Children Federation
Inner Cities Program
345 E. 46th Street
New York, New York 10017
                        212-697-0264

+Save the Children Federation
Meandrou Street 7
Athens 612, Greece


+Save the Children Federation
P.O. Box 1143
Jerusalem, Israel

+Save the Children Federation
P.O. Box 5179
Beirut, Lebanon

+Community Development Trust Fund of
  Tanzania
P.O. Box 9421
Dar es Salaam, Tanzania

+Save the Children Federation
P.O. Box 421
Dacca, Bangladesh

+SOS Children's Villages of India
P.O. Box 747
New Delhi 1, India

+Save the Children Federation
18 Mook Jung Dong
Chung-ku, Seoul, Korea

+Save the Children Federation
"Ayuda Estudiantil"
Apartado Aereo 14827
Bogota, Columbia

+Save the Children Federation
Calle Sanchez no. 6
Loma de Cabrera, Provincia de Dajabon
Dominican Republic

+Federacion Desarrollo Juvenil
  Communitario
Apartado 333
Tegucigalpa, D.C., Honduras

+Save the Children Federation
Office for Mexico
P.O. Box 1882
Calexico, California 92231

## COMMUNITY HUNGER APPEAL
See: National Council of Churches

## COMMUNITY NUTRITION INSTITUTE (CNI)
1910 K Street, N.W.
Washington, D.C. 20006      202-833-1730

Nonprofit public interest group. Training and
technical assistance services; workshops and
conferences on public policy issues related to
nutrition. Pub.: CNI Weekly Report, a newsletter on food and nutrition programs, policies, and events.

## COMMUNITY WAREHOUSE
2010 Kendall Street, N.E.
Washington, D.C. 20002      202-832-4517

Wholesale of bulk food staples to non- or low-
profit food distributors and buying club consumer cooperatives.

## CONCERN, INC.
2333 Wisconsin Avenue, N.W.
Washington, D.C. 20007      202-965-0066

Est. 1970. Disseminates to consumers information on the environmental impact of house-
hold products and practices; encourages manufacture of products less damaging to the environment. Pub.: Eco-Tips, irregular topical
newsletter; topics have included "Food, Chemicals, and Health."

## CONQUEST OF HUNGER PROGRAM
See: Rockefeller Foundation

## CONSORTIUM FOR INTERNATIONAL DEVELOPMENT (CID)
c/o Utah State University, UMC-35
Logan, Utah 84322      801-752-4100, ext. 7471

Consortium of six western universities - the
Universities of Arizona and California, Colorado State University, Oregon State University,
Texas Tech University, and Utah State University - concerned primarily with the problem of
increasing world food supplies through better
soil, water, and plant management. Continuation of the Council of United States Universities for Soil and Water Development in Arid
and Sub-Humid Areas (CUSUSWASH).

Examples of projects: technical and consulting
services designed to increase productivity of
farm corporations and production cooperatives
in Iran; improvement of production of basic
food crops and livestock products on small
farms in the intermountain valleys of central
Bolivia; assistance to the Government of
Niger for increased production of cereals.

## COOPERACIÓN
1931 Baugh Avenue
East St. Louis, Illinois 62205      618-271-6550

Provides technical assistance and financial and
material support to self-help agricultural projects in Honduras.

## COOPERATIVE FOR AMERICAN RELIEF EVERYWHERE (CARE)
660 First Avenue
New York, New York 10016      212-686-3110

Est. 1945. CARE is a federation of agencies,
including religious, nationality, labor, and
other groups interested in channeling food,
equipment, books, other self-help materials,
and development aid generally to needy people
overseas. It has programmed over $1 billion
worth of aid since it was founded. CARE oper-
rates currently in some 38 developing countries
in Asia, Africa, Latin America, and the Middle
East.

Food programs are a very large part of the CARE program.  Through its feeding and food-for-work programs, it is instrumental in feeding over 20 million people per day.  More than 90% of those fed are children served at preschool centers, primary schools, and other institutions.  Recipients also include pregnant and nursing women.  Linked with the child-feedings are projects to build nutrition centers, where children are fed while their mothers are instructed in basic nutrition and health care.

CARE also undertakes, in all of the countries in which it operates, to end the dependency of people on foreign imports of food.  Emphasis is on agricultural projects to increase food production and raise family incomes.  Projects include construction of schools, water systems, farm-to-market roads, rural electrification, irrigation systems, low-cost housing, clinics, and community centers.  In these projects, done in cooperation with local governments and other organizations, CARE provides adminis-tration, know-how, and materials not locally available.  For every donor dollar used, an average of $3 in cash or kind is contributed by host governments and people of each community.

Organized CARE food distribution programs are conducted in the following countries: Egypt, Bangladesh, Chad, Chile, Colombia, Costa Rica, Dominican Republic, Ecuador, Guatemala, Haiti, Honduras, Hong Kong, India, Indonesia, Israel-Gaza, Jordan, Macao, Mali, Niger, Pakistan, Panama, the Philippines, Sierra Leone, Sri Lanka, Tunisia, and Turkey. As needs arise and resources permit, CARE also sends food aid to Afghanistan, Belize, Kenya, Lesotho, Liberia, Nicaragua, Nigeria, Peru, and South Korea.

CARE's total annual budget in 1975 was about $169 million.  Field offices are maintained in all of the countries to which CARE provides assistance.  Domestic regional offices are maintained in Atlanta, Boston, Chicago, Colum-bus, Dallas, Detroit, Los Angeles, Milwaukee, New York City, Philadelphia, Pittsburgh, Seattle, Kansas City (Missouri), San Francisco, Washington, D.C., and Coral Gables (Florida).

Pub.: <u>World Report</u>, q.  Various pamphlets.

<u>COOPERATIVE LEAGUE OF THE U.S.A.</u>
  (CLUSA)
1828 L Street, N.W., Suite 1100
Washington, D.C. 20036          202-872-0550

Est. 1916.  National federation of cooperatives of all types and associations of cooperatives. Maintains a close relationship with the <u>Coopera-tive League Fund</u> (CLF), same address. CLUSA and CLF are both involved in activities to strengthen the cooperative movement and expand participation in coops both in the U.S. and abroad.

The League's major activity related to the world food situation is providing technical assistance to agricultural and consumer coops, usually under contract with AID, in developing countries.  The largest programs are in India (focusing on fertilizer, oilseed processing, and dairy improvement); Chile; Panama; Ecuador; and Costa Rica.  Other projects have involved Bangladesh, Turkey, and regional institutions in Latin America.

CLUSA's annual budget for such projects has run from $590,000 to $734,000 in recent years. There are advisory committees on fertilizer, agricultura credit, oilseeds processing, dairy, farm supply and marketing, farm machinery, livestock production and marketing, rice, grain, and fisheries.

Pub.:  The Fund issues <u>Fund Report</u>, q. CLUSA issues <u>Outreach International News</u>, q.; and a biennial progress report on overseas activities.

<u>COORDINATION IN DEVELOPMENT</u> (CODEL)
79 Madison Avenue
New York, New York 10016          212-685-2030

Est. 1969.  A consortium of some 30 church-related organizations (both Protestant and Roman Catholic).  Provides consultative and fund-raising services to its member organi-zations to improve their capacities for develop-ment work overseas.  Food production is a major area of interest.  Conducts field surveys and training projects.  Major support has been given by AID.

CORNELL UNIVERSITY
Center for International Studies
Ithaca, New York 14850          607-256-6370

Offers graduate-level professional training in
International Agriculture, International Nutrition, International Nutrition and Development
Policy, and research opportunities in those
fields.  Pub.: International Studies Newsletter,
annual.  Research reports.

CORNELL UNIVERSITY
New York State College of Agriculture and Life
   Sciences
Program in International Agriculture
261 Roberts Hall
Ithaca, New York 12850          607-256-2283

The Program in International Agriculture conducts training and coordinates research activities
in the various fields of agriculture as they
relate to world food problems and related subjects.  Pub.: ALS: International Agriculture,
quarterly newsletter.  Research mimeographs,
reprints, and bulletins.  Rural Development in
Tropical Latin America (1967).  Issues Emerging from Recent Breakthroughs in Food Production (1971).  Publications list available.

CORPORATE INFORMATION CENTER (CIC)
c/o Interfaith Committee on Social Responsibility in Investments (ICSRI)
475 Riverside Drive, Room 846
New York, New York 10027        212-870-2294

CIC is the research arm of ICSRI, conducting
research on church investment holdings and on
specific corporations.  Pub.: The Corporate
Examiner, monthly newsletter, which has
included information on agribusiness and the
world food crisis (see especially the November
1974 issue).

COUNCIL FOR AGRICULTURAL SCIENCE
   AND TECHNOLOGY (CAST)
c/o Department of Agronomy
Iowa State University
Ames, Iowa 50010

Umbrella group for 17 scientific societies.
Participated in the 1976 Food Day observance
(sponsored by the Center for Science in the

Public Interest, which see) by operating a
"National Food Day Dial-ogue" over a toll-
free telephone line, to answer questions about
chemicals, additives, nutrition, agricultural
production, and world hunger.  The event was
partially funded by the National Agricultural
Chemicals Association.

COUNCIL ON ECONOMIC PRIORITIES (CEP)
84 Fifth Avenue
New York, New York 10011        212-691-8550

Est. 1970.  Disseminates "unbiased and detailed information" on the policies and practices of American corporations in the areas of
military production, minority advancement,
environmental quality, and overseas investments.  Formed to provide information to
people who insist on social responsibility from
business corporations.  Coverage includes
reports on U.S. corporations involved in food
or agribusiness.  Pub.: CEP Newsletter, 10-
12 times a year; CEP Report, 3 times a year;
CEP Study, 3 times a year.  Minding the Corporate Conscience, annual review.

COUNCIL ON RELIGION AND INTERNATIONAL
   AFFAIRS (CRIA)
170 E. 64th Street
New York, New York 10021        212-838-4120

Est. 1914.  An independent nonsectarian foundation originally established as the Church
Peace Union with financial support from Andrew
Carnegie.  Its mandate is to work "for peace
and justice in international relations, and to
relate religious concerns and ethical insights
to the political and economic processes which
affect the world's people."

Maintains the Carnegie Center for Transnational
Studies, a program which explores the economic
relationships between business and developing
countries.  The Center's 1976-77 agenda concentrates on the topic, "Value Systems and the
World Food Crisis, with Special Reference to
the Transnational Corporation."

Pub.: Worldview, 10 times a year.  Disarmament News and International Views, mon.  Various booklets and special studies; publications
list available.

## CREDIT UNION NATIONAL ASSOCIATION (CUNA)
1730 Rhode Island Avenue, N.W.
Washington, D.C. 20036  202-659-2360

Est. 1934. Service organization of state credit union leagues. Provides support to its international affiliate, the World Council of Credit Unions, which aids groups of and individual credit unions in developing countries through financial assistance and technical advice. The international program includes small farmer production credit projects and rural credit unions working to improve the income of small farmers. Aid goes to several dozen countries in Africa, Asia, Latin America, and the Pacific. Pub.: Credit Union Magazine, mon.; various other publications.

## CROP
See: National Council of Churches

## CROP SCIENCE SOCIETY OF AMERICA (CSSA)
677 S. Segoe Road
Madison, Wisconsin 53711  608-274-1212

Est. 1955. Professional organization. Committees include: Borlaug Book Fund - Publications Donations Project; International Agronomy; Preservation of Genetic Stocks. Affiliated with the American Society of Agronomy. Pub.: Crop Science, bimon.

## DAIRY RESEARCH, INC. (DRINC)
6300 N. River Road
Rosemont, Illinois 60018  312-696-1870

Est. 1939. The research and product development arm of the U.S. dairy industry. Works with commercial companies to develop new and increased uses for milk and dairy products. Maintains an information service and library on dairy foods and processes. Pub.: Dairy Research Digest, mon.

## DIRECT RELIEF FOUNDATION (DRF)
P.O. Box 1319
Santa Barbara, California 93102
   805-966-9149

Est. 1945. Major activity is providing medical and related supplies, including food supplements, and medical personnel to some 50 countries in nearly all regions of the world. Food has also been sent for emergency relief, for example, to Guatemala after the 1976 earthquake.

DRF's Agricultural Development Program, conducted in cooperation with the Community Environmental Council of Santa Barbara, trains volunteers in the intensive garden farming method and assigns them for service in less developed countries "where farming costs escalate because of the price of artificial fertilizers, sprays, and mechanical farming methods." The intensive method is based on the use of simple hand tools, relatively unsophisticated irrigation systems (where needed); production of organic fertilizers by means of composts, small-scale animal husbandry, leaf litter, turf-loam and cover crops; sophisticated transplanting techniques; hedges for fencing; companion planting; crop rotation; and the development of complex, food-producing ecosystems that are most suited to existing natural ecosystems.

DRF's total annual budget is about $3 million. Pub.: What's Up at DRF, q.

## DIVINE WORD MISSIONARIES
Mission Office
Techny, Illinois 60082  312-272-7600

Missionary activities in Ghana, Indonesia, Papua New Guinea, Mexico, and India include agricultural education. Makes dairy products available in some areas.

THE THOMAS A. DOOLEY FOUNDATION
442 Post Street
San Francisco, California 94102
415-397-0244

Est. 1961.  A medical relief organization with
projects in Asia.  Vitamins and other nutritional
supplements are provided to host country programs.  Pub.: Sawadee, semiann.

EARTH METABOLIC DESIGN, INC.
P.O. Box 2016, Yale Station
New Haven, Connecticut 06520   203-776-4921

Est. 1972.  Applies what R. Buckminster Fuller
has called "Comprehensive Anticipatory Design
Science," i.e., conscious design of the total
environment using the principles of science.
Its World Food Strategy Project works on
strategies for developing the world's food
sources and systems to insure a regenerative
supply of food for all humans. Also concerned
with shelter, energy, and broad resources-
economics problems.  Seminars; lectures;
educational materials.  Pub.: Design Science
Primer (1976).  Ho Ping: Food for Everyone
(1976).  Regenerative Resource Economy (1976).

EAST-WEST FOOD INSTITUTE (EWFI)
1777 East-West Road
Honolulu, Hawaii 96822          808-949-2956

Part of the East-West Center, est. in 1960
by the U.S. Congress to "promote better
relations and understanding between the
United States and the nations of Asia and the
Pacific through cooperative study, training,
and research."  Five institutes with international, interdisciplinary academic and
professional staffs conduct the Center's
problem-oriented programs.  The Center is
directed by the Board of Governors of a
public, nonprofit educational corporation,
the Center for Cultural and Technical Inter-
change Between East and West, Inc.  The U.S.
Government provides basic funding.

The East-West Food Institute focuses attention
on the human, technical, and economic concerns of food.  Main program areas are:
(1) Agro-economic management (food production, diversification, and trade; water management for intensified agriculture; fertilizer);
systems of crop protection (pest management);
agriculture and food planning and administration (public program management; integrated
policymaking; information generation, use,
and processing); and community nutrition
(curriculum development; problems of nutri-
tionally-vulnerable groups).

The Institute cooperates with academic and
other research institutions in the U.S. and
Asia.  In addition to research, activities include postgraduate education; conferences,
workshops, and seminars; and curriculum
development.

Pub.:  The Center issues East-West Center
Magazine, q., and an Annual Report.  EWFI
issues Food Institute Newsletter and technical
and progress reports.

ENVIRONMENTAL FUND
1302 18th Street, N.W.
Washington, D.C. 20036          202-293-2548

An operating foundation concerned primarily
with the effect of continued population growth
on the environment.  Conducts research and
forums on the relationship of population growth
to such problems as hunger, inflation, and
resource depletion.

THE EPISCOPAL CHURCH OF THE U.S.
Domestic and Foreign Missionary Society
815 Second Avenue
New York, New York 10017          212-867-8400

Missionary activities in Liberia, Guatemala,
and the Philippines include rural development
projects, such as crop and livestock improvement and instruction in agronomy.

EXPLORATORY PROJECT FOR ECONOMIC
  ALTERNATIVES
2000 P Street, N.W., Suite 515
Washington, D.C. 20036

Est. 1976.  Nonprofit research group formed
to stimulate debate on new approaches to controlling inflation by stabilizing the costs of the
four basic consumer necessities: food, housing,
basic energy, and health care.  Published in
early 1977 a report, Toward a National Food
Policy, which finds that "low, stable food
prices can be guaranteed for American consumers, but only if we adopt programs to provide
a secure income for family farmers and dras-
tically restructure the U.S. food system in
accordance with resource and ecological
needs."

Concerning world food problems, the Project's
report recommends that U.S. aid focus on food
production in the Third World, and that sanc-
tions be applied to corporations pursuing cash-
crop or other projects abroad that disrupt
efforts to attain food self-sufficiency.

FARMERS AND WORLD AFFAIRS (FWA)
101 N. Seventh Street
Camden, New Jersey          609-963-0903

Est. 1956.  Conducts an exchange program of
farm leaders between the U.S. and developed
and developing countries.  Has conducted a
Food and Population Program in Maharashtra
State, India, emphasizing education in food
production and family planning.  Other countries involved include Egypt, Pakistan, Italy,
Ireland, and Denmark.  Pub.: FWA Newsletter,
3 times a year.

FAST FOR FAMINE RELIEF
See: National Beef Boycott Center

THE FERTILIZER INSTITUTE (TFI)
1015 18th Street, N.W.
Washington, D.C. 20036          202-466-2700

Est. 1970.  Major national association of manufacturers, importers, brokers, and dealers of
fertilizers and related equipment.  Works to
expand and encourage use of chemical fertilizers
and has been represented at major international
meetings on food problems.  Pub.: Fertilizer
Progress, bimon.; other publications.

FOOD ACTION CENTER
See:  The Action Center

FOOD CONSPIRACIES
403 W. School House Lane
Philadelphia, Pennsylvania 19144

Promotes the concept of neighborhood nonprofit
food cooperatives in the U.S.  Reference and
information services.  Pub.:" Food Conspiracies," booklet for sale.

FOOD CO-OP DIRECTORY
106 Girard Street, S.E.
Albuquerque, New Mexico 87106
                              505-265-7416

Est. 1974.  Nonprofit group which publishes
a Food Co-op Directory, listing some 2,500
consumer food cooperatives in the U.S. and
Canada.  Latest edition, 1977.

FOOD COOP PROJECT
Chicago Loop College
64 E. Lake Street
Chicago, Illinois 60601          312-269-8101

A national information clearinghouse for food
cooperatives, which conducts educational and
training projects on such topics as supermarket
practices, agribusiness, world trade problems.
Pub.: Food Coop Nooz, bimon.  Food Coop
Directory, semiann.  "How to Form a Food
Coop." Other publications.  (Send a stamped
envelope for information.)

FOOD DAY
See:  Center for Science in the Public Interest

FOOD RESEARCH AND ACTION CENTER
  (FRAC)
25 W. 43rd Street
New York, New York 10036          212-354-7866

Est. 1970.  A non-profit public interest law
firm and advocacy center working with the poor
and near-poor to end hunger and malnutrition in
the United States.  Offers legal assistance, organizing aid, training, and information to poor
people and their groups working to improve and
expand the federal food programs (food stamps,
school lunch/breakfast, day care, summer
feeding, WIC, and Nutrition Programs for the
Elderly).  Pub.:  Guide to the Food Stamp
Program (1976).  If We Had Ham, We Could
Have Ham and Eggs: A Study of the National
School Breakfast Program.  Guide to the National School Breakfast Program.  Out to Lunch: A
Study of USDA's Day Care and Summer Feeding
Programs.  More than Tea and Toast: A Guide
to Community Groups Organizing Nutrition Programs for the Elderly.

FORD FOUNDATION
320 E. 43rd Street
New York, New York 10017          212-573-4918

Est. 1936.  The Ford Foundation's support for
international agricultural research focuses on
finding and applying more efficient scientific and
technical means of increasing food production.
Most of this work is carried on at international
research centers established in cooperation with
the Rockefeller Foundation and now also given
support by several international aid sources
coordinated by the World Bank.

The centers are: International Rice Research
Institute (Philippines); International Maize and
Wheat Improvement Center (Mexico); Interna-
tional Institute of Tropical Agriculture (Nigeria);
International Center of Tropical Agriculture
(Colombia); International Potato Center (Peru).
Ford support for the fice centers totaled some
$56 million between 1960 and 1976.  In addition,
the Foundation supports the International Crop
Research Institute for the Semi-Arid Tropics in
India.

The Foundation also supports national programs to increase food production and for related purposes in Bangladesh, India, Indonesia, Malaysia, Pakistan, the Philippines,
Thailand, Argentina, Brazil, Dominican Republic, Chile, Colombia, Mexico, Peru, Uganda,
Nigeria, Dahomey, and Lebanon.

Field offices are maintained in countries in
which the Foundation has major projects.  Pub.:
Ford Foundation Letter, bimon.  "Current
Interests of the Ford Foundation," irreg.

FOREIGN POLICY ASSOCIATION (FPA)
345 E. 46th Street
New York, New York 10017          212-697-2432

Est. 1918.  Educational organization which
works to stimulate interest in international
relations and assist in development of greater
understanding of foreign policy issues confronting the U.S.  FPA has, from time to time,
published analyses of world food problems,
including Our Daily Bread, by Lester R.
Brown (1975); The Struggle Against World
Hunger, by D. Gale Johnson (1967), and "The
World Food Problem," in Great Decisions...
1975.  Also publishes Headline Series, 5
times a year.

FOSTER PARENTS' PLAN (FPP)
P.O. Box 400
Warwick, Rhode Island 02886       401-738-5600

Est. 1937.  Members are individuals and groups
who send contributions to assist needy children
and families in several developing countries,
and establish a personal relationship with them
through correspondence.  Assists more than
50,000 children and their families and communities.

Projects related to food include assistance to
fishing, farming, and food cooperatives; animal
husbandry; rice irrigation; fisheries; and a
"back to the farm" project to stem migration to
urban areas.  These are in Indonesia, the
Philippines, South Korea, and Bolivia.  Pub.:
Foster Parent Report, q.  Annual Report.

FOUNDATION FOR THE PEOPLES OF THE
  SOUTH PACIFIC (FSP)
158 W. 57th Street
New York, New York 10019     212-757-9740

Est. 1965.  Economic development projects
include food preservation in Western Samoa
and Tonga, nutrition in Papua New Guinea and
Fiji, and fisheries in the Solomon Islands.

FRIENDS OF THE EARTH (FOE)
124 Spear Street
San Francisco, California 94105
                             415-495-4770

Est. 1969.  A major activist environmental
organization affiliated with similar groups
abroad.  Has a continuing interest in such
issues as agribusiness, preservation of prime
agricultural land, food additives, and chemical
contamination of the environment.  Pub.: Not
Man Apart, fortnightly.


FRIENDS COMMITTEE ON NATIONAL
  LEGISLATION (FCNL)
245 Second Street, N.E.
Washington, D.C. 20002       202-547-4343

Est. 1943.  Autonomous political committee
related to the Religious Society of Friends
(Quakers).  Conducts background research,
legislative analysis, and lobbying and advocacy in favor of policies that it feels will help
the hungry in both the short term and the long
run.  Supports an increase in U.S. food aid
overseas, elimination of "food for politics" and
"food for war" practices, development of both
domestic and world food price systems which
encourage farmers to produce and are also
fair to consumers; establishment of a sizeable
worldwide grain reserve system, increasing
U.S. production incentives for nutritious food,
providing incentives to reduce wasteful consumption, and encouragement of land reform.
Pub.: FCNL Washington Newsletter, mon.
Pamphlets and legislative reports.  Publications list available.

FRIENDS OF CHILDREN
14 Brookside Road
Darien, Connecticut 06820     203-655-2218

Collects food (some 5,000 lbs. yearly) for
distribution to orphanages in Guatemala and
Korea.  Pub.: Newsletter, q.

FRIENDS OF THE THIRD WORLD
428 E. Berry Street
Fort Wayne, Indiana 46802     219-422-6821

Resource center providing technical assistance,
information, and organizing help to grassroots
organizations concerned with Third World
issues, including hunger, for fundraising,
development education, and volunteer action
projects.  Pub.: Perspective.

THE GLEANERS
635 Fulton
Cuba, Illinois 61427

Est. 1974.  Groups of students who collect
crops (mainly corn) left behind after fields
are harvested mechanically.  They pay nothing,
but sell what they collect and donate the pro-
ceeds to private agencies that provide food aid
abroad: CARE, Bread for the World, CROP,

Church World Service, and Heifer Project
International.  Started at Eureka College,
Illinois; now has groups at several midwestern
colleges.  (According to a story about the
Gleaners in the New York Times, Oct. 9, 1975,
about a fifth of the U.S. corn crop is missed
by combines and is left in fields to rot.)

GRAY PANTHERS
3700 Chestnut Street
Philadelphia, Pennsylvania 19104
                             215-EV 2-6644

Est. 1971.  National consciousness-raising
group that works to fight discrimination against
persons on the basis of chronological age.
Maintains a Hunger Task Force (Chairwoman:
Beverly Williams, AFSC, 407 S. Dearborn
Street, Chicago, Illinois 60605).  Pub.:
Network, q.

GREAT PLAINS WHEAT, INC. (GPW)
1030 15th Street, N.W.
Washington, D.C. 20005          202-659-1240

Est. 1959.  A federation of eight state wheat
growers' associations and commissions.  Works
to expand and develop markets for U.S. wheat
in the U.S. and abroad.  Places nutritionists
and other technicians in foreign countries.
Pub.: Great Plainsman, mon.

GPW is a market development cooperator with
the U.S. Department of Agriculture, and maintains four field offices abroad:

+Great Plains Wheat, Inc.
Edificio Avenida Central
Avenida Rio Branco 156, Salas 3314-3315
Rio de Janeiro ZC-21, Brazil
                              242-4413

+Great Plains Wheat, Inc.
c/o U.S. Feed Grains Council
5 Neofitou Douca Street
Athens 138, Greece          718-431

+Great Plains Wheat, Inc.
Coolsingel 6
Rotterdam, Netherlands      13-91-55

+Great Plains Wheat, Inc.
Apartado 62300
Caracas 106, Venezuela      33-12-61

HEIFER PROJECT INTERNATIONAL (HPI)
P.O. Box 808
Little Rock, Arkansas 72203     501-376-6836

Est. 1944.  Provides livestock, poultry, technical help, and related services to small
farmers abroad.  Main methods are to intro-
duce genetic improvement in farm animals and
to demonstrate and teach proper management.
Financed by voluntary contributions.  Maintains an International Livestock Center at the
1,200-acre Fourche River Ranch in Arkansas.

Projects in some 90 countries have been aided.
Annual budget is about $2 million.  Current
projects (1975 data) are in 11 Latin American
countries (42% of the budget), 6 Asian countries (20%), 6 African countries (18%), and
also in about 15 states in the U.S.  HFI has
regional offices in the U.S. at Plymouth,
Massachusetts; Goshen, Indiana; El Monte,
California; and Modesto, California. Pub.:
Sharing Life, q.

HOLY CROSS FOREIGN MISSION SOCIETY,
INC.
4301 Harewood Road, N.E.
Washington, D.C. 20017          202-526-2211

Missionary activity includes operating agricultural cooperatives and donating livestock,
equipment, and agricultural tools in Uganda
and Bangladesh.

HUDSON INSTITUTE (HI)
Quaker Ridge Road
Croton-on-Hudson, New York 10520
                              914-762-0700

Est. 1961.  Founded by futurist Herman Kahn.
A "think-tank" which seeks to provide "a broad,
workable conceptual framework within which
intelligent and successful policy is more likely
to be developed."  Projects directly related to
food have included Prospects for Mankind,
which has generated a book, World Food Prospects and Agricultural Potentials (1970), and a
study for the National Science Foundation of
medium- and long-term food prospects, which
emphasizes resources and technology, institutional factors which enhance or limit increased
food production, and the likelihood of increased
use of nonconventional sources of food "as de-
pendence on traditional agriculture decreases."

HUNGER TASK FORCE
65 S. Fourth Street
Columbus, Ohio 43215            614-464-1956

HUNGER WORKSHOP
P.O. Box 2474
Washington, D.C. 20013          202-544-4162

Purpose is to help people connect with the information they need on domestic and world hunger,
and with others involved in the field.  Reference
services; information center; publications.
Plans to incorporate as Hunger Information
Network.  Pub.: Hunger Workshop Notes, mon.

IMPACT
See: Interreligious Task Force on U.S. Food
  Policy

INSTITUTE FOR POLICY STUDIES (IPS)
1909 Q Street, N.W.
Washington, D.C. 20009          202-234-9332

Est. 1963.  A "center of intellectual activity in
which scholars and citizens can exchange ideas
and collaborate on some of the problems most
critically in need of new thought."  Pub.: The
Elements, mon., which frequently covers
aspects of the world food situation.

INSTITUTE FOR WORLD ORDER (IWO)
1140 Avenue of the Americas
New York, New York 10036        212-575-0055

Est. 1948.  Research, development, and promotion of a peace-world order curriculum for
all educational levels.  Makes available materials; conducts seminars, workshops, and in-
service courses for educators.

Its University Food Resource Center helps
universities and other educational institutions
to incorporate food and hunger issues into the
curriculum.  Pub.: Pamphlets, syllabi, etc.
See also: The Action Center.

INSTITUTE OF FOOD TECHNOLOGISTS (IFT)
221 N. LaSalle Street
Chicago, Illinois 60601         312-782-8424

Est. 1939.  Professional organization of technical personnel in food production, product
development, research, and product control.
Committees include: World Food Programs;

Expert Panel on Food Safety and Nutrition.
Pub.: Journal of Food Science, bimon.  Food
Technology, mon.

INSTITUTE OF INTERNATIONAL
  EDUCATION (IIE)
809 United Nations Plaza
New York, New York 10017        212-867-0400

Est. 1919.  Information clearinghouse and
consultative services on all aspects of educational and cultural exchange.  Among its activities, IIE provides administrative support for
researchers at ten international institutes of
agriculture.

INSTITUTE ON MAN AND SCIENCE (IMS)
Rensselaerville, New York 12147
                                518-797-3783

Est. 1963.  An educational center "where new
ideas about human problems and prospects are
examined in depth."  Projects have included a
conference on the food and energy situations.
Pub.: Newsletter, irreg.  The World Food and
Energy Crises: The Role of International Organizations, Proceedings (1974).

INTERFAITH COMMITTEE ON SOCIAL
  RESPONSIBILITY IN INVESTMENTS (ICSRI)
475 Riverside Drive, Room 566
New York, New York 10017        212-870-2294

Est. 1971.  Assists various boards and agencies of several Protestant churches to express
social responsibility with their investments.
Has negotiated with management of agribusiness
corporations about corporate responsibility
regarding world hunger issues, followed by
stockholder action and, in some cases, legal
action.  See also: Corporate Information
Center.

INTERNATIONAL ASSOCIATION FOR THE
  EXCHANGE OF STUDENTS FOR TECHNICAL
  EXPERIENCE/UNITED STATES, INC.
  (IAESTE/US)
American City Building, Suite 217
Columbia, Maryland 21044        301-997-2200

Program includes on-the-job training for
exchange students in agriculture from various
countries in Africa, Asia, South America,
and the Near and Middle East.

## INTERNATIONAL DEVELOPMENT
### FOUNDATION (IDF)
175 Clearbrook Road
Elmsford, New York 10523          914-592-3469

Est. 1962.  Projects have included technical
assistance to agricultural marketing programs
in Latin America involving small farmers.


## INTERNATIONAL EDUCATIONAL
### DEVELOPMENT, INC. (IED)
924 West End Avenue
New York, New York 10025          212-666-5264

Provides financial, technical, and material
assistance to various development programs
conducted overseas by the Society of Jesus
(Jesuits), including model farms, small loans,
farm equipment, and technical advice in agriculture in India, the Philippines, Argentina,
Belize, and Brazil.


## INTERNATIONAL EXECUTIVE SERVICE
### CORPS (IESC)
622 Third Avenue
New York, New York 10022          212-490-6800

Est. 1964.  Provides managerial and technical
assistance to food production and agricultural
projects through assignment of volunteer
executives (mainly recently-retired business
men and women and technologists) on a short-
term basis.  Projects have been in many
countries of Africa, Asia, Latin America, and
the Near and Middle East.  Pub.: International
Executive News, mon.


## INTERNATIONAL INDEPENDENCE
### INSTITUTE (III)
Exeter, New Hampshire 03833

"Dedicated to the revitalization of economic and
community life in the technologically underdeveloped areas of the world, particularly the
rural, by research, education, and the creative
use of economic instruments."  Projects include
the Earth Foods Center, concerned with nutritional standards for foods; Farm Centers Inter-
National (FCI), a pilot project in small-scale
credit involving some 1,000 Mexican farmers;
and International Foundation for Independence
(IFI), an international credit mechanism for
production loans to small producers.


## INTERRELIGIOUS TASKFORCE ON U.S.
### FOOD POLICY
110 Maryland Avenue, N.E.
Washington, D.C. 20002          202-543-2800

A coalition of representatives from over 20
Protestant, Roman Catholic, and Jewish agencies "who work together to facilitate the witness
of the American religious community for a responsible U.S. food policy."  The Taskforce
speaks for itself.  Seeks to serve the religious
community by providing reliable information
about and analyses of U.S. food policy and
policy options; by identifying and recommending
U.S. policy objectives and options which in the
judgment of the Taskforce are morally responsible and politically feasible; and by developing
and helping to implement political strategies by
which members and groups in the religious
community can be most effective.

Areas of interest include U.S. food aid (P.L.
480), U.S. economic aid and development assistance to other nations, U.S. domestic food
assistance programs, and U.S. agricultural
policy.

Information and recommendations developed by
the Taskforce are communicated through
IMPACT/Hunger, a bimonthly newsletter published by IMPACT, an interreligious federal
policy information and recommendation service,
and through organs of the participating agencies.

IOWA STATE UNIVERSITY
Center for Agricultural and Economic
  Development
East Hall
Ames, Iowa 50010

Est. 1957.  Research projects have included
studies of basic development issues, including
the role of agriculture in economic development
and interrelationships between domestic farm
policies and international trade and aid.

IOWA STATE UNIVERSITY
World Food Institute
102 E.O. Building
Ames, Iowa 50011                515-294-7699

Est. 1972.  Major goals are:  (1) to analyze
food and nutrition problems; (2) to generate
solutions to such problems and to suggest
means for implementing them; (3) training
of people to generate and implement solutions;
(4) to collect, analyze, and disseminate
information bearing on such problems; and
(5) to study interrelationships between the
U.S. (with particular emphasis on Iowa) and
other countries in the food and nutrition field.

The Institute held a World Food Conference of
1976 at Iowa State, which emphasized "The
Role of the Professional in Feeding Mankind."


IRI RESEARCH INSTITUTE
One Rockefeller Plaza
New York, New York 10020        212-581-1942

Est. 1950.  Provides technical assistance and
tarining to agricultural projects in Latin America, including an experimental farm in Brazil,
beef and dairy projects in Venezuela, and rice
production in Brazil.  Also conducts commodity
research in Spain. Pub.: Bulletin, irreg.

IRAN FOUNDATION
350 Fifth Avenue
New York, New York 10001        212-563-5920

Est. 1948.  Primarily engaged in providing
health and educational assistance to Iran; also
participates in the Meals for Millions program

JOINT DISTRIBUTION COMMITTEE
See: American Jewish Joint Distribution
  Committee

JOINT STRATEGY AND ACTION COMMITTEE,
INC. (JSAC)
475 Riverside Drive, Room 1700-A
New York, New York 10027        212-870-3105

Est. 1965.  A coalition of Protestant denominational mission agencies "which have decided to
work collaboratively in areas of overlapping or
mutual concern... an ecumenical vehicle or
style through which the churches work coopera-
tively on mutual agendas."  Several JSAC
task forces or work groups have been involved
with the hunger issue, including the Task
Force on Economic Responsibility, a group on
Alternate Life Styles, and the Native American
Ministries Task Force.  Pub.: JSCA Grapevine,
10 times a year (each issue deals with a special
topic; past issues have focused on "Today's
International Economic Disaster and Human
Survival" and "Crisis in Population and Hunger").

W.K. KELLOGG FOUNDATION
400 North Avenue
Battle Creek, Michigan 49016    616-965-1221

Est. 1930.  Program includes providing grants
for innovative demonstration projects to improve rural life, nutrition, and food supply.
Current grants emphasize improved food
production techniques, preparation of nutrition
professionals, and human nutrition education to
maintain or improve health.

Kellogg grants have gone to the Institute of
Nutrition of Central America and Panama
(INCAP), to a Study Commission on Dietetics,
to the International Center of Tropical Agriculture (Colombia), and to the Inter-American
Institute of Agricultural Sciences (Costa Rica),
as well as to domestic U.S. programs.  The
Foundation's total payments in fiscal year 1975
were $22.9 million.

## CHARLES F. KETTERING FOUNDATION
5335 Far Hills Avenue
Dayton, Ohio 45429                513-434-7300

Est. 1927. Foundation-sponsored projects
related to the food situation have included
conferences of leaders from the U.S., the
U.S.S.R, and developing countries; and
scientific research on getting more food from
plant crops, and the relationship between
climate and food production. The Foundation's
total payments in fiscal year 1976 were $4.8
million. Pub.: New Ways, q.


## LEAGUE FOR INTERNATIONAL FOOD
  EDUCATION (LIFE)
1155 Sixteenth Street, N.W., Room 705
Washington, D.C. 20036                202-331-1658

Est. 1968. A mechanism whereby U.S. professionals in fields related to food are able to help
disseminate technical information on food and
nutrition to the developing countries. LIFE is
a consortium of nine scientific and professional
organizations: American Association of Cereal
Chemists, American Chemical Society (through
its divisions of Agricultural and Food Chemistry
and Microbial Chemistry and Technology), American Institute of Chemical Engineers, American
Institute of Nutrition, American Oil Chemists'
Society, American Society of Agricultural Engineers, American Society of Agronomy, Institute
of Food Technologists, and Volunteers in Technical Assistance.

Operates under contract with the U.S. Agency
for International Development as a nutrition
information clearinghouse, to provide advice and
technical services, to identify experts for nutrition-related assignments in developing countries,
and to promote development of a technical assistance network among the consortium's societies,
private voluntary organizations, and the developing world.

Answers requests for technical information;
conducts workshops and seminars; maintains
extensive information files. Pub.: LIFE Newsletter, mon. Reference lists and special
reports; list available.


## LUTHERAN WORLD RELIEF (LWR)
360 Park Avenue South
New York, New York 10010                212-677-3950

Est. 1945. Overseas relief agency of the Lutheran churches of the U.S. Heavy emphasis on
agricultural development, including introduction
of improved seeds and new crops, encouraging
widespread fertilizer use where appropriate,
planting experimental and demonstration plots
to aid the discovery of better techniques, providing tools and oxen for cultivation and livestock
and poultry for improved breeding, and making
loans for farm purchases.

Also promotes farm cooperatives to strengthen
bargaining positions when buying or selling,
and assists in proding water resources through
digging of wells, building dams, and irrigation.
Runs some projects for emergency food relief
using P.L. 480 or food-for-work programs.
Most of the assistance is provided to indigenous church agencies which, in turn, help
local people to help themselves where possible.

In 1975, LWR shipped 14.2 million lbs. of food
abroad. Food-related development and relief
activities were active in Ethiopia, Mauritania,
Mozambique, Niger, Sudan, Tanzania, Togo,
Bangladesh, India, Viet-Nam, Jordan, Brazil,
Chile, and Guatemala. The organization's
total disbursements were $3.6 million.


## MARYKNOLL FATHERS
Maryknoll, New York 10545        941-7590

Missionary activities include conducting and
cooperating in programs in agricultural development, land reclamation, irrigation, extension, marketing, and similar projects, as
well as fisheries projects, in various developing countries, including Kenya, Tanzania,
the Philippines, South Korea, Taiwan, Bolivia,
El Salvador, Guatemala, Mexico, and Peru.

MARYKNOLL SISTERS OF ST. DOMINIC, INC.
Maryknoll, New York 10545      914-941-7575

Missionary activities include support for agricultural projects in various developing countries, including Tanzania, the Philippines, Bolivia, Guatemala, Peru, and the U.S. Trust Territory of the Pacific Islands.

MASSACHUSETTS INSTITUTE OF
  TECHNOLOGY (MIT)
System Dynamics Group
Cambridge, Massachusetts 02139
                       617-253-1550

Est. 1956. Development and teaching of system dynamics methodology; seminars, conferences, and workshops. Publications resulting from the Group's work have included The Limits to Growth, by Donella H. Meadows, et al. (1972).

MEALS FOR MILLIONS FOUNDATION (MFM)
1800 Olympic Boulevard
Santa Monica, California 90406
                       213-829-5337

Est. 1946. Primary objective is to assist impoverished communities in the prevention of hunger and malnutrition through self-help projects which focus on low-cost, high-nutrition foods. Through its early development of Multi-Purpose Food (MPF), the Foundation pioneered the concept of using low-cost vegetable and oil-seed residue sources of protein for this purpose. MFM focuses currently, however, on various agricultural, fisheries, and related projects. It provides technical and material assistance to produce foods; training and education through the International Institute of Protein Food Technology; research and development; and nutrition education.

Programs have been carried out in Bangladesh, Biafra, Brazil, Ceylon, Colombia, Ecuador, Hong Kong, India, Israel, Japan, Korea, Mexico, Pakistan, the Phillipines, and Taiwan. The 1975 budget was about $500,000. Field offices are maintained in Tucson, Arizona; Hazelwood, Missouri; Fairfield, Connecticut; Guayaquil, Ecuador; and Seoul, Korea. Pub.: Newsletter, q.

MEDICAL ASSISTANCE PROGRAMS (MAP)
P.O. Box 50
Wheaton, Illinois 60187          312-653-6010

Est. 1954. Program includes shipments of nutritional supplements donated by industry to contacts in 84 developing countries, both as part of the MAP medical programs and, from time to time, for emergency situations. Pub.: MAP International Report, mon.

MENNONITE CENTRAL COMMITTEE (MCC)
21 S. 12th Street
Akron, Pennsylvania 17501        717-859-1151

Est. 1920. MCC is the relief and service agency of North American Mennonite and Brethren in Christ churches, sponsoring 700 workers in 35 countries. Over 100 of its projects are directly related to food production. Pub.: Intercom, monthly. Development Monograph Series, irreg.

MICHIGAN STATE UNIVERSITY
Institute of International Agriculture
113 Agriculture Hall
East Lansing, Michigan 48823     517-355-0174

Part of the College of Agriculture. Conducts research in international aspects of agricultural science and related areas, including food, nutrition, rural development, and natural resources.

MILL HILL MISSIONARIES, INC.
Albany, New York 12203           518-456-6262

Missionary activities include financial, personnel, and material support to fishery and agriculture projects in various developing countries, including Cameroon, Kenya, Uganda, Zaire, Malaysia, the Philippines, India, and Pakistan.

MILLERS' NATIONAL FEDERATION (MNF)
1776 F Street, N.W., Suite 104
Washington, D.C. 20006           202-452-0900

Est. 1902. Members are millers of wheat, rye, and durum flour (they manufacture some 85% of the flour produced in the U.S.). Maintains a Flour Export Programs Division. A market development cooperator with the Foreign Agricultural Service, U.S. Department of Agriculture. Pub.: Hook-Up, biweekly.

MISSIONS HEALTH FOUNDATION (MHF)
P.O. Box 89
Independence, Missouri 64051     816-254-6205

Est. 1969.  Program includes sponsorship of
a nutrition center in Haiti and some support of
similar activities in other countries.

NATIONAL ASSOCIATION FOR FOREIGN
  STUDENT AFFAIRS (NAFSA)
1860 19th Street, N.W.
Washington, D.C. 20009          202-462-4811

Est. 1948.  Members are some 2,000 organizations dealing with international educational exchange.  Promotes and coordinates programs

to facilitate foreign nationals studying at U.S.
colleges and universities.  NAFSA's Global
Issues Committee has prepared and distributed
an information packet, "Global Issue: Hunger,"
which includes guides for planning educational
programs, and lists of materials, films, and
resource groups.  Pub.: Newsletter, 9 times
a year.

NATIONAL ASSOCIATION OF EVANGELICALS
  (NAE)
P.O. Box 28
Wheaton, Illinois 60187          312-665-0500

Est. 1942.  With some 3.5 million members,
NAE is a "channel for interchurch cooperation"
for more than 300 denominations, individual
churches from some other 30 groups, and
other evangelical organizations, including
colleges and seminaries.  NAE's World Relief
Commission promotes and conducts various
activities in developing countries, including
support to food production and rural development projects in Africa, South Korea, and
Bangladesh.  Pub.: United Evangelical Action,
q.

NATIONAL ASSOCIATION OF WHEAT
  GROWERS (NAWG)
1030 15th Street, N.W.
Washington, D.C. 20005          202-659-1533

Est. 1950.  Federation of eleven state wheat
growers associations.  Maintains a Committee
on International and Domestic Market Development.  Pub.: Report from Washington, weekly.

NATIONAL BEEF BOYCOTT CENTER
1345 Euclid Street, N.W.
Washington, D.C. 20009          202-667-6407

Objectives are to: "greatly reduce beef consumption; greatly reduce retailing feed-lot
beef by markets and increase grass-fed beef
(making available protein grain for human
need); educate the public as to the plight of
domestic ranchers whose low profit margins
are transferred to feedlot/packaging/retailing
middlemen, not to consumers; provide a nutritional education that tells the true facts
regarding meat, fats, sugars, etc.; provide
non-meat quality menus (including preparation
of grass-grazed beef)."

Collects money for purchase and distribution of
food to famine-stricken areas of the Third
World.  Educational work on hunger, global
maldistribution and abuse of resources and
food.  Personal response through fasting and
simple living.

Fast for Famine Relief, which is affiliated,
works with Africare, the Buddhist Peace Dele-
gation in Paris, and the
Committee to purchase, package, and deliver
foodstuffs.

NATIONAL COALITION FOR LAND REFORM
  (NCLR)
345 Franklin Street
San Francisco, California 94102   415-863-0339

Est. 1971. Works for a "more equitable distribution of land in rural America." Educational,
legal, and political action. Among its goals is
increasing the number of self-employed farmers, encouraging agricultural cooperatives,
diminishing use of toxic chemicals, and fighting
"corporate feudalism." Pub.: Newsletter, q.

NATIONAL CONFERENCE OF CATHOLIC
  CHARITIES (NCCC)
1346 Connecticut Avenue, N.W.
Washington, D.C. 20036          202-785-2757

Est, 1910. Central national organization for
Roman Catholic charities in the U.S. Concerns
include domestic food and nutrition policies.
Affiliated local charities are actively involved in
emergency food assistance in the U.S. and as
advocates for those in need of governmental
assistance. Pub.: Charities U.S.A., ten times
a year. Congressional Comment, 3 times a
year.

NATIONAL CORN GROWERS ASSOCIATION
  (NCGA)
P.O. Box 358
Boone, Iowa 50036               515-432-2703

Trade organization of growers, processors,
marketers, and exporters of corn (maize).
Purpose is to further the use, proper marketing,
protection, legislative position, tariff consideration, and efficient production of corn. Compiles
statistics on production and export of corn. Pub.:
Cornletter, mon.

NATIONAL COUNCIL OF CHURCHES OF
  CHRIST IN THE U.S.A. (NCC)
475 Riverside Drive
New York, New York 10027        212-870-2200

Est. 1950. NCC is a federation of 31 Protestant
and Eastern Orthodox denominations, with a total
combined membership of some 41 million. All
three of the Council's major divisions are involved in hunger issues, and in addition, there are
several "inter-unit" activities:

The Division of Church and Society (DCS) has
formed a DCS Working Group on Hunger to
coordinate its various hunger-related projects.
These include assisting migrant workers
obtain emergency food supplies through the
NCC Office of Migrant Services; and the Crusade
Against Hunger, which focuses on raising U.S
consciousness of domestic hunger and malnutrition and on increasing the effectiveness of
existing federal food programs through political
education and legal action. The National Farm
Worker Ministry provides subsistence support
for church people who work full-time with
farm workers; part of the program involves
emergency relief as needed. The Delta Ministry supports community development efforts in
the Mississippi River Delta. Its staff has
helped day care centers become eligible for
federal food programs and assistance, and
brought a suit against the U.S. Department of
Agriculture which led to an expansion of the
national supplemental food program by $30
million. The Interreligious Foundation for
Community Organization (IFCO) has been engaged in the war against hunger and disease in
the Sahelian region of Africa. One of its programs, Relief for Africans in Need in the
Sahel (RAINS) has contributed directly to
passage of legislation to appropriate U.S. funds
for the Sahelian relief effort; conducts public
education to make the American people aware
of the gravity of the crisis there; and maintains
an up-to-date file on the operations of various
international and national governmental and
private organizations involved in Sahelian
research and technical assistance.

The Division of Overseas Ministries (DOM)
deals with human hunger across a wide spec-
trum of concerns and activities, which range
from public policy concerns through development activity, to direct relief. The Division
encourages and channels ecumenical support
from U.S. churches to overseas Christian communities to support them in their programs to
deal with the root problems of hunger through
locally-determined programs. The Division
maintains close contact with the World Council
of Churches, and contributes to many of its
programs. Contacts are also maintained regularly with regional councils of churches (such as
the All Africa Conference of Churches) and
many national councils of churches throughout
the world.

Two agencies of the Division of Overseas Ministries in particular deal with specific issues related to hunger:

+Church World Service (CWS)
475 Riverside Drive
New York, New York 10027

212-870-2257

Est. 1946. The major overseas relief and development unit of the NCC. CWS operates a wide variety of programs that impact hunger concerns. These involve emergency relief at points of particular need, and technical and material assistance in such areas as community development, food production, land reclamation, and irrigation. It provides self-help loans, assists in nutrition and medical care, and provides health training.

These programs operate in some 40 countries in Africa, Asia, Latin America, Europe, and the Middle East. The total CWS budget in 1975 was $35 million.

CWS has helped in the filming of several national television features on world hunger and assists denominations in the promotion of the One Great Hour of Sharing, many funds from which are used in hunger programs.

++CROP, The Community Hunger
  Appeal of Church World Service
28606 Phillips Street
Elkhart, Indiana 46514

219-264-3102

Est. 1947. Conducts campaigns to raise money and other gifts to be used by Church World Service and other relief agencies in providing emergency food in times of disaster and seeds, tools, and other self-help aid for development projects.

CROP works through local committees of volunteers. Home-to-home canvasses are the most common means of raising funds; other methods include hunger walks, fasts for the hungry, special gifts from individuals and businesses, and friendship farmer programs.

National Council of Churches, Church World Service, CROP, contin.

CROP provides films, filmstrips, and other educational materials. It maintains regional offices in Springfield, Illinois; Indianapolis, Indiana; Des Moines, Iowa; Topeka, Kansas; Lansing, Michigan; Hagerstown, Maryland; Huron, South Dakota; Jefferson City, Missouri; Lincoln, Nebraska; Rocky Hill, New Jersey; San Francisco and Pasadena, California; East Longmeadow, Massachusetts; Columbus, Ohio; Camp Hill, Pennsylvania; Austin, Texas; Durham, North Carolina; and Madison, Wisconsin.

++Office of the Consultant on World
  Hunger, Church World Service
955 L'Enfant Plaza, S.W., Suite 4300,
  North Building
Washington, D.C. 20024

202-484-3950

Maintains liaison with U.S. government agencies on U.S. food and development policies and programs; major recent effort has concentrated on monitoring implementation by the U.S. Government of the resolutions of the World Food Conference of 1974.

CWS maintains field offices in some 15 countries in Africa, South Asia, and Latin America. It publishes a series of fact sheets on world hunger. CROP distributes educational packets, films and filmstrips (list available).

+Agricultural Missions (AM)
475 Riverside Drive
New York, New York 10027

212-870-2553

Est. 1930. AM is the NCC Division of Overseas Ministries' technical agency for agriculture and rural development. It offers training in agriculture, nutrition, cooperatives, and other forms of community organization, and consultant services to farm people and missionaries around the world. AM gives high priority to the development of rural networks to share information and encourage self-development.

National Council of Churches, Agricultural
Missions, contin.

It also seeks to raise awareness within the
churches about the world's agricultural
needs and causes of rural poverty and
hunger.  Pub.: Rural Missions, q.  Technical reports.

The Division of Education and Ministry (DEM)
is involved in hunger issues in several ways.
Its program on Education for Life and Mission
(Friendship Press) produces a variety of materials concerning hunger and development in
the U.S. and abroad.  These include: Some-
times They Cry; Can the World Share the
Wealth?; Wealth and Want in One World; Need
is Our Neighbor; How Churches Fight Poverty;
and New Hope for the Hungry?: The Challenge
of the World Food Crisis.  Study packets, filmstrips, and dramas are also distributed.

NCC's Washington Office (110 Maryland Avenue,
N.E., Washington, D.C. 20002, 202-544-2350)
facilitates and coordinates the Council's concerns with public policy.  It has arranged for
testimony before congressional committees on
drought and hunger in Africa, on a system of
consumer and marketing reserves for major
agricultural commodities, on the need for a
coordinated approach to the multifaceted problems of the world food crisis, and on the role
of voluntary agencies in helping to meet the
crisis.

NCC's Communications Commission (at the
New York address) works to get hunger issues
before the churches and the public at large
through mass media.  It has facilitated the
production of several national television programs on the subject in cooperation with other
units of the Council.

NCC's Commission on Justice, Liberation and
Human Fulfillment, through its Working Committee on Hunger, monitors the hunger programs of the churches to insure that the fundamental issues of justice and other root causes
of hunger are considered.

NCC's Commission on Faith and Order has been
concerned with the theological and ethical dimensions of the world hunger problem.

NCC publications include: Tempo, mon.  Spec-
trum/Journal, q.

NATIONAL COUNCIL OF FARMER
  COOPERATIVES (NCFC)
1129 20th Street, N.W.
Washington, D.C. 20036          202-659-1525

Est. 1929.  A federation of 133 national, regional, and state associations of 6500 farmers'
marketing and purchasing cooperatives serving
a total farm membership of 3 million.  Works
to protect the interests of farmer cooperatives
and the farm coop movement.  Maintains a
Committee on Marketing and Foreign Trade.
Pub.: Washington Councilor, weekly.  Washington Situation, mon.

NATIONAL COUNCIL ON HUNGER AND
  MALNUTRITION IN THE UNITED STATES
1000 Wisconsin Avenue, N.W.
Washington, D.C. 20007          202-338-5515

Est. 1968.  Seeks to mobilize private resources
in the campaign against hunger and malnutrition in the U.S.  Currently inactive.

NATIONAL DAIRY COUNCIL (NDC)
111 N. Canal Street
Chicago, Illinois 60603          312-372-3156

Est. 1915.  Trade association which conducts
programs of nutrition research, nutrition education, and public relations in the U.S. on the
uses of milk and milk products.  Pub.: Dairy
Council Digest, semimon.  Nutrition News,
semimon.  Dairy Councilor, q.

NATIONAL FISHERIES INSTITUTE (NFI)
1730 Pennsylvania Avenue, N.W.
Washington, D.C. 20006          202-785-0500

Est. 1945.  Umbrella trade association of
producers, processors, distributors, wholesalers, importers, and canners of fish and
shellfish.  Major activities are government and
public relations on behalf of the industry and
greater consumption of fish and fish products
in the U.S.  Also conducts a modest scholarship program, which has sponsored research
on such topics as textured vegetable protein
and minced fish blends.  Pub.: Flashes, weekly.

NATIONAL FOOD AND CONSERVATION
  THROUGH SWINE, INC. (National FACTS)
  (FACTS)
217 Fourth Avenue
Haddon Heights, New Jersey 08035
                                609-547-0751

Est. 1970.  An organization of people who collect food waste and feed it to hogs.  Maintains
that it is the "oldest anti-pollution and conservation" oriented industry in the U.S., since
some six million tons of food waste are re-
cycled each year through swine and into pork
and pork products.  Works to protect the industry through legislative action.  Pub.: Newsletter, q.

NATIONAL FOOD STAMP INFORMATION
  COMMITTEE
1910 K Street, N.W.
Washington, D.C. 20006

Publishes informational literature about the
federal Food Stamp Program and its participants, including "The Facts About Food
Stamps."

NATIONAL 4-H FOUNDATION OF AMERICA
7100 Connecticut Avenue, N.W.
Washington, D.C. 20015          301-656-9000

Est. 1948.  The national 4-H program is sponsored by the U.S. Department of Agriculture,
state land-grant universities, and county governments.  (The four H's are head, heart, hands,
and health.)  It involves about 5 million youths
9-19 years old, and fosters development of good
character and citizenship, as well as skills in
agriculture, homemaking, and community service.  (Information about the 4-H Program itself
can be had from the Extension Service, U.S.
Department of Agriculture, Washington, D.C.
20250.)

The National 4-H Foundation was organized as a
separate organization to carry on programs with
private funding.  Its projects include international exchange programs for farm youth, and
youth programs in developing countries.  Pub.:
Annual Review.  Pamphlets.

NATIONAL GRAIN AND FEED ASSOCIATION
501 Folger Building
Washington, D.C. 20005          202-783-2024

Est. 1896.  Trade association of wholesalers
and retailers of grain and feed for livestock
and related purposes.  Maintains a Committee
on International Trade.  Pub.: National Newsletter, weekly.  Feed and Feeding Digest, mon.

NATIONAL GRAIN TRADE COUNCIL (NGTC)
725 Fifteenth Street, N.W.
Washington, D.C. 20005          202-783-8945

Est. 1930.  Council of grain dealers.  Concerns
include grain exports.

NATIONAL PEANUT COUNCIL (NPC)
7900 Westpark Drive, Suite 713
McLean, Virginia 22101          703-893-5038

Est. 1941.  Trade association of growers,
shellers, manufacturers, and brokers in the
peanut industry.  Promotes exports of peanuts
and peanut products as a market development
cooperator with the U.S. Department of Agriculture.

NATIONAL PLANNING ASSOCIATION (NPA)
1606 New Hampshire Avenue, N.W.
Washington, D.C. 20009          202-265-7685

Est. 1934.  "An independent, private, nonprofit,
nonpolitical organization that conducts research
and policy studies relating to the full and efficient use of the productive resources of the
United States and in the international economy."
NPA's Agriculture Committee has adopted
statements on U.S. farm policy in the light of
the world food situation.  Pub.: Looking Ahead
& Projection Highlights, 10 times a year, which
has included coverage of world food issues and
related topics.  New International Realities,
3 times a year.  Various policy reports, including A Farm, Food and Land Use Policy for the
Future (1975).

NATIONAL SOYBEAN PROCESSORS
  ASSOCIATION (NSPA)
1133 Fifteenth Street, N.W., Suite 206
Washington, D.C. 20005          202-452-8040

Est. 1930.  Trade organization of producers of
soybean oil and meal.  Sponsors the Food

Protein Council (111 E. Walker Drive, Chicago, Illinois 60606), which publishes menus and other information about food preparation using soybean products in meal planning. Has also served as an export marketing cooperator with the U.S. Department of Agriculture for short-term projects.

NEAR EAST FOUNDATION (NEF)
54 E. 64th Street
New York, New York 10021          212-838-3500

Est. 1915. Assists people of developing nations, through technical assistance, to launch self-help programs for rural development and improvement. Originally focused on the plight of Armenian refugees from Turkey, NEF since 1964 has devoted most of its resources to some 15 countries in Africa, with financial support from the U.S. Agency for International Development, and with individual contributions from some 10,000 Americans. Assistance is also provided to projects in Iran, Jordan, Lebanon, and Greece. Examples of projects: assisting in setting up a cooperative livestock marketing program in Botswana; training Malawi students and faculty in agricultural science and laboratory techniques. The total NEF budget in 1975 was about $1.4 million. Pub.: Near East Foundation News, semiann.

NETWORK
224 D Street, S.E.
Washington, D.C. 20003          202-544-1371

"A religious lobby for social justice" operated by Roman Catholic religious. Global hunger is a principal concern. Supports the "Pastoral Plan of Action on the World Food Crisis" of the National Conference of Catholic Bishops (1974). Supported mainly by contributions from individual congregations. Legislative research for congressional testimony and action; intern program; workshops; phone alerts. Pub.: Network Newsletter, mon. Network Quarterly. Issue packets, pamphlets, and an organizing manual.

NEW DIRECTIONS (ND)
2021 L Street, N.W.
Washington, D.C. 20036          202-452-1050

Est. 1976. Formed to lobby in the U.S. Congress on global issues. Current priorities are: safe energy, reducing arms sales, and "making the world's food system work for everyone." Concerning food, ND seeks improved and expanded U.S. development efforts "in certain very specific and concrete ways." Measures supported are: aid to integrated rural development in the neediest nations; improved and increased aid to the neediest nations; increased support for policies and programs that reduce population growth and ameliorate problems of population distribution; and full U.S. food production. Pub.: Citizen Force, bimon. newspaper.

NEW WORLD COALITION
419 Boylston Street, Room 209
Boston, Massachusetts 02116    617-266-6120

Main goal is to create a basis for sustained support of grass-roots initiatives for self-determination in the U.S. and overseas. Operates the Peoples' Development Fund, which supports various projects, including a nutrition-fishery program in Zambia, which trains and equips fishermen living along the Zambezi River. Related to the New Internationist (England).

NORTH AMERICAN EXPORT GRAIN
 ASSOCIATION (NAEGA)
26 Broadway
New York, New York 10004          212-269-7673

Est. 1920. Members are U.S. and Canadian companies which export grain. Pub.: Bulletin, irreg.

NUTRITION FOUNDATION
888 17th Street, N.W.
Washington, D.C. 20006          202-872-0778

Est. 1941. Sponsors research and educational projects in the science of nutrition. Pub.: Nutrition Reviews, mon. Nutrition Education Materials (index). Booklets. Publications list.

OVERSEAS DEVELOPMENT COUNCIL (ODC)
1717 Massachusetts Avenue, N.W.
Washington, D.C. 20036          202-234-8701

Est. 1969.  Seeks to increase American under
standing of the problems faced by the developing countries and the importance of those
countries to the U.S.  Its functions are to "keep
the urgency of the challenges of development
before the American public and responsible
authorities; to serve as a forum for individuals
directly concerned with development to share
ideas through conferences, seminars, and discussions; to conduct studies of its own on
current and emerging problems; and to distri-
bute information and knowledge about development as widely as possible.

The world food situation has been a major
interest, focusing on policies necessary to
carry out the recommendations of the World
Food Conference.

Pub.: Communique on Development Issues
series, including "World Food Insecurity: Has
Anything Happened Since Rome?" (1975); "The
Changing Face of Food Scarcity" (1975); and
other reports.  Development Paper series.
Monograph series.  ODC publications are
available individually or on a subscription
basis (list on request).

OXFAM-AMERICA
474 Centre Street
Newton, Massachusetts 02158    617-965-3917

Est. 1970.  A development assistance and emergency relief organization which is part of a
worldwide network known as OXFAM, a name
derived from the Oxford Committee for Famine
Relief, organized in England in 1942 to aid
war refugess.  The U.S. committee raises
funds for international projects, usually small,
rural development efforts often overlooked by
larger agencies.  Among its projects have been
a Nationwide Fast for a World Harvest (1974)
and "Plant a Seed for Change" (1975).  Distributes literature and films on development
topics, including hunger and nutrition.

PARTNERS OF THE AMERICAS
2001 S Street, N.W.
Washington, D.C. 20009          202-332-7332

Est. 1964, by the U.S. Agency for International
Development as a private-citizen people-to-
people component of the Alliance for Progress.
It works by linking people in a state in the U.S.
with a state, region, or country of Latin
America.  Once joined in this partnership, they
work together as volunteers on mutual self-
help projects in a variety of fields, including
agriculture, nutrition, and community development.  In 1975, partners in 24 states conducted
a total of 65 projects in these fields with a value
of $450,000.

Examples of projects: Alabama Partners has
worked in Guatemala to develop a fish restock-
ing program; Michigan Partners has conducted
intensive in-service training for all agricultural
extension officers in Belize; Vermont Partners
has donated bulls for a livestock breeding project in Honduras; Ohio Partners has helped to
set up a program to supply fish protein to low-
income farmers in Parana State, Brazil.  Pub.:
The Partner, bimon.

THE PEOPLE-TO-PEOPLE HEALTH
 FOUNDATION, INC. (PROJECT HOPE)
2233 Wisconsin Avenue, N.W.
Washington, D.C. 20007          202-338-6110

Est. 1958.  An international medical education
organization which works to bring the skills and
techniques of the U.S. medical professions to
developing countries.  Program includes nutrition education.  Operates HOPE ship plus land-
based projects in the Caribbean, South America,
and Tunisia.  Pub.: Hope News, q.

THE PHILADELPHIA MACROANALYSIS
 SEMINARS
c/o Movement for a New Society
4719 Cedar Avenue
Philadelphia, Pennsylvania 19143
                         215-SA 9-1928

Works to develop and spread seminars using
"macroanalysis, the process by which concerned people study the big picture of social
reality and try to apply the findings to their
social actions and their life style."  Projects
have included seminars on the U.S. Food for

Peace program.  Training of seminar organi-
zers.  Pub.: On Organizing Macroanalysis
Seminars: A Manual.

PLENTY
Route 1, Box 156
Summertown, Tennessee 38483  615-964-3574

Est. 1974.  The international charitable wing
of the Farm, the largest spiritual intentional
community, which has over 1,000 "voluntary
peasants" on 1,750 acres in Middle Tennessee.
Provides food relief supplies, materials, and
technical assistance to projects in Guatemala,
Honduras, Mexico, and Bangladesh.  Pub.:
Farm Reports, semiann.

POPULATION CRISIS COMMITTEE (PCC)
1835 K Street, N.W.
Washington, D.C. 20006          202-659-1833

Est. 1965.  Primary purpose is to work as a
"catalyst for constructive population programs
and policies."  Food and Population Program
stresses the important links between the two
issues.  Emphasis is on raising funds to
support agencies working in the field.  Pub.:
Population Crisis, q.  Population, irregular
series of briefing papers.

POTATO ASSOCIATION OF AMERICA (PAA)
13 Brainerd Drive
Cranbury, New Jersey 08512     609-655-3458

Est. 1913.  Research organization of the
potato industry and specialists in the field.
Maintains an International Relations Committee.
Pub.: American Potato Journal, mon.

POULTRY AND EGG INSTITUTE OF
  AMERICA (PEIA)
521 E. 63rd Street
Kansas City, Missouri 64110     816-361-5775

Est. 1971.  Activities include promoting
exports of poultry and eggs and their products.
A market development cooperator with the
Foreign Agricultural Service, U.S. Department
of Agriculture.

+International Trade Development Board,
  Poultry and Egg Institute of America
425 13th Street, N.W., Suite 929
Washington, D.C. 20004     202-347-3991

PRESBYTERIAN CHURCH IN THE UNITED
  STATES (PCUS)
Taskforce on World Hunger
341 Ponce de Leon Avenue, N.E.
Atlanta, Georgia 30308

Hunger has been a denominational priority of
the PCUS since 1969.  Taskforce conducts
workshops and conferences, administers funds
for pilot projects in the U.S. and overseas,
provides resources and action suggestions,
and maintains a network of people working on
the issue.  Pub.: "Hunger and What You Can
Do."

PRIVATE AGENCIES COLLABORATING
  TOGETHER (PACT)
777 United Nations Plaza
New York, New York 10017     212-697-6222

A consortium of independent, private, voluntary agencies which works to promote a coordinated approach to planning for overseas development programs.  In the area of food production
and agricultural development, PACT agencies
are assisting in development of small and me-
dium scale rural agribusinesses, livestock
development, soybean production, nutrition
research, development of a soy-based food
product, agricultural extension, and rural
self-help projects.  Programs operate in
Ghana, Kenya, Liberia, the Philippines,
Dominican Republic, Ecuador, El Salvador,
Honduras, and Nicaragua.

PROJECT HOPE
See: People-to-People Health Foundation, Inc.

PROTEIN GRAIN PRODUCTS INTERNATIONAL
1030 15th Street, N.W.
Washington, D.C. 20005          202-785-2052

Promotes exports of protein grains.  A market
development cooperator with the Foreign
Agricultural Service, U.S. Department of
Agriculture.

PUBLIC WELFARE FOUNDATION
2600 Virginia Avenue, N.W.
Washington, D.C. 20037          202-965-1800

Program includes providing grants for various
agricultural development projects in developing
countries, e.g., education and training; irrigation systems; technical assistance. Recent
food-related activities have been in Mali, Mauritania, Niger, Brazil, Mexico, Panama, and
Peru.


RESOURCES FOR THE FUTURE (RFF)
1755 Massachusetts Avenue, N.W.
Washington, D.C. 20036          202-462-4400

Est. 1952. Purpose is "to advance research
and education in the development, conservation,
and use of natural resources, and in the improvement of the quality of the environment.
Most of its studies are in the social sciences,
and are broadly concerned with the relationships of people to the natural environment."
Studies related to the world food situation have
included research on management issues
arising from efforts to accelerate food production both in the U.S. and in developing
countries. Pub.: Resources, three times a
year. Books, monographs, and working
papers, including (for example), Agricultural
Development and Productivity: Lessons from
the Chilean Experience (1970).


RICE COUNCIL FOR MARKET
  DEVELOPMENT (RCMD)
P.O. Box 22802
Houston, Texas 77027            713-623-6700

Est. 1956. Rice trade organization; members
are in Arkansas, Louisiana, Mississippi, and
Texas. Provides worldwide advertising and
promotion services. A market development
cooperator with the U.S. Department of Agriculture, Foreign Agricultural Service.

     +Rice Council for Market Development
     European Operations
     Weinbergerstrasse 48
     8006 Zurich, Switzerland    01/34-40-10


ROCKEFELLER BROTHERS FUND
30 Rockefeller Plaza
New York, New York 10020        212-247-8135

The Fund supports food-related activities as
part of its Environmental Program. Grants in
this field have included funding for the Center
of Concern and Aspen Institute for Humanistic
Studies (which see), substantial support for
Worldwatch Institute, and an experimental
project to blend advanced technology and traditional farming practices in a search for ways
people can learn "to live more gently upon the
earth." In the future, the Fund will look increasingly "for opportunities to deal with conservation and population problems as they are
related to a cluster of basic considerations -
food, the use of capital, and the prevention of
pollution - and as they are influenced by
economic systems and governed by values."


THE ROCKEFELLER FOUNDATION (RF)
1133 Avenue of the Americas
New York, New York 10036        212-869-8500

Est. 1913. One of the Foundation's seven
major program areas is "Conquest of Hunger,"
which has the aim of improving the supply and
quality of basic foods and the quality of life of
the rural poor in developing countries. Major
support has been given to 9 international agricultural research institutes sponsored by the
Consultative Group on International Agricultural
Research. Other grants have been provided
to numerous projects in various countries to
improve the nutritional quality and yield of
basic food crops through breeding, plant
protection, and collection of genetic materials,
and to improve animal health and production;
to broaden the food production base through
research on biological engineering of plants
and animals and through new techniques for
management of living aquatic resources; to
strengthen institutional capabilities; to identify
strategies for improving the standard of living
for small farmers; and to increase understanding
of the socio-economic aspects of food production and distribution.


In 1975, the Foundation had total appropriations
of $45.5 million. Field offices are maintained
in 17 countries. Pub.: RF Illustrated, 3 times
a year. Working Papers series, including
Climate Change, Food Production, and Interstate

Conflict (1976); The World Food Situation: A New Initiative (1975); The Role of Animals in the World Food Situation (1975); Strategies for Agricultural Education in Developing Countries (1976); and others.

THE SALVATION ARMY
120 W. 14th Street
New York, New York 10011 212-243-8700

Est. 1865 (1880 in U.S.). An international religious and charitable movement organized along military lines. Social welfare activities include distributing food in the U.S. and overseas. Works through the International Salvation Army (which see) in development projects overseas. Pub.: The War Cry, weekly.

SAVE THE CHILDREN FEDERATION
See: Community Development Foundation

SELF HELP
116 Sixth Street, S.E.
Waverly, Iowa 50677 319-352-4483

Est. 1959. Supplies new and rebuilt agricultural and industrial equipment at the lowest possible cost to developing countries through missionary and government aid projects.

SEVENTH-DAY ADVENTIST WORLD
 SERVICE
6840 Eastern Avenue, N.W.
Washington, D.C. 20012 202-723-0800

International relief and development arm of the General Conference of Seventh-Day Adventists. Projects include food production, nutrition, manufacturing, storage, and feeding in various Third World countries.

SHAKERTOWN PLEDGE GROUP
W. 44th Street at York Avenue S.
Minneapolis, Minnesota 55410 612-926-6159

Est. 1973. Information and resource center for "those who are interested in radical simplicity and searching out new ways of life in a rapidly changing world." Promotes the Shakertown Pledge, a document developed at a meeting of religious retreat center directors in Shakertown, Kentucky. The Pledge is a commitment to "lead an ecologically sound life...to occupational responsibility...[and] to leading a life of

creative simplicity and to sharing my personal wealth with the world's poor." Public education on "contrasumption," including food. Workshops; public events. Maintains a Simple Living Network and contacts with similar groups abroad. Pub.: Creative Simplicity, mon. Pamphlets (list available).

SIERRA CLUB
530 Bush Street
San Francisco, California 94108

   415-981-8634

Est. 1892. A major national conservation organization with an active international program. Concerns have included preservation of prime agricultural lands (especially in California) and superfarms (especially in North Carolina); and environmental aspects of international development programs. Pub.: Sierra Club Bulletin, mon. National News Report, weekly. Books and special reports (list available).

 +Office of International Environment
  Affairs, Sierra Club
 800 Second Avenue
 New York, New York 10017

   212-867-0080

 Pub.: International Report, twice a month.

SMITHSONIAN SCIENCE INFORMATION
 EXCHANGE (SSIE)
1730 M Street, N.W., Room 300
Washington, D.C. 20036 202-381-4211

Est. 1949. Collects, indexes, stores, and disseminates data about basic and applied research projects in all areas of the life and physical sciences, including 35 categories in the agricultural aciences. Provides search services and selective dissemination of information. Pub.: SSIE Science Newsletter, 10 times a year. Research Information Packages in the Agricultural Sciences.

SOCIETY FOR NUTRITION EDUCATION (SNE)
2140 Shattuck Avenue, Suite 1110
Berkeley, California 94704 415-548-1363

Est. 1968. Professional organization of nutrition educators from the fields of dietetics, home economics, medicine, public health, and education at all levels. Overall goal is "to promote good nutrition for all by making nutrition education more effective.  It will be promoted at all levels: international, national, state, and local. "

Educational activities include developing and promoting concepts for teaching, both in and out of schools; helping to implement the recommendations on nutrition education from the White House Conference on Food, Nutrition and Health and the National Nutrition Study; working for effective use of mass media; and establishing standards.

Research activities include promoting or sponsoring research in nutrition education;  making research findings known; identifying research needs and establishing priorities; exploring sources of funding; and developing consultation resources.

Sponsors conferences, workshops, and symposia.  Maintains the National Nutrition Education Clearing House (NNECH), a collection, evaluation, and cataloging facility at the Berkeley address, which provides library, bibliographic, and consulting services.

Pub.:  Journal of Nutrition Education, q.  SNE Communicator, q.  Nutrition Education Resource Series.  Nutrition Education Resource Pamphlets.  Audiovisual aids.  List available.

SOUTHERN BAPTIST CONVENTION
460 James Robertson Parkway
Nashville, Tennessee 37219    615-244-2495

The church's Christian Life Commission works to raise consciousness about social justice issues, including world hunger, among its members, by preparing and distributing resource materials, consulting with agencies active in the field, and providing speakers.

Its Foreign Mission Board (see below) includes agricultural and nutrition projects in missionary activities in Africa, Asia, Latin America, and the Middle East.

+Southern Baptist Convention
Foreign Mission Board
3806 Monument Avenue
Richmond, Virginia 23230   804-353-0151

STANFORD UNIVERSITY
Food Research Institute
Stanford, California 94305      415-497-3653

Institute est. 1921.  A major research and teaching facility concerned primarily with economic analysis of the production, distribution, and consumption of food on a global scale; study of agricultural commodities, marketing systems, and futures markets; and examination of international commodity trade, development finance, and demographic trends, with special emphasis on income growth and distribution in developing countries.  Holds seminars, meetings, and conferences; library; offers courses.  Also involved in developing a new curriculum in human nutrition at Stanford.

Pub.:  Food Research Institute Studies, 3 times a year.  Miscellaneous Publications series.  Studies in Commodity Economics and Agriculture Policy series.  Studies in Tropical Development series.  Books and special studies. Publications catalog available.

SUDAN INTERIOR MISSION, INC.
Cedar Grove, New Jersey 07009
           201-857-1100

Projects include technical help and supplies for agricultural projects in Ethiopia and Niger.

SYNAGOGUE COUNCIL OF AMERICA (SCA)
432 Park Avenue South
New York, New York 10016   212-686-8670

Est. 1926.  Umbrella organization for organizations representing Orthodox, Conservative, and Reform Jews in the U.S.  Maintains committees on International Affairs, Social Justice, the UN, and UNESCO.  In 1975, SCA issued a Resolution on Hunger outling policies and strategy alternatives to stimulate Jewish involvement in the world hunger crisis.  Pub.: Analysis, semimon.  Action Memo, bimon.

## TECHNOSERVE, INC.
36 Old King's Highway South
Darien, Connecticut 06820

Provides technical services to local enterprises in developing countries through encouragement, analysis, management help and training, transfer of technology, and assistance in locating capital funds. Program includes aiding associations of farmers and farm cooperatives in Ghana, Kenya, and Honduras.

## UNION OF AMERICAN HEBREW CONGREGATIONS (UAHC)
838 Fifth Avenue
New York, New York 10021

Est. 1873. The central congregational body of Reform Judaism in the Western Hemisphere. Department of Social Action works to raise members' awareness of social issues, including discrimination, poverty, and hunger. It has issued a Passover Pledge of Conscience urging members to make personal commitments, such as eating less meat and using less fertilizer. Works with the Commission on Social Action of Reform Judaism in a comprehensive world hunger program. Pub.: Keeping Posted, biweekly (which has devoted an entire issue to Jewish dimensions of world hunger). RJA Voice, q. To Deal Thy Bread to the Hungry, an action workbook.

## UNITARIAN UNIVERSALIST SERVICE COMMITTEE (UUSC)
78 Beacon Street
Boston, Massachusetts 02108    617-742-2120

Est. 1963. A non-sectarian international social action organization related to the Unitarian Universalist Association. Overseas projects include nutrition activities. Pub.: World Service, q.

## UNITED CHURCH OF CHRIST (UCC)
Board for World Ministries
475 Riverside Drive
New York, New York 10027    212-870-2637

Provides support to a variety of rural development projects in Africa, Asia, and Latin America, including agricultural extension, demonstration farms, fisheries development, development of dairy herds, animal husbandry, poultry production, and agricultural cooperatives.

## UNITED METHODIST COMMITTEE ON RELIEF (UMCOR)
475 Riverside Drive
New York, New York 10027    212-749-0700

Est. 1940. Overseas development and relief agency of the United Methodist Church. Raises funds for projects in some 55 countries, as well as the U.S. Provides financial and personnel support to various agencies (including Methodist missionaries) in food-related activities, including land reclamation, irrigation, development of water supplies and agricultural cooperatives, agricultural extension, crop diversification, and training of agricultural personnel. Food-related projects are in Niger, Sudan, Bolivia, Haiti, Honduras, Nicaragua, Peru, Bangladesh, India, Jordan, and Pakistan. Pub.: Inasmuch, semiann.

+Center for the Study of Power and Peace
110 Maryland Avenue, N.E.
Washington, D.C. 20002

Charged with developing educational action resources on world hunger for use by local church organizations and secular groups. Pub.: World Hunger Packet.

<u>UNITED NATIONS ASSOCIATION OF THE
UNITED STATES OF AMERICA</u> (UNA-USA)
345 E. 46th Street
New York, New York 10017     212-697-3232

Est. 1964. A council of organizations which
"seeks, through information, education, and
research, to strengthen this country's capacity
for advancing the ideals of the United Nations."
World food issues, particularly as they involve
the United Nations System, have been a major
interest. The Washington office (below) conducts research and disseminates information
on U.S. Government funding of, and activities
related to, UN specialized agencies which deal
with aspects of the food problem. Pub.:
<u>The Inter-Dependent,</u> mon. newspaper.

    +Washington Office, UNA-USA
    411 E. Capitol Street, S.E.
    Washington, D.C. 20003    202-547-6645

<u>THE UNITED PRESBYTERIAN CHURCH IN
THE U.S.A.</u>
The Program Agency
475 Riverside Drive
New York, New York 10027    212-870-2316

Provides personnel and financial support to
programs in agricultural extension, agricultural credit, water resource development, land
reclamation, and settlement. Supports agricultural institutes, training centers, and a college.
Projects have been aided in Kenya, Sudan,
Zaire, Zambia, Taiwan, Thailand, India,
Nepal, and Guatemala.

<u>UNITED STATES CATHOLIC CONFERENCE</u>
(USCC)
1312 Massachusetts Avenue, N.W.
Washington, D.C. 20005    202-659-6600

Est. 1919. Civil entity of Roman Catholic
bishops in the U.S. Its <u>Office of International
Justice and Peace,</u> part of the USCC Department of Social Development and World Peace,
formulates policy on world hunger issues, and
carries on programs of legislative and administrative action and public education in the field.

A special USCC organization, the <u>Campaign
for Human Development,</u> is an education and
action program which attempts to increase the
awareness of the American people about

poverty and hunger in the U.S. and which
raises and distributes funds to domestic development projects, including community-owned
food cooperatives and farm and cattle cooperatives. CHD was started in 1970. Total grants
during 1971, 1972, and 1973 were $14.7 mil-
lion.

USCC foreign food activities are carried out by
Catholic Relief Services - USCC, Inc., <u>which
see.</u>

Pub.: <u>Our Daily Bread</u> (3 vols.), outlining
Catholic policies and programs on hunger
issues. Office of International Justice and
Peace issues essays; educational materials
for schools, parishes, and dioceses; reprints;
and copies of USCC testimony before Congress
(list available). The Campaign for Human
Development issues a <u>Newsletter,</u> q., and
various booklets, flyers, posters, and films
(list available).

<u>UNITED STATES COMMITTEE FOR UNICEF</u>
331 E. 38th Street
New York, New York 10016    212-686-5522

Est. 1947. Purpose is to support the United
Nations Childrens Fund (UNICEF) and to inform
the American people about UNICEF programs
to combat world hunger and about the world
food crisis generally and its effect on children
of the developing countries. Pub.: <u>News of
the World's Children,</u> q. <u>Youth Newsletter,</u> q.

<u>U.S. FEED GRAINS COUNCIL</u> (USFGC)
1030 15th Street, N.W., Suite 540
Washington, D.C. 20005    202-659-1640

Organization of some 70 grain producers, processors, dealers, exporters, and feed supplement manufacturers. Promotes development
of overseas markets for U.S. corn, grain
sorghum, oats, barley, alfalfa, feed additives,
and other feedstuffs. Maintains 10 offices
abroad:

    <u>+U.S. Feed Grains Council</u>
    157 Nanking East Road, 7th Floor
    Section 2, Taipei, Taiwan   561-6401

    <u>+U.S. Feed Grains Council</u>
    26, quai Louis-Bleriot
    7506 Paris, France    578-0194

+U.S. Feed Grains Council
Ballindamm 9
Hamburg 1, West Germany  33-87-86

+U.S. Feed Grains Council
5 Neofitou Douca Street
Athens 138, Greece          718-431

+U.S. Feed Grains Council
Via XX Settembre 5
00187 Rome, Italy           487034

+U.S. Feed Grains Council
P.O. Box 97
Kasumigaseki Building, 31st Floor
2-5 Kasumigaseki 3-chome
Chiyoda-ku, Tokyo, Japan  581-9456

+U.S. Feed Grains Council
Coolsingel 6
Rotterdam, Netherlands      134-525

+U.S. Feed Grains Council
Edificio España
Grupo 4, Planta 11, Oficinas 8 y 9
Madrid 13, Spain            2489090

+U.S. Feed Grains Council
28 Mount Street
London W1Y 5RB, England

+U.S. Feed Grains Council
Paik Nam Building, Room 902
188-3 Euljiro 1-KA, Chung-ku
Seoul, Korea                23-5192

UNITED STATES NATIONAL STUDENT
  ASSOCIATION
See:  The Action Center

UNIVERSITY OF CALIFORNIA
Task Force on World Food Problems
c/o Department of Agricultural Engineering
Davis, California 95616      916-752-1421

Conducts research on energy requirements for
food production (using California as an example),
machinery systems for food production, and
food processing.

UNIVERSITY OF CALIFORNIA, BERKELEY
Giannini Foundation of Agricultural Economics
207 Giannini Hall
Berkeley, California 94720      415-642-3345

Foundation est. 1928.  Research and public
service in agricultural economics, natural
resource economics, ' nd rural institutions,
focusing mainly on the U.S. and especially
California, but also on foreign agricultural
trade.  Library.  Pub.: research monographs
and reports.

UNIVERSITY OF CALIFORNIA, LOS ANGELES
School of Public Health
Center for Health Services
Division of Population, Family, and
  International Health
Los Angeles, California 90024    213-825-4053

Conducts research on nutrition in developing
areas, both in the U.S. and overseas.

UNIVERSITY OF CHICAGO
Community and Family Study Center
1126 E. 59th Street
Chicago, Illinois 60637          312-753-2965

Center est. 1961.  Program includes training
and research in communication for nutrition and
agricultural development.  Library of communications materials.

UNIVERSITY OF WISCONSIN
Climate/Food Project
Madison, Wisconsin 53706

Conducts research on the global food production
system.

UTAH STATE UNIVERSITY
Office of International Programs
Logan, Utah 84321                801-752-4100

Operates agricultural development projects,
under contracts with the U.S. Agency for International Development, in various countries,
including Bolivia, Iran, Cameroon, and Mali.
Pub.: IP Newsletter.

VEGETARIAN SOCIETY OF NEW YORK
1133 Broadway
New York, New York 10010  212-349-1242

Est. 1931. Members are some 350 persons
who do not eat fish, fowl, or flesh. Public
education; promotes research in the field of
vegetarianism; library. Pub.: Vegetarian
Courier, mon.

VOLUNTEER DEVELOPMENT CORPS (VDC)
1629 K Street, N.W.
Washington, D.C. 20006  202-223-3349

Sends volunteers to provide short-term technical help to agricultural cooperatives and to
governmental agencies involved in cooperative
development on request.

VOLUNTEERS FOR INTERNATIONAL
 DEVELOPMENT (VID)
P.O. Box 4543
Stanford, California 94305  415-497-3228

Est. 1958. Recruits volunteers for various
United Nations development projects overseas,
including projects related to hunger. Affiliated
is Volunteers in Asia (same address). Areas
served are in Asia, Africa, and Latin America.

VOLUNTEERS IN TECHNICAL ASSISTANCE
 (VITA)
3706 Rhode Island Avenue, N.W.
Washington, D.C. 20822  301-277-7000

Est. 1960. Provides volunteer professionals
to assist individuals and development organizations requesting technical assistance for social
and economic development projects in planning,
implementation, and problem-solving. Maintains a roster of specialists to whom it sends
inquiries from around the world for solution.
In special cases, VITA arranges for short-
term assignment overseas of experts.

Technical Information Service gathers and
tests data which are made available through
publications and local affiliates. "Appropriate
technology" is emphasized. Local affiliates in
the Philippines, Brazil, El Salvador, Honduras,
and Nicaragua. Pub.: VITA News, 8 times a
year. Various pamphlets and reports.

WESTERN WHEAT ASSOCIATES, U.S.A.,
INC.
200 S.W. Market Street, Suite 985
Portland, Oregon 97201  503-223-8123

Promotes exports of wheat from the Western
U.S. A market development cooperator with
the Foreign Agricultural Service, U.S. Department of Agriculture.

 +Western Wheat Associates
 Washington Office
 1030 15th Street, N.W., Suite 1008
 Washington, D.C. 20005  202-659-1737

WOMEN, FOOD AND POPULATION
1835 K Street, N.W., Suite 200
Washington, D.C. 20006

Women's group whose objective is to pressure
the world's governments for female equality,
production of more food, and a better life for
children.

WORLD EDUCATION (WE)
1414 Sixth Avenue
New York, New York 10019  212-838-5255

Est. 1951. Provides "professional assistance
to programs for the functional education of
adults in nearly twenty countries on four continents. Working in partnership with private
and governmental agencies, World Education
helps to plan, implement, support, and evalu-
ate innovative educational programs, especially
those related to literacy, food production, and
family planning."

Operates projects in Ethiopia, Colombia, India,
Honduras, Kenya, Tanzania, Thailand, the
Philippines, Ecuador, El Salvador, Ghana,
Indonesia, Bangladesh, and the U.S. Pub.:
World Education Reports, q. World Education
Monographs series. Training materials and
workshop reports. Publications list available.

WORLD HUNGER EDUCATION/ACTION
 TOGETHER (WHEAT)
475 Riverside Drive, Room 634
New York, New York 10027  212-870-2331

WHEAT is a collaborative effort of several
Protestant denominations to "mobilize persons
concerned about hunger." It "seeks to create

a broad base of persons in the churches who understand the root causes of hunger and are committed to first steps in a long-term response to the problem." Individuals are asked to make a covenant to: (1) commit themselves to intensive study of the problem of hunger and the issues it raises; (2) become directly involved in dealing with hunger issues in their own communities; (3) support advocacy efforts at the state and national levels for public policy changes on food and related issues; (4) provide financial support for church food efforts; and (5) change their own lifestyles toward reduced and less wasteful food and energy consumption.

WHEAT is coordinated by the National Council of Churches, but is not a Council program. It works closely with Bread for the World, the Interreligious Taskforce on U.S. Food Policy, and the Interfaith Center on Corporate Responsibility. Pub.: Brochures.

WORLD NEIGHBORS (WN)
5116 N. Portland Avenue
Oklahoma City, Oklahoma 73112
                              405-946-3333

Est. 1951. Provides assistance to developing nations through community development programs at the village level. Food production activities are part of WN's "total development" concept, which also encompasses family planning, public health, small industries, and leadership training.

Food-related services include agricultural extension services, including soil conservation; water supply projects; promoting fruit and vegetable growing and improved seeds; fish raising; education in nutrition and family gardening; improved fertilizers; rural leadership training in agriculture and follow-up extension work; revolving loan funds to assist agricultural production, land purchases, and fish pond construction; improvement of marketing systems for agricultural products; provision of farm implements; seed distribution; livestock production; agricultural resettlement.

WN operates in some 30 countries in Africa, Latin America, and East and South Asia. It is supported from private sources - mainly individuals, but also foundations, churches, and other organizations. Pub.: World Neighbors Newsletter, q.

WORLD PEACE THROUGH LAW CENTER
400 Hill Building
Washington, D.C. 20006          202-347-7992

Est. 1963. Membership organization of lawyers and law students; seeks to build law rules and legal institutions for world peace. The Center's biennial World Conferences have included discussions of food issues. Pub.: World Jurist, bimon.; other periodicals, pamphlets, conference documents, and reference books.

WORLD VISION INTERNATIONAL (WV)
919 W. Huntington Drive
Monrovia, California 91016          213-357-1111

Est. 1950. An interdenominational Christian humanitarian agency supported primarily by churches and individual contributions. Program includes assistance to orphans, Christian colleges and Bible schools, hospitals, etc., as well as to various development projects.

Relief program, administered through World Vision Relief Organizations (WVRO), involves feeding of some 90,000 children in 38 countries, and food for refugees in several areas.

Development assistance is given to agricultural projects in Ethiopia, the Gambia, Kenya, Niger, Senegal, Upper Volta, India, Indonesia, South Korea, the Philippines, and Thailand. Projects include agricultural credit; seeds; livestock; irrigation; agricultural equipment; teacher training; fishery cooperatives; and grain production.

Project FAST (Fight Against Starvation Today) encourages family and church group participation in various WV hunger projects. Methods include urging people to consider periodic "famine luncheons" or fasts.

Total WV disbursements in 1975 were $20.6 million, of which $5.7 million was for child care; $4.9 million for emergency aid (including food and medicine); and $924,000 for development projects.

Field offices are maintained in Dacca, Bangladesh; Belo Horizonte, Brazil; Addis Ababa, Ethiopia; Kowloon, Hong Kong; Madras, India; Malang, Java, Indonesia; Nairobi, Kenya; Seoul, Korea; Makati, Rizal, Philippines; and Bangkok, Thailand.

Area offices in the U.S. are at Midland Park, New Jersey; Atlanta, Georgia; Grand Haven, Michigan; Portland, Oregon; and Monrovia, California.

Pub.: World Vision Magazine, mon. Christian Leadership Newsletter, mon. World Hunger Bulletin, mon. WV sponsored a national television special on world hunger in August 1977.

WORLD WITHOUT WAR COUNCIL, INC. (WWWC)
175 Fifth Avenue
New York, New York 10010  212-674-2085

Est. 1961. A joint effort of national and regional peace, labor, religious, veterans, educational, and public affairs organizations "to achieve a disarmed world under law, safe for free societies and democratic values." Coordinates work of affiliated councils in Northern California; the Midwest; the Northwest; Eugene, Oregon; and Portland, Oregon. Policy statements have been issued on world hunger. Pub.: Perspective, bimon. World Hunger Crisis Kit (1975).

WORLDWATCH INSTITUTE
1776 Massachusetts Avenue, N.W.
Washington, D.C. 20036  202-452-1999

An independent research organization funded by private foundations and UN and U.S. Government agencies. "As an 'early warning system,' Worldwatch identifies issues which may develop into crises during the years immediately ahead. Focusing global attention on these problems, Worldwatch presents decision-makers with a range of public policy alternatives. The approach to problem solving is international and interdisciplinary. It reflects the Worldwatch view that the com-

plexity of tomorrow's important problems requires solutions not to be found within the narrow confines of national frontiers and traditional academic perspectives." Current projects include study of "economic, demographic, and political discontinuities facing the world in the last quarter of this century."

Pub.: Worldwatch Papers series, including The Politics and Responsibility of the North American Breadbasket, by Lester R. Brown (1975).

YOUNG MEN'S CHRISTIAN ASSOCIATION OF THE UNITED STATES (YMCA)
291 Broadway
New York, New York 10007  212-349-0700

Est. 1851. Through its International Division, the YMCA provides financial support and the services of U.S. Y personnel to indigenous YMCAs in some 30 countries in Africa, Asia, and Latin America to assist and advise their community development projects, which include training in improved farming methods, extension services, and irrigation projects in Ethiopia, Senegal, South Korea, and Sri Lanka. Pub.: YMCA Today.

YOUNG WOMEN'S CHRISTIAN ASSOCIATION OF THE U.S.A. (YWCA)
600 Lexington Avenue
New York, New York 10022  212-753-4700

Est. 1855. Through its International Division, contributes to agricultural development projects in Africa funded by the World YWCA in Geneva, Switzerland.

# Part 5.
# Canadian Organizations

# A. FEDERAL GOVERNMENT

CANADIAN INTERNATIONAL DEVELOPMENT
  AGENCY (CIDA)
122 Bank Street
Ottawa, Ontario K1A 0G4          613-996-7761

CIDA is heavily involved in both food . ... and
agricultural and fisheries development projects in developing countries.  Canada's
"Strategy for International Development Cooperation, 1975-1980" commits the country to
"a substantial program of food aid, including
the provision of one million tons of grain per
year." However, the Government has stated
that while "we are doing what we can to fend
off the threat of starvation in those areas most
severely affected by the crisis of recent years
... Canada's international development policies
will henceforth give a much higher priority to
programs designed to enhance agricultural
productivity."

Total CIDA disbursements for all development
purposes totaled $760 million (all figures are
in Canadian dollars).  About two-thirds ($503
million) was used for bilateral programs in
some 70 Third World Countries.  Bilateral
projects related to food production "concentrate on areas where Canadian expertise and
capabilities are considerable or can be easily
expanded," such as provision of fertilizer,
research in dryland farming, water resource
evaluation and development, planning and provision of storage and bulk handling facilities,
development of wheat farming and cattle and
dairy farming, fisheries and forestry management, soil sciences, animal breeding, animal
nutrition, and crop storage and processing.

Other bilateral programs involve scholarships,
providing skilled Canadian personnel, and
shipments of fertilizers.

CIDA has major bilateral food aid or food-
related development projects in Bangladesh,
India, Malaysia, Sri Lanka, Algeria, Morocco,
Tunisia, Upper Volta, Mali, Mauritania, Niger,
Chad, Senegal, Rwanda, Zaire, Madagascar,
Ghana, Tanzania, Kenya, Guyana, the Leeward
and Windward Islands, El Salvador, Honduras,
and Peru.

Technical assistance  is  provided to a number
of multilateral agencies, including the UN
Development Program, UNICEF, the World
Health Organization, and the Commonwealth
Fund for Technical Cooperation.  Multilateral
food aid is given primarily through the World
Food Program of the UN.

Capital assistance is given to several multilateral agencies involved in agricultural and
other food-related projects, including the
World Bank Group, Asian Development Bank,
Caribbean Development Bank, African Development Bank, and Inter-American Development
Bank.

In addition, CIDA supports international insti-
tutes of agricultural research through the
Consultative Group on International Agricultural
Research; and programs of two national non-
governmental organizations: the Canadian
Executive Service Overseas (CESO) and the
Canadian University Service Overseas (CUSO).

Pub.: Canada: Strategy for International Deve-
lopment Cooperation, 1975-1980 (1975).  Annual
Review.  Cooperation Canada, bimon. magazine.
Contact, mon. newsletter.

CANADIAN WHEAT BOARD
423 Main Street
Winnipeg, Manitoba R3C 2P5

A federal agency which is the sole marketing
authority for interprovincial and international
commerce in wheat, oats, and barley grown in
a designated area that includes Manitoba,
Saskatchewan, Alberta, eastern British Columbia, and the western edge of Ontario; it also
controls exports of those grains generally.
Maintains marketing offices in London, Tokyo,
and Brussels.

DEPARTMENT OF AGRICULTURE (Agriculture
  Canada)
Sir John Carling Building
Ottawa, Ontario K1A 0C5          613-994-5533

The Department carries on a wide-ranging
program of research, information, policy
development, and regulatory activities focused
on Canadian agriculture.

Its International Liaison Service (613-994-5571) is responsible for matters relating to international agriculture. It collects and reports on agriculture policy trends abroad and evaluates their impact on Canadian agriculture and trade; maintains liaison for the Canadian Government with such international agencies as FAO, OECD, and the World Food Program; provides technical assistance in agriculture to the Canadian International Development Agency; and participates in the work of the Inter-American Institute of Agricultural Sciences. The Service publishes Agriculture Abroad, a bimonthly digest of agricultural policies and programs in various countries; and Spot News from Abroad, weekly.

DEPARTMENT OF THE ENVIRONMENT
  (Environment Canada)
Ottawa, Ontario K1A 0H3    613-997-2136

The Department's Fisheries and Marine Service has as among its objectives to maintain and increase stocks of fish in Canadian marine and inland waters; to work with the fishing industry to develop better equipment for catching and processing fish; to conduct research in the marine sciences; and to help in the domestic and foreign marketing of Canadian fishery products.

DEPARTMENT OF EXTERNAL AFFAIRS
Lester B. Pearson Building
Ottawa, Ontario K1A 0G2    613-992-2148

The Aid and Development Division of the Department's Bureau of Economic and Scientific Affairs is responsible for formulating foreign policies related to international aid and development.

DEPARTMENT OF INDUSTRY, TRADE
  AND COMMERCE
Place de Ville
Ottawa, Ontario K1A 0H5    613-992-7404

Includes a Grains Marketing Office, which is responsible for promoting export markets for Canadian grains.

DEPARTMENT OF HEALTH AND WELFARE
  (Health and Welfare Canada)
Place Vanier, Tower B
355 River Road
Ottawa, Ontario K1A 0K9    613-993-9884

The Department's International Welfare Branch provides technical assistance in social development to Canadian and international development agencies; and advises and participates in programs for disaster relief in other countries.

INTERNATIONAL DEVELOPMENT
  RESEARCH CENTRE (IDRC)
P.O. Box 8500
Ottawa, Ontario K1G 3H9    613-996-2321

IDRC is a public corporation est. in 1970 by an act of the federal Parliament "to initiate, encourage, support, and conduct research into the problems of the developing regions of the world and into the means for applying and adapting scientific, technical, and other knowledge to the economic and social advancement of those regions, and, in carrying out those objects, (a) to enlist the talents of natural and social scientists and technologists of Canada and other countries; (b) to assist the developing regions to build up the research capabilities, the innovative skills, and the institutions required to solve their problems; (c) to encourage generally the co-ordination of international development research; and (d) to foster co-operation in research on development problems between the developed and the developing regions for their mutual benefit."

While supported financially by the Canadian Government, IDRC is an international organization governed by a Board of Governors composed of 10 Canadians and 10 non-Canadians (including 6 from developing countries). Its staff is also international in character.

Research to improve food production and nutrition is a foremost concern of IDRC, and during fiscal year 1975, the Centre's Agriculture, Food and Nutrition Sciences Division received about $5.4 million out of the total budget of $16.7. Support in this field is balanced between international agricultural research centers and smaller groups of researchers in a series of countries.

Emphasis is placed upon research in crops, farming systems, and reforestation in arid and semi-arid lands; multiple cropping with rice; use of agricultural wastes and byproducts in animal feed; fish farming and shellfish culture; fish preservation and processing; postharvest systems of protection, processing, and distribution; and the needs of the rural housewife and her family.

Recent projects have included, for example, grants to the Nigerian Government to develop a suitable milling system for producing bread, noodles, infant foods, and other products from local grains; to the Southeast Asian Fisheries Development Centre in the Philippines for aquaculture studies; and to various Mexican institutions to test cattle feeding systems using sugarcane and cane byproducts, and to study the consequences.

Pub.: Annual Report.  Interface: IDRC Review, annual.  Monograph Series, in English, French, and Spanish (list available).  IDRC maintains five regional offices:

+Office for Asia
International Development Research
  Centre
Tanglin P.O. Box 101
Singapore 10, Singapore

+Centre de Recherches pour le Développement International (Office for West Africa)
B.P. 11007
Dakar C.D. Annexe, Senegal

+Centro Internacional de Investigaciónes para el Desarollo (Office for Latin America and the Caribbean)
Apartado Aereo 53016
Bogota, D.E., Colombia

+Office for North Africa and the Middle East
International Development Research
  Centre
5 Latif Mansour Street
Cairo, Egypt

+Office for East Africa
International Development Research
  Centre
P.O. Box 30677
Nairobi, Kenya

SCIENCE COUNCIL OF CANADA
150 Kent Street
Ottawa, Ontario K1P 5P4          613-992-9991

The Council's overall responsibilities are to assess Canada's scientific and technical resources and to improve public awareness of issues involving science and technology.  Its major projects include developing a food policy for Canada within the context of "a world short of food."  Pub.: Issues in Canadian Science Policy, irreg. journal.  Reports.

# B. OTHER ORGANIZATIONS

Note:  A number of the private organizations listed in the United States section of this book are binational in character or have substantial memberships in Canada.  We have tried to include as many as possible in this section, but see also the U.S. listings for other such groups.

THE ANGLICAN CHURCH OF CANADA
The Primate's World Relief and Development
  Fund
600 Jarvis Street
Toronto, Ontario M4Y 2J6

ASSOCIATION QUEBECOISE DES ORGANISMES DE COOPERATION INTERNATIONALE
(Quebec Association of Organizations for International Cooperation ) (AQOCI)
4824, Côte des Neiges
Montreal, Quebec

Members are some 20 private organizations concerned with international development.  Serves as "a forum for opinion, action, and services;" seeks greater involvement by the Quebec provincial government in international development projects.

BRITISH COLUMBIA INTER-CHURCH
 COMMITTEE FOR WORLD DEVELOPMENT
 EDUCATION
150 Robson Street
Vancouver, British Columbia

CANADIAN CATHOLIC CONFERENCE
90 Parent Avenue
Ottawa, Ontario K1N 7B1

CANADIAN CATHOLIC ORGANIZATION FOR
 DEVELOPMENT AND PEACE
67 Bond Street, Suite 305
Toronto, Ontario M5B 1X5

CANADIAN COALITION FOR A JUST SOCIAL
 ORDER
Formed to work on public education efforts
about the New International Economic Order
and other development issues. For information, contact Gatt-Fly, or the Canadian Council
for International Cooperation (see index).

CANADIAN COUNCIL FOR INTERNATIONAL
 COOPERATION (CCIC)
75 Sparks Street
Ottawa, Ontario K1P 5A5          613-235-4331

Est. 1968. Made up of some 80 Canadian non-
governmental organizations involved in international development; works to mobilize
greater Canadian participation in world development efforts. Held a major Canadian Conference on the World Food Crisis in 1974.

THE CANADIAN COUNCIL OF CHURCHES
40 St. Clair Avenue, East
Toronto, Ontario M4T 1M9         416-921-4152

CANADIAN HUNGER FOUNDATION
75 Sparks Street
Ottawa, Ontario K1P 5A6          613-237-0180

Provides self-help assistance to developing
countries in agriculture, forestry, fisheries,
and nutrition. Also conducts educational and
information programs in Canada on the world
food problem, appropriate technology, and
related matters.

CANADIAN INSTITUTE OF FOOD SCIENCE
 AND TECHNOLOGY
10 Elgin Street, Room 46
Ottawa, Ontario K1P 5K6

CANADIAN INTER-CHURCH COMMITTEE
 FOR WORLD DEVELOPMENT
600 Jarvis Street, Room 223
Toronto, Ontario M4Y 2J6         416-922-0591

CANADIAN NATIONAL COMMITTEE FOR THE
 INTERNATIONAL UNION OF NUTRITIONAL
 SCIENCES
c/o Institut de Dietetique et de Nutrition
Université de Montréal
Case Postal 6128
Montréal, Quebec H4Y 1B9

CANADIAN UNICEF COMMITTEE
737 Church Street
Toronto, Ontario M4W 2M8

Support group for the United Nations Children's
Fund (UNICEF).

CANADIAN UNIVERSITY SERVICE
 OVERSEAS (CUSO)
151 Slater Street
Ottawa, Ontario K1P 5H5          613-237-0390

An independent Canadian development agency
that provides full-time volunteer skilled personnel for Third World development projects;
supports such projects through financial and/or
material contributions; and promotes public
education in Canada on "the causes of inequita-
ble development." Operates throughout Latin
America, Asia, Oceania, and Africa, with over
800 volunteers. About 47% of its projects are
related to agriculture and food. Total 1975
budget was $8 million. Pub.: Forum, bimon.

CHRISTIAN REFORMED WORLD RELIEF
 COMMITTEE OF CANADA
P.O. Box 235
Grimsby, Ontario L3M 4G3         416-643-2507

For description, see index for Christian Reformed World Relief Committee, USA

CITIZENS' ASSOCIATION TO SAVE THE
 ENVIRONMENT (CASE)
6002 W. Saanich Road, R.R. 7
Victoria, British Columbia V8X 3X3
                         604-652-3487

Concerns include community nutrition programs
in Canada and a "new food ethic" for developed
countries that reflects the needs of developing
countries, including modification of eating
habits and "de-escalation of the role of red
meat in our diets." Position papers.

COOPERATIVE FOR AMERICAN RELIEF
 EVERYWHERE (CARE)
CARE of Canada
1312 Bank Street
Ottawa, Ontario K1S 5H7

For description, see index for Cooperative for
American Relief Everwhere, USA.

DEVELOPMENT EDUCATION CENTER (DEC)
121-A Avenue Road
Toronto, Ontario M5R 2G3          416-964-6560

Develops and distributes educational materials
on the problems of the Third World and of
development in Canada. Has held seminars on
food issues. Reference Library. Pub.: DEC
Literature List, annual, including numerous
publications, films, and slide-tape shows.

DEVELOPMENT EDUCATION LIBRARY
 PROJECT
c/o Oxfam-Ontario
174 Carlton Street
Toronto, Ontario

Projects have included a Third World Bibliography & Resource Guide.

FOOD FOR THE HUNGRY
P.O. Box 67800
Vancouver, British Columbia V5X 3L8
                         604-324-7885

Food relief and self-help food development
projects. Has worked in Kenya, Ethiopia,
Niger, Mauritania, Senegal, Bangladesh, India,
Costa Rica, Haiti, Honduras, Panama, Nicaragua, Viet-Nam, and Guatemala. Also known
as Dominion Food for the Hungry Society.

GATT-FLY
600 Jarvis Street
Toronto, Ontario M4Y 2J6          416-921-4615

A project sponsored by five Canadian churches
(Anglican, Lutheran, Presbyterian, Roman
Catholic, and United). Works to promote
world justice by advocating alternative econo-
nomic policies, particularly in the areas of
trade and monetary reform. The food issue
has been a main focus. Pub.: GATT-Fly
Notes, irreg. newsletter.

INTER-CHURCH COMMITTEE FOR WORLD
 DEVELOPMENT EDUCATION
600 Jarvis Street, Room 219
Toronto, Ontario M4Y 2J6          416-922-0591

LATIN AMERICAN WORKING GROUP (LAWG)
P.O. Box 6300, Station A
Toronto, Ontario M5W 1P7          416-533-4221

Est. 1966. Research and public education on
Latin American issues, especially as they
relate to Canada's role in and relationship to
the region through official and business links.
Pub.: LAWG Newsletter, 10 times a year.

LUTHERAN COUNCIL IN CANADA
Canadian Lutheran World Relief
365 Hargrave Street, Suite 500
Winnipeg, Manitoba R3B 2K3
     See also: Lutheran World Relief.

MENNONITE CENTRAL COMMITTEE
 (CANADA)
201-1483 Pembina Highway
Winnipeg, Manitoba R3T 2C8        204-475-3550

Sponsors agricultural and rural development
projects overseas; development education in
Canada. See also: Mennonite Central Committee (USA)

NORTH AMERICAN EXPORT GRAIN
 ASSOCIATION
See index

ONTARIO INSTITUTE FOR STUDIES IN
  EDUCATION (OISE)
Third World Studies Project
252 Bloor Street, W.
Toronto, Ontario M5S 1VS

Maintains a Third World Resource Library.
Pub.: Underdevelopment: Canada and the
Third World: A Guide to Resources for Study and
Action (1973).

THE PRESBYTERIAN CHURCH IN CANADA
Committee on Inter-Church Aid, Refugee,
  and World Service
50 Wynford Drive
Don Mills, Ontario M3C 1J7

REGINA COMMITTEE FOR WORLD
  DEVELOPMENT
217-808 Smith Street
Regina, Saskatchewan SR4 2K8      306-522-8780

THE SALVATION ARMY
6 Murray Street
Ottawa, Ontario K1N 5N4

See: Salvation Army listing in international
  section

TASKFORCE ON THE CHURCHES AND
  CORPORATE RESPONSIBILITY
600 Jarvis Street
Toronto, Ontario M4Y 2J6      416-923-1758

A national inter-church ecumenical group.
Assists member churches and agencies to share
information and research.  Baby foods have
been a concern.

TEN DAYS FOR WORLD DEVELOPMENT
600 Jarvis Street, Room 219
Toronto, Ontario M4Y 2J6      416-922-0591

An annual event, which is a joint development
education program of the Anglican, Lutheran,
Presbyterian, Roman Catholic, and United
churches in Canada.  Goals are to increase
understanding among church members and
Canadians generally of world development needs
and to encourage action in response.  Holds
mass media events during a particular "Ten
Days" each year.  Theme for 1977 "Days" is
food.  Pub.: Tabloids, 2 or 3 a year.  Pamphlets and leadership kits.

UNITARIAN SERVICE COMMITTEE OF
  CANADA
2624 33rd Street, S.W.
Calgary, Alberta T3E 2T5

See also: Unitarian Universalist Service
  Committee (USA)

THE UNITED CHURCH OF CANADA
Committee on Education for Mission and
  Stewardship
85 St. Clair Avenue, East
Toronto, Ontario M4T 1M8

UNITED NATIONS ASSOCIATION IN CANADA
63 Sparks Street
Ottawa, Ontario K1P 5A6        613-232-5751

Concerned with Canada's role in the UN.
Distributes informational materials on UN
programs.  Seminars and meetings on development issues.  Pub.: Bulletin, bimon.

# Part 6.
# Organizations of
# Other Countries

Note: Listed in this part of the directory are selected national organizations outside North America that are concerned with food problems. The emphasis is on church groups, aid and educational organizations in donor countries, and nutrition institutions.  This is by no means a comprehensive listing; our information for this first edition is necessarily incomplete, and our purpose here is to provide points of contact in countries giving or receiving food-related aid.

## ALGERIA

Comité Chrétien de Service en Algerie (Christian Service Committee in Algeria) (CCSA)
60, rue Larbi Ben M'Hidi
Algiers, Algeria                    63-64-80
    Rural development projects.

## ARGENTINA

Asociación Argentina de Nutrición (Argentine Nutrition Association)
Santa Fe 1171
Buenos Aires, Argentina

Salvation Army
Rivadavia 3257
Buenos Aires, Argentina          89-06-21

## AUSTRALIA

Australian Development Assistance Agency
Canberra, A.C.T., Australia
    The government overseas aid organization.

Australian Council of Churches
Division of World Christian Action
P.O. Box 111
Sydney, N.S.W., Australia        26-2901

Community Aid Abroad (CAA)
75 Brunswick Street
Fitzroy, Victoria 3065, Australia
    Est. 1953.  Raises funds for development, including agricultural, projects abroad, and emergency food aid; education of the Australian public about world hunger.

Shakertown Pledge Group
c/o B. Hodgkin, 7 Tivey Place
Highes, A.C.T. 2605, Australia
    Contact for SPG (U.S.); see index.

## AUSTRIA

Oesterreichischer Missionsrat (Austrian Missions Council)
Gumpendorfer Str. 129
Vienna VI, Austria                  57-34-30

Austrian Society of Nutrition Research
c/o Physiologisches Institut der Universitaet Wien
Schwarzpanier Str. 17
1090 Vienna, Austria

## BANGLADESH

Bangladesh Agricultural Research Council
130/C Road #1, Dhanmandi Residential Area
Dacca-5, Bangladesh

Christian Commission for Development in Bangladesh (CCDB)
P.O. Box 367
Dacca, Bangladesh                   21-62-82

Institute of Nutrition
University of Dacca
Dacca-2, Bangladesh
    Has received financial support from the Ford Foundation.

Nutrition Society of Bangladesh
c/o Institute of Nutrition, University of Dacca
Dacca-2, Bangladesh

## BELGIUM

Ministry of Development Cooperation
Brussels, Belgium
    The government's overseas development agency.

International Cooperation for Social and Economic Development (CIDSE)
59-61, avenue Adolph Lacomble
1040 Brussels, Belgium              02-36-57-98

Institut Belge de l'Alimentation et de la Nutrition (Belgian Institute of Food and Nutrition) (IBAN)
172, avenue de Cortenbergh
1040 Brussels, Belgium

National Komitee voor Gezonde en Rechvaardige
 Voeding
Geldmunt 18
9000 Ghent, Belgium
    Citizens' group concerned that promotion of
    packaged baby foods in developing countries
    is leading to malnutrition.

BOTSWANA

The Botswana Christian Council
Development Department
P.O. Box 355
Gaberone, Botswana                 486

BRAZIL

Sociedade Brasileira de Nutricão (Brazilian
 Nutrition Society)
c/o Prof. A. Vieira de Mello
Instituto de Nutricão, Universidade Federal
 de Pernambuco
Cidade Universitaria
50000 Recife, Pernambuco, Brazil

Ecumenical Commission on Service (CESE)
Caixa Postal 041
40000 Salvador, Bahia, Brazil

Instituto de Nutricão (Institute of Nutrition)
Universidade Federal de Pernambuco
50000 Recife, Pernambuco, Brazil
    Has received financial support from the
    Ford Foundation.

Comissão Nacional de Alimentacão (National
 Food Commission) (CNA)
Av. Rio Branco
Rio de Janeiro, G.B., Brazil

Instituto de Tecnologia Agricola e Alimentar
 (Agricultural and Food Technology Institute)
Rua Jardin Botanico
1024 Rio de Janeiro, G.B., Brazil

Conselho de Desenvolvimento da Pesca
 (Fisheries Development Council)
Rio de Janeiro, G.B., Brazil

BULGARIA

International Union of Nutritional Sciences
c/o Prof. Dr. Boris Ivanoff Slarkoff
Boul. G. Kinkhoff 18
Sofia, Bulgaria

BURMA

The Burma Christian Council
Christian Service Committee
20 Signal Pagoda Road
Rangoon, Burma                 13290

BURUNDI

Alliance des Eglises Protestantes du Burundi
 (Alliance of Protestant Churches of Burundi)
B.P. 17
Bujumbura, Burundi

CAMEROON

Fédération des Eglises et Missions
 Evangéliques du Cameroun (Federation of
 Evangelical Churches and Missions in the
 Cameroon)
Commission pour le Developpement (Commis-
 sion for Development)
B.P. 790
Yaounde, Cameroon

CHILE

Sociedad Chilena de Nutrición (Chilean
 Nutrition Society)
Vicuña Mackenna 20, C. 6084
Santiago, Chile

CHINA, REPUBLIC OF

Taiwan Christian Service
No. 6 Jen-ai Road, Section 4
Taipei, Taiwan, Republic of China   77-31-71

COLOMBIA

Instituto Nacional de Nutrición (National
 Institute of Nutrition)
Carretera 3, no. 18-24, A.A.
15609 Bogota, D.E., Colombia

CYPRUS

Cyprus Ecumenical Team
c/o T. Thankachen
59 Irinis Street
Limassol, Cyprus

CZECHOSLOVAKIA

Czechoslovak National Committee of Nutrition
Czechoslovak Academy of Sciences
Budějovická 800
Prague, Czechoslovakia

DENMARK

Afdelingen for Internationalt Udviklings-
  samarbejde (Danish International Development Agency) (DANIDA)
Amaliegade 7
1256 Copenhagen K, Denmark
    The Danish Government's overseas deve-
    lopment agency.  Contributes to interna-
    tional food-related projects and conducts
    bilateral development activities.

Danish Nutrition Society
c/o Royal Danish School of Pharmacy
2100 Copenhagen Ø, Denmark

International Forum
Skt. Peders Straede 30
1453 Copenhagen K, Denmark
    Promotes Danish aid to developing coun-
    tries; also criticizes it because the current
    program mainly "carries the condition that
    the receiver must spend all the money in
    Denmark."

Danish National Committee
Lutheran World Service (LWS)
Nørregade 11
H65 Copenhagen K, Denmark     01-17-59-49
    See:  Lutheran World Service.

DOMINICAN REPUBLIC

Servicio Social de Iglesias Dominicanas
  (Social Service of Dominican Churches) (SSID)
Emiliano Tejera 6, No. 659
Santo Domingo, Dominican Republic

ECUADOR

Instituto Nacional de Nutrición (INN)
Avenida Colombia
Quito, Ecuador

Centre for Social Studies (CES)
Colon 413, 2 piso (alto)
Apartado 981
Guayaquil, Ecuador               5-13795

EGYPT

Food Science and Nutrition Laboratory
National Research Centre
Cairo, Egypt

Ecumenical Advisory Council for Church
  Services in the Egyptian Arab Republic
Anba Rueis Building, Ramses Street, Abbasyia
Cairo, Egypt                    821274

Coptic Evangelical Organization for Social
  Services
P.O. Box 50
Minia, Egypt                 2003-33-711

ETHIOPIA

Inter-Church Aid Committee
Ethiopian
P.O. Box 503
Addis Ababa, Ethiopia           16524

FIJI

Fiji Council of Churches
P.O. Box 35
Suva, Fiji

FINLAND

Finnish National Committee of the Lutheran
  World Federation
Vuorikatu 22-A
Helsinki 10, Finland            13-334
    See:  Lutheran World Service.

FRANCE

Ministry of Cooperation
Paris, France
    Overseas development agency.

Office de la Recherche Scientifique et Technique
  Outre-Mer (Office of Scientific and Technical
  Research Overseas) (ORSTOM)
24, rue Bayard
75008 Paris, France
    Quasi-official; maintains centers in French
    and ex-French territories; food projects.

Centre National de Coordination des Etudes et
  Recherches sur la Nutrition et l'Alimentation
  (National Center for Coordination of Studies
  and Research on Nutrition and Food)
71, boulevard Pereire
75017 Paris, France

CIMADE (Service Agency of the Protestant
  and Othodox Churches in France)
176, rue de Grenelle
75007 Paris, France                705-9399

United Towns Organization
13, rue Racine
75006 Paris, France
     Links towns in France with towns in deve-
     loping countries (e.g., Dreux with Kou-
     dougou in Upper Volta) for development,
     including agricultural projects. "Not an
     act of charity, but a display of international
     solidarity."

GERMANY, FEDERAL REPUBLIC OF

Ministry of Economic Cooperation
Kaiserstrasse 185-197
53 Bonn, West Germany
     The West German Government's overseas
     development agency.  Contributes to
     international food-related development
     projects.

Deutche Gesellschaft fuer Ernaehrung (German
  Society for Nutrition)
Feldbergstrasse 28
6000 Frankfurt/Main, West Germany

Arbeitsgemeinschaft Christlicher Kirchen in
  Deutchland (Council of Christian Churches
  in Germany)
P.O. Box 174025
6 Frankfurt/Main, West Germany   77-05-21

Arbeitsgemeinschaft fuer Weltmission (Council
  for World Mission)
Mittelweg 143
2-Hamburg 13, West Germany   0411-41-70-21

Christoffel Blindenmission
Nibelungenstrasse 124
614 Benshiem-Schoenberg, West Germany
     Part of HEED Bangladesh, which see.

Shakertown Pledge Group
c/o Peter Davids, Bibelschule Wiedenest
Postfach 2201
5275 Bergneustadt 2, West Germany
     Contact for SPG (U.S.); see index.

GHANA

Christian Service Committee
Christian Council of Ghana
P.O. Box 3262
Accra, Ghana                    76678

GREECE

Holy Synod of the Church of Greece
ICA and Foreign Relations Committee
14 Ioannou Gennadiou Street
Athens 140, Greece              738-671

GRENADA

Grenada Inter-Church Council for Social
  Welfare
P.O. Box 329
Market Hill, St. George's, Grenada
                                2765

GUATEMALA

Junta Evangelica de Servicio Social y Cultural
  (Evangelical Council for Social and Cultural
  Service) (JESSYC)
Apartado 904
Guatemala City, Guatemala       84-953

Instituto de Nutrición de Centroamérica y
  Panamá (Institute of Nutrition of Central
  America and Panama)
Carretera Roosevelt, Zona 11, A, 1188
Guatemala City, Guatemala

GUYANA

Guyana Council of Churches
Demerera, East Coast, Guyana

HAITI

Service Chretien d'Haiti (Christian Service of
  Haiti)
P.O. Box 285
Port-au-Prince, Haiti

## HONDURAS

Comisión Nacional de Alimentación y Agricultura (National Commission of Food and Agriculture) (CNAA)
Tegucigalpa, Honduras

## HUNGARY

Hungarian Society of Nutritional Sciences
c/o Institute of Nutrition
Gyali u. 3/a
1097 Budapest IX, Hungary

## ICELAND

Hjalparstofnun Kirkjunnar (Icelandic Church
  Relief)
Klapparstig 27
Reykjavik, Iceland          24440

## INDIA

Action for Food Production (AFPRO)
C-52 N.D. South Extension 11
New Delhi 49, India          62-16-51

Ecumenical Church Loan Fund (ECLOF)
4 Sunkurama Chetty Street
Madras 1, India

Christian Service Agency (CAS)
National Christian Council of India
Christian Council Lodge
Nagpur, M.S., India

Churches' Auxiliary for Social Action (CASA)
c/o National Council, YMCA
Massey Hall, Jai Singh Road
New Delhi 1, India

Indian National Committee for the International
  Union of Nutritional Sciences
c/o Dr. C. Gopalan
Indian Council of Medical Research
New Delhi 110016, India

Tamil Nadu Nutrition Project
Krishi Bhavan, Dr. Rajendra Prasad Road
New Delhi 110001, India
       Supported by the Ford Foundation.

## INDONESIA

Nutrition Society of Indonesia
P.O. Box 8 KBB
Kebayoran baru, Indonesia

Council of Churches in Indonesia
P.O. Box 2357
Jakarta, Indonesia          82317

## IRAN

Food and Nutrition Institute of Iran
P.O. Box 3234
Teheran, Iran

Iran Inter-Church Committee
P.O. Box 1505
Teheran, Iran

## ISRAEL

Ministry of Foreign Affairs
International Cooperation Division
Jerusalem, Israel
       Administers the foreign aid program.

Israel National Committee on the International
  Union of Nutritional Sciences
c/o Prof. Y. Birk, School of Agriculture
Hebrew University of Jerusalem
P.O. Box 12
Rehovot, Israel

## ITALY

Societa Italiana di Nutrizione Umana (Italian
  Society of Human Nutrition)
Cattedra di Scienza dell'Alementazione
Viale Forlanini 1
27100 Pavia, Italy

## JAMAICA

Caribbean Conference of Churches
P.O. Box 527
Kingston 10, Jamaica          936-5636

Shakertown Pledge Group
c/o Maribel Todd, P.O. Box 39
Highgate, St. Mary, Jamaica
       Contact for SPG (U.S.); see index.

JAPAN

Japan International Cooperation Agency
No. 42, Honmura-Cho, Ichigaya, Shinjuku-ku
Tokyo, Japan
> The Japanese Government's overseas
> development agency.

National Committee on Food and Nutrition
Science Council of Japan
22-34, Roppongi, 7-chome, Minato-ku
Tokyo, Japan

National Christian Council of Japan (NCCJ)
Division of Service
551, Totsuka-machi, 1-chome, Shinjuku-ku
Tokyo 160, Japan                 031-203-0372

Organization for Industrial, Spiritual, and
  Cultural Advancement - International
  (OISCA-International)
6-12 Izumi 3-chome, Suginami-ku
Tokyo 168, Japan
> Voluntary group, often known by its motto,
> "Food First." Provides technical assis-
> tance to Asian countries (Bangladesh,
> Indonesia, Pakistan, Thailand, Cambodia,
> Laos, the Philippines, Viet-Nam, India,
> Malaysia, and Sri Lanka), through sending
> Japanese experts. Focus is on food pro-
> duction. Provides technical training to
> farmers from other Asian countries at
> facilities in Japan.

JORDAN

Near East Council of Churches
Committee for Refugee Work (East Jordan)
P.O. Box 1295
Amman, Jordan                    41802

KENYA

National Christian Council of Kenya
P.O. Box 45009
Nairobi, Kenya                   22264

Joint Refugee Service of Kenya
P.O. Box 45627
Nairobi, Kenya

KOREA, REPUBLIC OF

Korean Nutrition Society
c/o Department of Nutrition and Biochemistry
College of Medicine, Korea University
4, 2-ga, Myong-yoon-dong, Jong-ro-ku
Seoul, Korea

National Christian Council of Korea
P.O. Box 134, Kwang-wha-moon P.O.
Seoul, Korea                     74-1367

LEBANON

Lebanese Food and Nutrition Society
c/o Animal Production Office
Verdun Street
Beirut, Lebanon

Joint Christian Committee for Social Service
  in Lebanon
P.O. Box 6496
Beirut, Lebanon

LESOTHO

Lesotho Christian Council
P.O. Box 547
Maseru, Lesotho

LIBERIA

United Ecumenical Organization (UEO)
King Sao Boscoe Street
Monrovia, Liberia

MADAGASCAR

Service Social des Eglises Protestantes à
  Madagascar (Social Service of Protestant
  Churches in Madagascar)
21, rue Gourbeyre Amparibe (B.P. 80)
Tananarive, Madagascar           50944

MALAWI

Christian Service Committee
P.O. Box 949
Blantyre, Malawi                 30671

## MALAYSIA

Council of Churches of Malaysia and Singapore
21 Jalan Abdul Samad, Brickfields
Kuala Lumpur, Malaysia          204273

## MEXICO

Sociedad Mexicana de Nutrición (Mexican Society
  of Nutrition)
c/o Instituto Nacional de la Nutrición
Viaducto Tlalpan y San Fernando
Mexico 22, D.F., Mexico

Intercultural Documentation Center (CIDOC)
Apartado 479
Cuernavaca, Morelos, Mexico      2-35-90
        Headed by Msgr. Ivan Illich.

Coordination of Initiatives for Human Develop-
  ment in Latin America (CIDAL)
Apartado 42, Suc. "A"
Cuernavaca, Morelos, Mexico      2-40-04

## MOROCCO

International Service for Peace (EIRENE)
13, rue Berchoux
Casablanca, Morocco              25-20-41

## NETHERLANDS

Ministry of Development Assistance
The Hague, Netherlands

Dutch Society for Nutrition and Food Technology
c/o Dr. C.C.J.M. van der Meijs
Ministerie van Landbouw en Visserij
1e van den Boschstraat 4
The Hague, Netherlands

Interchurch Coordination Committee for
  Development Projects (ICCO)
Cornelis Houtmanstraat 2
Utrecht, Netherlands             030-711824

Stichting Toekomstbeeld der Techniek (Future
  Shape of Technology Foundation)
Prinsessegracht 23
The Hague, Netherlands           070-646800
        Est. 1968. Research institute; the future
        of "feeding the world" has been a major
        topic.

Gast aan Tafel (Guest at Your Table)
NOVIB
Van Blankenburgstraat 6
The Hague, Netherlands
        An innovative program to provide Dutch
        citizens with information about the world
        food problem and to raise funds for food
        projects in the Third World. Pub.: Onze
        Wereld, fortnightly (in Dutch). Pamphlets.

## NEW ZEALAND

CORSO, Inc.
P.O. Box 4719
Wellington, New Zealand          859585

Also known as the Freedom from Hunger
Campaign. Raises and disburses funds for
emergency food aid and feeding of children,
and agricultural development projects in
Indonesia, South Korea, Bangladesh, Thailand,
Sri Lanka, India, and the South Pacific.
Grants in 1974 totaled NZ$445,000.

National Council of Churches in New Zealand
Christian World Service
P.O. Box 297
Christchurch, New Zealand        69-274

## NICARAGUA

Comite Evangelico pro Ayuda a los
  Damnificados (Evangelical Committee for Aid
  to the Damnified) (CEPAD)
Apartado Postal 9091
Managua, D.H., Nicaragua

## NIGERIA

Nutrition Society of Nigeria
c/o Department of Biochemistry
University of Ibadan
Ibadan, Nigeria

Christian Council of Nigeria
Social Action Department
P.O. Box 5017
Lagos, Nigeria

## NORWAY

Direktoratet for Utviklingshjelp (Norwegian
  Agency for International Development)
  (NORAD)
Postboks 8142
Oslo-Dep., Oslo 1, Norway
      The Norwegian Government's overseas
      development agency.

Kirkens Nødhjelp (Norwegian Church Relief)
Kinkegatan 5
Oslo 1, Norway                          41 42-19

Fremtiden i Vare Hender (Future in Our Hands)
Postboks 5304 Majorstua
Oslo 3, Norway
      Citizens' movement concerned with world
      hunger and resource depletion.  Pub.:
      Ny Livsstil (New Lifestyle).

## PAKISTAN

West Pakistan Christian Council
P.O. Box 357
Lahore, Pakistan                        54830

## PAPUA NEW GUINEA

Melanesian Council of Churches
P.O. Box 356
Lae, Papua New Guinea

## PHILIPPINES

Development Academy of the Philippines (DAP)
P.O. Box 5160
Makati, Rizal, Philippines
      Policy studies; research and development;
      development planning; training.  Program
      includes projects in agriculture and
      fisheries.  Pub.: Breakthrough, bimon.
      Agriculture & Natural Resources Develop-
      ment in the Philippines for the Year 2000
      (1975).

National Christian Council in the Philippines
Division of Self-Development
P.O. Box 1767
Quezon City, Manila, Philippines
                                        99-8636

Nutrition Foundation of Philippines, Inc.
107 E. Rodriguez Boulevard
Quezon City D-502, Manila, Philippines

## POLAND

Institute of Food and Nutrition
Powsinska Street 61/63
Warsaw 34, Poland

## RHODESIA

Christian Council of Rhodesia
P.O. Box 3566
Salisbury, Rhodesia                     28500

## RWANDA

Conseil Protestant du Rwanda (Protestant
  Council of Rwanda)
B.P. 79
Kigali, Rwanda

## SENEGAL

Service Oecuménique d'Entraide (Ecumenical
  Aid Service)
B.P. 5070
Dakar, Senegal

## SIERRA LEONE

United Christian Council
P.O. Box 404
Freetown, Sierra Leone

## SINGAPORE

See also: Malaysia

Ecumenical Church Loan Fund (ECLOF)
29 Victoria Park
Singapore 1, Singapore

## SOUTH AFRICA

National Food Research Institute
P.O. Box 395
Pretoria, South Africa

South African Council of Churches
Inter-Church Aid
P.O. Box 31190
Braamfontein, Transvaal, South Africa

SPAIN

Ecumenical Church Loan Fund (ECLOF)
Calle Raimundo Lulio 2
Madrid 10, Spain                    25-71-424

SRI LANKA (CEYLON)

National Christian Council of Sri Lanka
490 Havelock Road
Colombo 6, Sri Lanka

SUDAN

Sudan Council of Churches
Relief and Rehabilitation Commission
P.O. Box 469
Khartoum, Sudan                     42859

SWAZILAND

Swaziland Conference of Churches
P.O. Box 333
Mbabane, Swaziland

SWEDEN

Styrelsen för Internationell Utveckling
  (Swedish International Development
  Authority) (SIDA)
Birger Jarlsgatan 61
105 25 Stockholm, Sweden
    The Swedish Government's overseas deve-
    lopment agency.

Swedish National Committee for Nutrition
c/o Department of Nutrition
University of Uppsala
P.O. Box 551
751 22 Uppsala, Sweden

Svenska Missionsradet (Swedish Missionary
  Council)
P.O. Box 6302
113 81 Stockholm, Sweden       08-15-18-30

Lutherska Värlsförbundet (Lutheran World
  Federation)
Fack, 181 20 Ligingö 1, Sweden

Formedlingscentralen for Framtidsstudier AB
  (Swedish Association for Futures Studies)
P.O. Box 5073
102 42 Stockholm, Sweden       8-22-07-60
    Est. 1971. Studies have included research
    on long-term prospects for food supplies.
    Pub.: Futures Studies News, 10 times a
    year.

SWITZERLAND

Swiss Society for Nutrition Research
c/o Prof. J.C. Somogyi
Institut fuer Ernaehrungsforschung
Seestrasse 72
8803 Rueschlikon-Zurich, Switzerland

Hilfswerk der Evangelischen Kirchen der
  Schweiz (Service Agency of the Protestant
  Churches of Swizerland) (HEKS)
Postfach 168
8035 Zurich, Switzerland       01-26-66-00

Erklaerung von Bern (Declaration of Bern)
Gartenhofstrasse 27
8004 Zurich, Switzerland       01-39-69-00
    Action and information on food production
    and consumption in Switzerland, including
    how they relate to world hunger and deve-
    lopment problems. Pub.: Rundbrief, 3-4
    times a year.

Jochgruppen Haus
3432 Lutzelfluh, Switzerland     034-6132-87
    Retreat center; developing a simple style
    of life. Contact with Shakertown Pledge
    Group, U.S. Pub.: Wegweiser, 3 times
    a year.

TANZANIA

Christian Council of Tanzania
P.O. Box 2537
Dar es Salaam, Tanzania         21886

TRINIDAD AND TOBAGO

Christian Council of Trinidad and Tobago
Opposite Gopaul Avenue, Diego Martin Road
Diego Martin, Trinidad          637-4449

TUNISIA

Service Oecuménique en Tunisia (Ecumenical
   Service in Tunisia)
10, rue Eve-Nohelle
Tunis, Tunisia                          248-294

UNION OF SOVIET SOCIALIST REPUBLICS

Institute of Nutrition
Ustinsky pr. 2/14
Moscow G-240, U.S.S.R.

UNITED KINGDOM

Ministry of Overseas Development
Eland House, Stag Place
London S.W. 1, England

British National Committee for Nutritional
   Sciences
The Royal Society
6 Carleton House Terrace
London SW1Y 5AG, England

The British Council of Churches
10 Eaton Gate
London S.W. 1, England          01-730-9611

Scottish Churches Council
41 George IV Bridge
Edinburgh EH1 1EL, Scotland

Cyngor Eglwysi Cymru (Council of Churches
   for Wales)
55 Aberfan Road
Aberfan, Merthyr Tydfil, Glamorganshire
Wales

Christian Aid
P.O. Box 1
London SW1W 9BW                 01-720-0614

Baby Foods Action Group
103 Gower Street, Basement
London WC1E 6AW, England
      Concerned that promotion of commercial
      baby foods in developing countries is lea-
      ding to malnutrition.

Bible and Medical Missionary Fellowship
352 Kennington Road
London S.E. 1, England          01-735-8227
      Participates in HEED Bangladesh.

Counter Information Services (CIS)
52 Shaftsbury Avenue
London W.1, England
      Provides "alternative, critical information"
      about the activities of business corporations.
      Studies have included one on the activities
      of a multinational food firm in developing
      countries.

Haslemere Group
467 Caledonian Road
London N7 9BE, England
      Research and action on the relationship
      between economic and political developments
      in the U.K. and in the Third World.  Has
      published studies of the sugar and banana
      markets, and Death of the Green Revolu-
      tion (1973).

Help the Aged
8-10 Denman Street
London W1A 2AP, England
      Raises funds to send to relief organizations
      in some 80 countries for assistance to the
      aged.  Pub.: Yours, mon.

International Food Information Service
Shinfield, Reading, England

Leprosy Mission
50 Portland Place
London W1N 3DG, England     01-637-2611
      Participates in HEED Bangladesh.

London Vegetarian Centre
53 Marloes Road
London W8 6LD, England      01-937-7739

New Internationalist Publications, Ltd.
Stage House, High Street
Benson, Oxford, England
      Publishes the New Internationalist, a mon-
      thly magazine on "the people, the ideas,
      the action in the fight for world develop-
      ment." Sponsored by Christian Aid, Oxfam,
      and Third World First.

Oxfam
See listing under International Non-Governmental
   Organizations

Regions Beyond Missionary Union
Harley House, 99 Thurleigh Road
London SW12 8TY, England          01-673-1288

Shakertown Pledge Group
c/o Janet Sheperd
"Karen," Oddingly near Droitwich
Worcester, England
          Contact for SPG (U.S.); see index.

The Soil Association
Walnut Tree Manor, Haughley
Stowmarket, Suffolk 1P14 3RS, England
          Promotes organic agriculture.

Tear Fund
1 Bridgeman Road
Teddington, Middlesex TW11 9AJ, England
          Participates in HEED Bangladesh.

Third World First
4 Marston Ferry Road
Oxford, England          58725
          Works to build awareness and stimulate
          action among university students in the
          U.K. on food and other issues of world
          development.

War on Want (WOW)
467 Caledonian Road
London N7 9BE, England          01-609-0211
          Raises funds for and conducts relief and
          development programs abroad; public
          education to create a greater awareness of
          the causes of underdevelopment. Projects
          in Africa, Asia, and Latin America. Bud-
          get for the 1975 fiscal year was £768,000.
          Pub.: Frontline, q. Hope for the Hungry:
          World Hunger Crisis Kit. The Profits of
          Doom: An Investigation into the 'World
          Food Crisis! (1976). Pamphlets. List of
          publications available.

University of Sussex
Institute of Development Studies (IDS)
Brighton BN1 9RE, England          0273-66261
          Est. 1966. National center for teaching
          and research on Third World development
          and relationships between rich and poor
          countries. Projects include studies
          focused on irrigation benefits, crop
          storage economics, and population growth
          and rural poverty. Library. Pub.: IDS
          Bulletin, q. Communications Series.



          Discussion Papers. Books, bibliographies,
          and other publications (list available).

The Vegetarian Society (U.K.) Ltd.
Parkdale, Dunham Road
Altrincham, Cheshire, England

Voluntary Committee on Overseas Aid
  and Development (VCOAD)
Parnell House, 25 Wilton Road
London S.W.1, England          828-7611
          Coordination of British voluntary aid
          and development programs overseas.
          Pub.: Action for Development, mon.

World Development Movement (WDM)
Bedford Chambers, Covent Garden
London WC3E 8HA, England          836-3672
          Public education on problems of world
          development; stimulates support of
          British overseas development programs.
          Pub.: Booklets, pamphlets, posters (list
          available). Examples: "Producer Power:
          The Third World Hits Back" (1975). "Food
          in Our Time - But Not Just Yet: A Report
          on the World Food Conference" (1974).
          "The Party's Over: Grain - for the Rich
          World's Animals or the Poor World's
          People?" (1975). SPUR, monthly newsletter.

EXTERNAL TERRITORIES:

Belize:

Christian Social Council
P.O. Box 508
Belize City, Belize

British Solomon Islands:

Solomon Islands Christian Association
P.O. Box 357
Honiara, British Solomon Islands

Hong Kong:

Hong Kong Christian Council
Division of Christian Service
Metropole Building, 4th Floor
57 Peking Road
Kowloon, Hong Kong          678-034

EXTERNAL TERRITORIES (Contin.):

Southern Rhodesia:

See: Rhodesia

URUGUAY

Ecumenical Church Loan Fund (ECLOF)
Casilla de Correo 693
Montevideo, Uruguay

VENEZUELA

Instituto Nacional de Nutrición (National
  Institute of Nutrition)
Caracas, Venezuela

WESTERN SAMOA

Fellowship of Christian Churches in Samoa
P.O. Box 57
Nuku'alofa, Western Samoa

YUGOSLAVIA

Union of Societies for Improvement of
  Nutrition of the Yugoslav Peoples
Ul. Kosovska 18
11000 Belgrade, Yugoslavia

ZAMBIA

Christian Council of Zambia
P.O. Box 315
Lusaka, Zambia                    73287

# Indexes

# INDEX OF SUBJECTS

This index is intended to supplement the User's Guide (pages ix-xxv); please consult the User's Guide for complete directory references.

# INDEX OF ORGANIZATIONS

INDEX - ORGANIZATIONS

# INDEX OF ACRONYMS AND INITIALISMS

INDEX - ACRONYMS & INITIALISMS